LANDSCAPES OF HATE

Spaces and Practices of Justice series

Series editor: **Agatha Herman**, Cardiff University

The Spaces and Practices of Justice series focuses on the intersections between spaces and practices to provide innovative and important interventions on examples of real-world (in)justice. The series explores food justice, scholar-activism, social movements, gender, sexuality, race, childhood, labour, trade, domestic spaces, environmental relations and consumption to open out different approaches to questions of justice grounded within everyday experiences and spaces.

Forthcoming in the series:

Arctic Justice: Environment, Society and Governance
Corine Wood-Donnelly and **Johanna Ohlsson**, May 2023

The Practice of Collective Escape: Politics, Justice and Community in Urban Growing Projects **Helen Traill**, June 2023

Environmental Justice and Peacebuilding: Integrating Nature in Policy and Practice **Rebecca Farnum**, July 2023

Researching Justice: Engaging with Questions and Spaces of (In)Justice through Social Research **Agatha Herman** and **Joshua Inwood**, November 2023

Find out more at
bristoluniversitypress.co.uk/spaces-and-practices-of-justice

LANDSCAPES OF HATE

Tracing Spaces, Relations and Responses

Edited by
Edward Hall, John Clayton and
Catherine Donovan

BRISTOL
UNIVERSITY
PRESS

First published in Great Britain in 2022 by

Bristol University Press
University of Bristol
1–9 Old Park Hill
Bristol
BS2 8BB
UK
t: +44 (0)117 374 6645
e: bup-info@bristol.ac.uk

Details of international sales and distribution partners are available at bristoluniversitypress.co.uk

British Library Cataloguing in Publication Data
A catalogue record for this book is available from the British Library

ISBN 978-1-5292-1517-5 hardcover
ISBN 978-1-5292-1519-9 ePub
ISBN 978-1-5292-1520-5 ePdf

Cover design: blu inc
Front cover image: iStock/Rhoberazzi
Bristol University Press use environmentally responsible print partners.
Printed and bound in Great Britain by CPI Group (UK) Ltd,
Croydon, CR0 4YY

Dedicated to all those harmed, but not
defined, by hate.

Contents

List of Figures

About the Authors

Rick Bowler is Senior Lecturer in Community and Youth Work at the University of Sunderland. Rick's work involves sharing time between teaching, research and outreach. His pedagogical interests focus on transformative approaches to critical youth work practice. Rick has extensive community youth work experience connecting therapeutic with socio-cultural explanations to the lifeworld of young people. His doctoral study focused on anti-racist youth work practice in monocultural settings. He draws upon an intersectional critical race theory lens to trouble the white standards that perpetuate British racism. Rick and Amina Razak have researched and published together since 2016.

Kath Browne is Professor of Geography at University College Dublin. Her research has focused on social justice and inequalities, specifically around gender and sexualities. She has worked with those marginalized because of their sexual and gender identities, exploring how lives can be ameliorated in ways that take place seriously. She has also worked on those who are opposed to sexual and gender equalities, with Catherine Jean Nash and Andrew Gorman-Murray, developing the concept of heteroactivism. She currently leads Beyond Opposition, an ERC consolidator project that seeks to investigate the experiences of people who do not support some or all of the changes to sexual and gender equalities in the 21st century and explore new ways of engaging difference, differently.

Alice Butler-Warke is a human geographer and Lecturer in Sociology in the School of Applied Social Studies at Robert Gordon University. Her research interests are related to experiences of and representations of urban space, stigma, and online communities. She is especially interested in the intersection between media and power. Alice completed her PhD at the University of Leeds in the School of Geography where she undertook a Critical Discourse Analysis of press coverage of Toxteth during the 20th century. Recently, she has undertaken research around the contentious history of Portland Stone in the built environment.

John Clayton is Senior Lecturer in Human Geography in the Department of Geography and Environmental Sciences at Northumbria University. John is a social geographer, interested in the connections between space, identities and inequalities. His research centres around geographies of 'race', ethnicity, multiculture and racism, particularly in the British context. This includes work on everyday multiculturalism, experiences of work for 'new migrants' and emotions of diaspora. Current work focuses on the geographies of 'hate relationships' and cuckooing (home takeovers).

Ellen Daly is Research Fellow at Anglia Ruskin University's Policing Institute for the Eastern Region. Ellen's interdisciplinary research focuses on criminal justice responses to sexual violence and specifically explores intersectional narratives in rape trials. Her research interests further extend to policing and justice responses to violence more broadly, and she is particularly interested in how the intersections of gender, age, (dis)ability and social class shape victims' journeys through the justice system.

Catherine Donovan is Professor of Sociology and Head of Department at Durham University. Most of her research in the last 15 years has focussed on interpersonal violence: comparing love and violence in heterosexual and same sex relationships (Donovan and Hester, 2014, Policy Press); the use of violence and abuse in the relationships of LGB and/or T+ people (Donovan and Barnes, 2020, Palgrave); HE student experiences of violence and abuse; and hate relationships – where individuals/families are repeatedly targeted by perpetrators living in close proximity to them and impacts are similar to coercive control in domestic abuse.

Matthew Durey is Senior Lecturer in Social Sciences and a member of the Centre for Applied Social Sciences at the University of Sunderland. His research interests include cultural and creative industries, arts and culture in postindustrial society, everyday urban geographies, and the theory and practice of social research.

Bianca Fileborn is Senior Lecturer in Criminology and Australian Research Council Discovery Early Career Research Award Fellow in the School of Social and Political Sciences, University of Melbourne. Their current work examines victim-centred justice responses to street harassment, sexual violence at music festivals, and sexual violence and LGBTQ+ communities. Bianca is the author of *Reclaiming the Night-time Economy: Unwanted Sexual Attention in Pubs and Clubs* (Palgrave, 2016), and co-editor of *#MeToo and the Politics of Social Change* (Palgrave, 2019).

Denise Goerisch is Assistant Professor of Integrative Studies at Grand Valley State University, Michigan. Her research interests include college affordability, faculty labour and university culture. She has published in *The Professional Geographer*, *Children's Geographies*, and *Gender, Place and Culture*. She co-authored *The True Costs of College* (Palgrave, 2020), which examines the unforeseen costs associated with attending college in the US.

Edward Hall is Reader in Human Geography at the University of Dundee. His research focuses on disability and learning disability, including studies on social exclusion, inclusion and belonging, social care and personalization, creative arts, environmental hazards and hate crime. He is currently working on a collaborative project on community housing, with universities and housing organizations in Canada.

Peter Hopkins is Professor of Social Geography at Newcastle University, and Distinguished International Professor at Universiti Kebangsaan Malaysia. His current research focuses on Islamophobia, refugee youth experiences and intersectionality.

Zoë James is Professor of Criminology at the University of Plymouth. Her key research interests lie in examining hate from a critical perspective with a particular focus on the harms of hate experienced by Gypsies, Travellers and Roma. Zoë's research has explored how mobility, accommodation, policing and planning have impacted on the lived experience of Gypsies, Travellers and Roma. Zoë is Co-Director of the International Network for Hate Studies and has published and presented her work nationally and internationally, most recently authoring a monograph *The Harms of Hate against Gypsies and Travellers: A Critical Hate Studies Perspective* (Springer, 2020).

Stephen J. Macdonald is Professor of Social Work in the Department of Sociology at Durham University. Stephen has published in the areas of disability and social exclusion, including issues concerning diagnosis, disengagement, digital exclusion, crime, victimization, loneliness/isolation and homelessness. His work is underpinned by social models of disability. He is currently working on three research projects: disability hate crime; online disability hate speech; disability and cuckooing (home takeovers).

Katie McBride is Lecturer in Criminology at the University of Plymouth. Before joining academia, Katie worked within the public and third sectors on the development and delivery of policy and practice to address inequalities and discrimination experienced by marginalized communities. Her key research interests focus on critically analysing hate and specifically the harms of hate experienced by trans individuals. Katie's research utilizes ethnographic participatory methods to redress the balance of power in research and academia. Her research has explored how adverse childhood experiences, communities of support and structures of governance have impacted on the lived experience of trans individuals.

Catherine Jean Nash is Adjunct Professor in the Department of Geography, Queen's University and Professor Emerita, Brock University, Ontario. Her research interests include sexualities/queer/feminist geographies, as well as mobilities and digital sexualities. She is currently working with Kath Browne examining transnational oppositions to LGBTQ rights in Canada, the UK and Ireland, and with Andrew Gorman-Murray on new mobilities, digital life and the transformations in LGBT and queer neighbourhoods in Sydney, Australia, and Toronto, Canada. She has published in a wide range of national and international journals, has authored numerous book chapters and is co-editor of several books and compendia.

Amina Razak is Research Associate in the Inclusive Newcastle Knowledge Centre, Newcastle University. Amina's research interests focus on gender, ethnicity and racism. Her doctoral thesis focused on masculinities and South Asian young men, in particular Bangladeshi and Pakistani men, their new masculinities and experiences of racism. Amina has extensive experience in public sector and academic research and has co-worked on a number of research projects with Rick Bowler at the University of Sunderland.

Nicola Roberts is Associate Professor of Criminology at the University of Sunderland. Her research interests are focused on students' experiences of interpersonal violence, and their perceptions and strategies of safety, on and off-campus. Her publications include 'The makings of an exclusive community: students' perceptions of dangerous others' (*Higher Education: The International Journal of Higher Education Research*, 2022) and, with C. Donovan and M. Durey, 'Gendered landscapes of safety: how women construct and navigate the urban landscape to avoid sexual violence' (*Criminology and Criminal Justice*, 2022).

Olivia Smith is Senior Lecturer in Criminology and Social Policy from Loughborough University. Olivia is part of the British Society of Criminology's Victims' Network and acts as Research Events Co-ordinator for the Violence Against Women and Girls Research Network, as well as being Director of Research for Loughborough's Criminology, Sociology and Social Policy Division. Olivia specializes in justice responses to prejudicial violence, for example hate crime and gender-based violence, and is an Advisor to the Victims' Commissioner for England and Wales on these matters.

Fiona Vera-Gray is Reader at the Child and Woman Abuse Studies Unit at London Metropolitan University. She researches violence against women, specifically sexual violence. She has published widely on public sexual harassment including two full-length monographs, *Men's Intrusion, Women's Embodiment: A Critical Analysis of Street Harassment* (Routledge, 2016) and *The Right Amount of Panic: How Women Trade Freedom for Safety* (Policy Press, 2018).

David Wilkin, having been a victim of disability hate crime in his childhood, has served as the Lead Coordinator of the Disability Hate Crime Network, an associate with Disability Rights UK and has worked as a hate crime consultant for the UK government. He is now an Honorary Fellow at the University of Leicester for his hate crime research and an Associate Lecturer at the Open University in the UK. David holds a passion for reducing disability hate crime. He is the author of *Disability Hate Crime* (Springer, 2019).

Series Preface

Agatha Herman

Justice refers to a broad concern with fairness, equity, equality and respect. Just from the daily news, it is readily apparent how questions of justice or, in fact, the more obvious experiences of *injustice* shape our everyday lives. From global trade to our own personal consumption; living or dying through war and peace; access to education; relations in the workplace or home; how we experience life through a spectrum of identities; or the more-than-human entanglements that contextualize our environments, we need to conceptualize and analyze the intersections between spaces and practices of justice in order to formulate innovative and grounded interventions.

The Spaces and Practices of Justice book series aims to do so through cutting across scales to explore power, relations and society from the local through to international levels, recognizing that space is fundamental to understanding how (in)justice is relationally produced in, and through, different temporal and geographical contexts. It is also always practised, and a conceptual focus on these 'doings and sayings' (Shove, 2014) brings a sense of the everydayness of (in)justice but also allows for analysis of the broader contexts, logics and structures within which such experiences and relations are embedded (Jaeger-Erben and Offenberger, 2014; Herman, 2018).

References

Herman, A. (2018) *Practising Empowerment in Post-Apartheid South Africa: Wine, Ethics and Development*, London: Routledge.

Jaeger-Erben, M. and Offenberger, U. (2014) 'A practice theory approach to sustainable consumption', *GAIA*, 23(S1): 166–74.

Shove, E. (2014) 'Putting practice into policy: reconfiguring questions of consumption and climate change', *Contemporary Social Science*, 9(4): 415–29.

Preface

This edited collection marks the emergence of a distinctive spatial interpretation of 'hate', a term increasingly dominant in policy rhetoric and academic study, to describe injustice, prejudice and discrimination towards marginalized social groups, as well as acts of violence and abuse aimed at members of those groups. Although the geographies of hate incidents have been documented, there has been limited work to date on the role of place and space in the construction, circulation and lived experience of hateful actions. This book seeks to address this absence by providing a collection of interdisciplinary, yet spatially oriented, contributions, that critically explore the multiple and intersecting landscapes of hate. The chapters trace the spatial and relational situations and contexts through which hate is produced, experienced, and responded to.

We would like to offer huge thanks to all of the contributing authors. The book was proposed and started before the COVID-19 pandemic. The disruption and difficulties experienced by the authors during this time were significant, and we are very grateful for both their enduring commitment to and patience with what turned out to be an extended process of publication. All of the authors have responded to our comments very generously and in a timely fashion, ensuring that editing the collection has been a very positive experience. We would also like to acknowledge that the idea of this collection emerged from a session at the Royal Geographical Society (with the Institute of British Geographers) Annual Conference 2018, which involved several contributors who do not appear here. Despite their absence, their work inspired and informed us along this journey.

We would like to thank Agatha Herman, editor of the *Spaces and Practices of Justice* book series, for the initial invitation, and Emily Watt, Anna Richardson and Freya Trand at Bristol University Press who provided excellent advice and support throughout the publishing process. In particular, we would like to thank them for their understanding of the challenges encountered by the editors and authors during the pandemic.

Introducing Landscapes of Hate

Edward Hall, John Clayton and Catherine Donovan

Introduction

In the wake of the England men's football team's defeat in the European Championships final in July 2021, three young Black players – Marcus Rashford, Jadon Sancho and Bukayo Saka – received significant racist abuse on social media after failing to score in the penalty shoot-out. In a post a few days after the match, Saka wrote that he 'knew instantly the kind of hate that I was about to receive' (BBC News, 2021a). There were swift responses from England manager Gareth Southgate ('racist abuse is "unforgivable"'; BBC Sport, 2021), Prime Minister Boris Johnson ('those responsible should be banned from attending football matches'; BBC News, 2021b), sections of the media and members of the public. Eleven people who posted racist messages were arrested (BBC News, 2021c). However, another England player, Tyrone Mings, highlighted the hypocrisy in some reactions, claiming that the UK Home Secretary's refusal to criticize fans, who earlier in the tournament booed England players 'taking the knee', had 'stoked the fire' of racism (BBC News, 2021d).

This vignette is an illustrative snapshot of the form, extent, experience and response to 'hate' in the UK (largely the geographical focus of this collection); together these constitute what we refer to as 'landscapes of hate'.

First, this case shows that hate can be understood not only as discriminatory actions against an individual but also as directed at social groups and reinforced through divisive politics. Harmful attitudes, beliefs and practices oriented towards contingently demonized 'others' are not confined to the violent actions of a small number of extremists. Rather they are sanctioned and even encouraged by rhetoric and policy that produce the conditions necessary for hostile environments. Second, alongside other forms of discrimination, such forms of hate are a commonplace experience for many Black, Asian and other racialized people (as well as people of faith, disabled people and people from lesbian, gay, bisexual, transgender and queer [LGBTQ+] communities), despite the surprise and shock commonly expressed by those unaffected. Third, hate is expected to lead to a criminal justice response, albeit limited in extent due to the challenge of identification of perpetrators (especially when online). Fourth, hate represents an apparent contradiction between portrayals of society as tolerant and inclusive, and evidence of increasing hostility and harassment against marginalized groups (including the rise in hate crimes reported to the police; Allen and Zayed, 2021). In the UK, as in many other national contexts, despite legislative and policy action, hate is ever more prominent in the lives of many communities.

This edited collection seeks to address this apparent impasse, by broadening the examination and discussion of hate from a commonly singular focus on hate crime (Hall, 2013; Chakraborti and Garland, 2015), and the exceptional and extreme acts often associated with it (Sherry, 2011; Roulstone and Mason-Bish, 2013). To do so, we place hate within the framework of social, cultural, and political *landscapes* of experiences, emotions, attitudes, actions, and responses, by individuals, communities, places, organizations, institutions and governments. We employ the notion of landscapes to broaden the perspective out from the immediate incident of hate – in the vignette discussed earlier the posting of racist social media messages – to the spaces, contexts and relations through which such incidents emerge, are experienced, and responded to (Hall, 2019). In so doing we look to further understand the embeddedness of hate in the fabric of society. Bukayo Saka knowing 'instantly' that he would receive racist abuse can be seen as personal experience of the enduring character of English racism, the uneven racialized burdens placed on a Black England football player, the partial acceptance of him as part of a national community, and the apparent inevitability of such treatment in a society where racism and other forms of discrimination are commonplace. In this sense, the language of 'landscapes' enables connections to be made between broader social and political contexts, and those spaces and situations through which forms of hate and responses to it, play out.

We also employ the terminology of landscapes to reflect the scope of this collection, which seeks to consolidate and extend the emerging geographical study and critique of hate (Flint, 2004; Listerborn, 2014; Clayton et al, 2016; Hopkins, 2016; Hall, 2019; Legg and Nottingham Citizens, 2021; Edwards and Maxwell, 2021). So long dominated by criminology (Perry, 2001; Gerstenfeld, 2013; Hall, 2013) and, more recently, sociology (Roulstone and Mason-Bish, 2013), hate has been framed predominantly as incidents impacting specific individuals and groups and understood as requiring a criminal justice response. In contrast, we consider hate's widespread, embedded nature, the 'ordinariness' of most perpetrators (Iganski, 2008), and the social, cultural and political contexts implicated in the construction of and/or collusion with landscapes of hate at a range of scales. Together these give form to situated yet related experiences of harm.

The contributors are drawn from across a range of disciplines, including geography, criminology, sociology and youth work. They explore hate through a range of lenses from the systemic (James and McBride), the institutional (Goerisch), the discursive (Browne and Nash; Butler-Warke), the criminal/legal (Vera-Gray and Fileborn), the material (Clayton et al; Daly and Smith), the atmospheric (Durey et al), the emotional (Wilkin), as well as thinking 'beyond hate' (Bowler and Razak; Hall). Contributors also consider dimensions of hate in relation to specific and intersectional communities including 'race' and religion (Bowler and Razak; Butler-Warke; Clayton et al; Goerisch), sexuality (Browne and Nash; Clayton et al), gender and transgender identities (Durey et al; Vera-Gray and Fileborn: James and McBride), Gypsy and Traveller identities (James and McBride), disability (Clayton et al; Hall; Daly and Smith; Wilkin) and social class (Butler-Warke). However, all contributions, in different ways, argue for the potential of thinking through hate as intrinsically spatial and part of the landscapes we inhabit.

Why is it important to think about hate now?

Hate and hate crime have received much scholarly attention in recent years, in parallel with an expanding suite of legislative and policy actions in the UK and internationally. We will address the concept of 'hate' in the following section, but here set out why this edited collection is a timely and distinctive addition to the academic study of hate.

There is undoubted evidence of an increased presence of hateful extremism, in relation to 'race', religion, sexuality, transgender and disability, in the UK and other countries (European Commission Against Racism and Intolerance, 2020; The Guardian, 2021; BBC News, 2022), including the rise in prominence and actions of far-right groups and extremists, and in the context of the so-called 'culture wars' (Duffy et al, 2019). This is deeply troubling and should be actively monitored and contested. However, arguably of greater significance and concern is what was experienced by the England football players (discussed earlier) and many others in minoritized groups; that is, widespread and predominantly non-physically violent abuse in a range of online and in-person contexts, to such an extent that it has become everyday, even 'mundane' (Chakraborti et al, 2014; Hall, 2019). There is, of course, a connection between these different forms of hate. Both can be placed on what Kelly (1988) has called, in relation to violence against women, a 'continuum of violence', which Hollomotz (2013: 53; see also Daly and Smith, Chapter 7) also uses to talk about violence against disabled people. Similarly, Hall (2013) makes the distinction between 'hate' as the increasingly dominant, catch-all term, and what he sees as the root causes of hate – prejudice or hostility – with 'pure hate' as it would commonly be understood (that is, as extreme abjection) as 'just one small part of this spectrum' (Hall, 2013: 9).

Extremist views arguably create both the context for, and the normalizing of, everyday discriminatory acts; and, conversely, these often seemingly 'mundane' acts provide the basis for, or condoning of, extremist views. We argue it is problematic to see forms of hate as solely committed by those with (openly) extremist views (Hardy, 2017). Rather, most hate crime offenders, or for that matter those subject to processes of radicalization (Luger, 2022), are 'ordinary people' showing hostility in the 'everyday' course of their lives (Iganski, 2008: 23, cited in Hall, 2019: 252). This everyday hate characterizes many of the contributions in this collection and shows that while they may appear 'low-level' in criminal justice terms, such acts can have profound impacts on the mental and physical health and wellbeing of victimized individuals and communities (for example, in this collection, Wilkin; James and McBride; Clayton et al; Goerisch; Daly and Smith; and Durey et al). This collection argues for an expansion of the hate discourse to recognize the extent and significance of these actions and the long-term and embedded discrimination, exclusion and abjection, that sustains them. Hate has become central in the discourse of discrimination and prejudice, but in the process has been largely individualized.

The collection is timely too in terms of the socio-cultural and political context, in the UK and elsewhere. A rise in populist, authoritarian and in some cases fascist parties, the so-called 'culture wars', deeply entrenched discrimination identified by the Black Lives Matter movement, 'Trumpism', and the misogynist 'Incel' movement, are all aspects of, arguably, a fragmentation of the socially liberal consensus of the mid-1990s (Beckett, 2018). The 'reawakening of hate' is targeted towards many minoritized groups and women (Sternberg, 2020). Actions include austerity-promoted labelling of disabled people as 'parasite[s]' and 'spongers' (Burch, 2018; Power and Bartlett, 2018); the creation of a 'hostile environment' by the UK government for those already settled and those wishing to settle in the UK (Webber, 2019); the 2016 UK Brexit referendum to leave the European Union; the recent UK 'Sewell Report' that, in response to the Black Lives Matter protests, stated that 'geography, family influence, socio-economic background, culture and religion have more significant impact on life chances [of BAME communities] than the existence of racism' (Committee on Race and Ethnic Disparities, 2021: 8); and resistance to legislation on 'hate speech' in relation to sexuality, for example, in Ireland (as examined by Browne and Nash, Chapter 10).

Throughout this period, the number of hate crimes reported in the UK, and in other countries, has increased steadily (Home Office, 2020; The Guardian, 2021), with a surge just after the Brexit referendum (NPCC, 2016). As many incidents are not reported (see Hall, Chapter 12), it is widely acknowledged that hate is an everyday experience for many individuals and communities.

Austerity has, arguably, in large part underpinned the emergent landscapes of hate in the last decade in the UK, generating a discourse of and a legitimacy for discriminatory attitudes against disabled people, migrants and others who receive (limited) support and protections from the state (Burch, 2018; Healy, 2020). Long-standing discriminatory attitudes, deeply embedded within the UK's social, political and material landscapes, have (re)emerged and flourished. Austerity has also reduced or completely ended funding to community and national voluntary organizations that provide support, presence and community mediation for those groups most affected by both socio-economic pressures and potential hostile attitudes and actions (Clayton et al, 2016). Many disabled people, people with mental health conditions, those experiencing drug problems and families in crisis, are now both labelled as a problem *and* increasingly exposed to hateful actions. At the same time as austerity budgets have impacted on the fabric of civil society, governments have progressed rapidly with hate crime legislation and policy, including broadening the initial identification of 'race' as a 'protected characteristic' to include more groups, and reinforcing the criminal justice system and the police as the appropriate response (Home Office, 2016). The dominance of the law and criminal justice across the landscapes of hate is arguably problematic as, while it signals intent, it also directs attention to the extremes, and away from both those in positions of relative power and the hostile views and actions of 'ordinary' people (Iganski, 2008: 23; see also Vera-Gray and Fileborn, Chapter 3).

To return briefly to the vignette that began the chapter, the extensive online abuse of the three football players is without question 'unforgivable' (to quote the England team manager), but the reaction to it is arguably also problematic, with no real expectation that online abuse of players will end; and no real interrogation of or reflection on – by politicians, the media, fan's groups or society more widely – the personal and collective responsibility for such racist acts. The time has come for a different interpretation of hate, and, in turn, new ways of responding to its outcomes. This collection seeks to contribute to this critical moment in the story of hate.

We are acutely aware that the collection is confined mainly to UK contexts (exceptions are the chapters by Browne and Nash, Chapter 10; and Goerisch, Chapter 9). However, even with this caveat, the collection provides a rallying cry for the field of hate crime and hate studies to further open up to geographical interrogation, and to reframe hate as a collective societal, rather than an individual criminogenic, problem. We offer the collection as a provocation to others to critically engage with the key arguments made and to reflect on the usefulness of these arguments across different national contexts.

Bringing into view the culpability of the broader landscapes in which hate is experienced enables a social and structural set of solutions to be considered (see Hall, Chapter 12). In addition, many of the contributors consider the ways in which those who are victimized are engaged in preventing, negotiating, agitating and confronting, as well as being fearful within and harmed through, landscapes of hate. The construction of those who are victimized as agentic also provides a perspective that can suggest innovative ways of addressing hate, such as in Goerisch's chapter (Chapter 9) where Hmong students at a US university take over an underused set of rooms to create their own safe space. And in Butler-Warke's chapter (Chapter 4), where a community housing group campaign and deliver an independent and community-led redevelopment project in Liverpool's Toxteth area. Also, in Bowler and Razak's chapter (Chapter 11), where young people are provided with safe spaces to enable them to 'speak out and see beyond' racism in their local communities. It is this refusal to be stigmatized and the subsequent inhabiting of transformative identities (see Donovan et al, 2019) that provides hope for change.

Critiquing 'hate'

'Hate' has become the discourse of harassment, violent abjection, and discrimination, over the past 20 years in the UK, US and elsewhere. However, importantly, in this chapter, and in some of the others that follow, the notion of hate as a way to interpret the actions, experiences, emotions and responses, of people affected, and to shape ways forward, is increasingly subject to examination and critique (see James and McBride, Chapter 2; and Daly and Smith, Chapter 7). Haslam and Murphy (2020) argue that hate has multiple meanings, with the public and those affected often having quite different understandings and usages of the term (see also Chakraborti, 2010).

Hate in relation to discrimination and harassment, and the legislation to tackle it, has its origins in the era of the US civil rights movement of the 1960s, and the associated violence against African Americans (Hall, 2013). Hate was invoked to identify the actions and consequences of white supremacist groups, and to (eventually) force the enactment of policies and legislation to counter it. The legislation that accompanied these civil actions adopted 'hate' and from then on the term has become embedded in public and policy discourse (Hall, 2013; see also Jacobs and Potter, 1998; and Chakraborti and Garland, 2015). Significantly, legislation in the UK has never explicitly used the term 'hate' (only very recently adopted in Scotland (Hate Crime and Public Order (Scotland) Act 2021). However, government policy, police forces, third sector organizations, media, and many people and communities affected by harassment, have readily taken on the term 'hate', seeing in it the potential to catch people's attention, to encapsulate in a simple term the many actions experienced, and to attach a label that conveys how fundamentally wrong and damaging these actions are. Hate is also often distinguished from discrimination and exclusion; these are commonly seen as social and structural, while hate carries a distinctive affective and visceral force, which may for some better capture what they and their communities experience. Indeed, rather than a focus on whether (or not) hate is a motivating factor of perpetrators, many have argued for the often traumatic experiences of victims (see Bowler and Razak, Chapter 11, in relation to racialized minority groups; and Wilkin, Chapter 8, regarding disabled people) to be central in the conceptualization of hate (crime) (Iganski, 2008; Hardy and Chakraborti, 2020), with several authors having published victim-centred accounts of, for example, transphobic (Colliver, 2021) and disablist (Sherry, 2010) hate.

What distinguishes hate is the broader targeting and impact on groups and communities, and the fear this generates. To fully understand hate, therefore, demands more than a focus on individual victims' experiences, crucial though these are. The groups, communities, locations and contexts of those individuals affected, are as much part of the picture of what hate is (see Clayton et al, Chapter 6); indeed, shifting the focus away from the individual can relieve the pressure on those directly affected. For example, Daly and Smith (Chapter 7) argue for the use of the term 'disablist' rather than 'disability' to describe hate directed at disabled people, to both capture what they term the 'pervasive low-level fear' (p 119) many experience and to recognize the 'underlying structural inequalities and embedded disablist attitudes' (p 123) that is a context generative of hateful actions and fear. Developing such an argument is crucial as the tide of current, dominant thinking is flowing in the opposite direction; for example, the UK Sewell Report's (Committee on Race and Ethnic Disparities, 2021) 'downplayed structural racism' (*The Guardian*, 2022), placing the emphasis instead on 'individual instances' (Committee on Race and Ethnic Disparities, 2021: 9) motivated by racist attitudes. There is a need, and perhaps an opportunity, now to reclaim the term 'hate' as both an inter-subjective lived experience and as a structural, spatial and situated process.

The work of Ahmed (2001: 347–8) critiques the dominance of psychological understandings, conceiving of hate not as residing in, but as distributed across, bodies, 'circulat[ing] between signifiers in relationships of difference and displacement' in what she refers to as 'an affective economy'. In doing so, she argues, we can 'consider how [hate/emotions] work, in concrete and particular ways, to mediate the relationship between the psychic and the social' and by extension the spatial (Ahmed, 2001: 349). Rescaling hate or abjection from the individual to the social and locational context is further examined by Tyler (2013: 23), who places abjection, what she calls 'disgust reactions', within the broader social contexts or 'prevailing belief systems'. As such, abjection is 'always contingent and relational, revealing less about the disgusted individual, or the thing deemed disgusting, than about the culture in which disgust is experienced and performed' (Tyler, 2013: 23). Disabled people, who experience significant and rising levels of hate, have long been seen as objects of disgust or 'scapegoats' (Shakespeare, 1994: 298): 'It is not just that disabled people are different, expensive, inconvenient, or odd: it is that they represent a threat' (see also Donovan et al, 2019, for a parallel account of how gay male and lesbian sexuality have been constructed as threatening to children, family life, norms of morality and, subsequently, society). Sociologists have then explained acts of hate as responses to broader senses of threat or 'strain' (Hall, 2013). Importantly, Hall (2013) cites Perry (2003) in her assertion that such responses to socio-cultural and economic strain are not confined to people in marginal or non-powerful positions. We build on Perry's (2001: 1) account of hate as 'embedded in the structural and cultural context ... a socially situated, dynamic process, involving context and actors, structure and agency', by emphasizing the complexity and multi-scalar nature of acts of hate. James and McBride (Chapter 2), for example, connect characteristics of neoliberal capitalism – what they see as increasing discrimination and exclusion – to the 'systemic violence' experienced by marginalized groups, specifically Gypsies, Travellers and transgender (trans) communities. The distinctive landscape interpretation of hate presented here examines closely the *spaces* (from micro to local and national, in-person and online) and the *relationships* (between potential victims and perpetrators of hate), within which hate is experienced, produced and responded to.

Criminal justice/legal dimensions of hate

Criminal justice has become a central strand of the hate discourse, hence the now almost automatic appending of 'crime' to references to hate. A legislative, police and court response to hate-related harassment and violence is the major tool of public policy towards hate (see Hall, Chapter 12). Hate crime and associated legislation was first explicitly referred to in the US in the 1990s (with the passing of the Hate Crime Statistics Act 1990), although its origins, as discussed previously, were in the 1960s civil rights movement (Hall, 2013). The language of hate was adopted in the UK soon after, in the wake of the murder of the Black teenager Stephen Lawrence by a group of young white men in London in April 1993, for no other reason other than that Stephen was Black. Evidence of racisms and racist violence in UK society became recognized in the 1970s and 1980s (Hall, 2013), and many Black people had been murdered before, but the violent and overtly racist killing of Stephen Lawrence struck a powerful chord. Further, the inadequate and incompetent response of the police to the murder, evidenced in the landmark Macpherson inquiry (1999), was concluded to be a product of 'institutional racism' in the Metropolitan Police force. In this 'watershed moment' (Hall, 2013: 34), hate crime was placed on the political agenda and in the discourses of violent discrimination.

In the years that followed, there were a number of other high-profile murders, attacks and deaths which, given the profile of the Lawrence murder and the Macpherson inquiry, were identified and interpreted through the lens of hate – including the so-called 'Nail Bomber' David Copeland who targeted LGBTQ+ and Black and Asian communities in London (Donovan and Hester, 2011); the murder of Sophie Lancaster in 2007, linked to her 'alternative gothic appearance' (Garland, 2010: 159); and the deaths of Fiona Pilkington and her disabled daughter, Francecca Hardwick, in 2007, after years of harassment (The Guardian, 2009). In the UK, existing legislation addressing discrimination, including the Race Relations Act 1965, the Human Rights Act 1998 and the Disability Discrimination Act 1995, was built upon with subsequent laws to address crimes motivated by prejudice. The Crime and Disorder Act 1998 and the Anti-Terrorism, Crime and Security Act 2001, respectively, recognized racially and religiously aggravated harassment or physical violence, with both laws introducing 'enhanced sentencing' for these offences (Law Commission, 2021: 14). Significantly, the term 'hate' is not used in any of this 'hate crime' legislation, recognition perhaps of its implication of extremism and violence, when the legislation can also be applied to actions further along the continuum, including hostility and verbal abuse.

As hate crime legislation became embedded as the discourse of how to interpret and respond to harassment and violence, other groups who historically had similar experiences were included – often through campaigns – in the legislation (the groups included became known as 'protected characteristics'). The Criminal Justice Act 2003, for example, referred to disability and sexual orientation as potential 'aggravating factors' when deciding on sentencing; the Legal Aid, Sentencing and Immigration Act 2012 extended this to transgender identity in 2012 (Law Commission, 2021: 14). Hate crime legislation has three aspects to it that are unique when compared with other crimes. First, hate incidents encompass any act believed to be motivated by hate regardless of whether the act is, in itself, a crime. The public is encouraged by the police and public campaigns to report any incident they believe is motivated by hate. Through reporting it is hoped that such incidents will be stopped from occurring in future (see

Hall, Chapter 12). Second, for the purposes of reporting, the definition of hate lies with the person reporting – who may or may not be the person victimized – if they believe the incident was motivated by hate. Third, a hate incident and/or crime might be deemed to take place even if the person victimized does not belong to any of the protected characteristics but is perceived to do so by the perpetrator(s). Such conditions for the legislation have meant that there is some confusion about the terms 'hate crime' and 'hate incident', the usefulness of reporting and the complexities involved in establishing a motive of hate.[1]

As discussed earlier, the first piece of UK legislation to specifically refer to hate was introduced in Scotland in 2021: The Hate Crime and Public Order (Scotland) Act. The Act (in response to a review of hate legislation by Lord Bracadale; Scottish Government, 2021) brings together existing legislation related to protected characteristics – disability, 'race', religion, sexual orientation and transgender identity – and adds age, for the first time in the UK. Significantly, gender was discussed as a potential additional protected characteristic but ultimately was not included (a working group was established to further consider the issue; BBC News, 2021e). The debate over including gender as a protected characteristic is insightful for the broader discussion of the adoption and employment of the term 'hate'. In March 2021, the UK government, in response to the murder of Sarah Everard in London, stated that police forces should record violence motivated by a person's sex or gender (BBC, 2021f).[2] The identification of violence against women as a hate crime, equivalent to 'race' or disability, has been viewed by many as a necessary extension of laws to protect women from violence, and also, as an evaluation of the Nottinghamshire Police misogyny crime pilot concluded, to start 'shifting attitudes' (BBC News, 2018; Mullany and Trickett, 2018). However, the evaluation found a still significant level of verbal and physical harassment, and violence, at the end of the pilot period in which misogynist hate crime could be reported, suggesting the potential limited impacts of such a policy on attitudinal change. Vera-Gray and Fileborn (Chapter 3) argue that 'shifting attitudes is much more related to public awareness campaigns about what misogyny is and why it is incompatible with a fair and just society, than about including it as a form of hate crime' (p 50). There are also those who have experienced hate behaviours, but do not recognize them as being motivated by hate. For example, while for some disabled people the term hate powerfully captures the affective experience of being targeted, many others do not recognize the harassment they experience as hate or related to hostility to their disability. Instead, they see a range of factors involved, including intersectional aspects of their identity, social contexts and relationships (Hall, 2019). The language of hate, to whom it might be applied and for what ends, are all very much part of ongoing debates within the field of hate studies.

Landscapes of hate

The concept of 'landscape' has an established history in cultural geography, with a particular concern with representation, and the symbolic and ideological production of such representations (Mitchell, 2000). Mitchell proposes that a reinvigorated focus on landscape must also more explicitly recognize the manner in which physical landscapes of everyday life are produced and destroyed by and, in turn, reproduce, material societal injustices:

> Landscape was more than a way of seeing, more than a representation, more than ideology – though it was very deeply all of these. It was a substantive, material reality, a place lived, a world produced and transformed, a co-mingling of nature and society that is struggled over and in. (Mitchell, 2003: 792)

Landscape, then, draws our attention not only to the material world around us and our relationships with it, in a deeply uneven and unequal social world, but also to the ways in which those worlds are seen, read and used. We therefore refer to landscapes of hate (in the plural) as simultaneously different ways of seeing, identifying and employing hate as embedded within spaces of everyday life – and to offer insights into the complex and circulating 'assemblage' of people, places, attitudes, ideologies, structures, materialities and emotions, that constitute how hate is produced, felt and responded to. Everyday landscapes are sensed through emotions of fear and safety (see Durey et al, Chapter 5), imagined through processes of historical policy-led stigmatization (see Butler-Warke, Chapter 4) and materialize through tangible and meaning-laden physical spaces of urban life (see Clayton et al, Chapter 6; and Wilkin, Chapter 8) in ways that can reproduce but also challenge harmful societal divisions. These elements may be familiar features of lived and represented landscapes or may be more hidden and need to be exposed through careful scholarly work.

In this collection, we adopt the term 'landscapes' to critically reflect on the concept of hate and to move beyond criminological and victimology perspectives on the incidence of hate and the experiences of victims (though see chapters by Wilkin, Chapter 8; Daly and Smith, Chapter 7; Durey et al, Chapter 5; James and McBride, Chapter 2; Bowler and Razak, Chapter 11; and Goerisch, Chapter 9, whose work centres the experiences of those victimized by hate). There has been little consideration of the immediate and broader contexts and spaces within which incidents and experiences of hate occur, and the role that these contexts and spaces play in the production and experience of these incidents. The contexts include the prevailing discriminatory social attitudes of the time related to government policy and deeper-seated assumptions about the right of presence and behavioural norms, for example, related to 'race', disability and sexuality. There has always been a powerful spatial aspect to these attitudes – about people, groups and behaviours deemed to being 'out of place' and often in fear in particular socio-spatial environments (for example, Valentine, 1989; Pain, 1997) – and many of the (explanations for) hateful responses have had a spatial aspect, including the defence of territory (Perry, 2001; Hall, 2013). The spatial has always been present, but never fully and properly engaged with, in hate studies, as an active agent in the production and experience of hate.

The concept of landscapes allows us to carefully consider space in relation to hate, not only as the context within which negative social attitudes and actions occur, but also as constitutive of these social attitudes and relations. It also allows us to think about the ways in which processes, practices and experiences of hate are reproduced through particular spatial configurations and are also always situated within wide-reaching imaginaries, relations and networks. Milligan and Wiles (2010: 736) use the notion of landscapes to describe the complex geography of care to 'teas[e] out the interplay between those socio-economic, structural, and temporal processes that shape the experiences and practices of care at various spatial sites and scales, from the personal and private through to public settings, and from local to regional and national levels, and beyond'. Hence, landscapes are not simply backdrops, but are 'both product and productive of social and political-institutional arrangements' and in sum refer to 'the complex embodied and organizational spatialities that emerge from and through the relationships of [care]' (Milligan and Wiles, 2010: 740).

Flint (2004) and Iganski (2008) provide two contrasting perspectives on the landscapes of ('race') hate, both addressing the central role of space in the production, expression and experience of hostility. Flint (2004) focuses his examination on the maintenance of 'white privilege' in the US through explicit and overt acts of hate committed by those adopting or associated with far-right ideologies in their 'defence of territory', from harassment and even murder, to exclusionary housing policies. In his book's introduction, Flint (2004: 2) 'does not deny the damage inflicted by everyday intolerance and discrimination', but his (and many of the contributors to his collection) focus is on those he describes as 'defenders of whiteness' and the manner in which their ideologies and actions 'facilitate ... the norms of our society'. Iganski (2008) focuses on the 'everyday intolerance' noted previously, examining the places and environments within which people, and in particular those from different ethnic minority groups, encounter each other in streets and neighbourhoods. In a study of London, UK, Iganski (2008) demonstrates that it is the nature and dynamics of these encounters – who, how many, when and where – that shape the likelihood and incidence of hate. It is not inevitable – despite the evidence from hate crime reporting of 'hotspots' or clusters – that hate will occur, just that certain combinations of people, place, time and contexts (material and representational) create the potential for acts of hostility (see Hall, 2019: 254).

Landscapes is a valuable concept too because of its acknowledgment of the inherent and ongoing transformation of the representational and material elements, as landscapes are reshaped, remade and reinterpreted by those who occupy them. Mitchell's (2003) coda in the quote cited earlier refers to 'struggle'. Much of the hate (crime) literature centres on the harassment and violence experienced, with little on how individuals and communities respond to and 'struggle' over these incidents and the wider contexts that shape them. Hall and Bates (2019) refer to both hate and 'belonging' in the title of their article, examining how people with learning disabilities, in response to their experiences of fear and uncertainty in spaces of the city, navigate and negotiate their way through and around streets and public spaces to build alternative, positive landscapes of belonging (see also Clayton et al, Chapter 6). There is hope that hate is not inevitable – it may be expected, it may be embedded, but it does not mean it cannot be effectively challenged, navigated or prevented. Daly and Smith (Chapter 7) identify hate as an issue of rights: 'It is about freedoms and the ability to take up space' (p 131). Struggles over landscapes – contesting, re-imagining and re-materializing spaces, identities and representations – are very much part of this assertion of rights in the context of hate. It is a refusal to be written out of and/or be rendered invisible in landscapes, even when it can feel that those landscapes were never constructed with them in mind as equal citizens.

We therefore look to acknowledge both those aspects of everyday life that are defined by hate (in its immediate embodied, material, structural and institutional forms), and the potential to resist, work against and go beyond hate (however temporary or permanent this may be). James and McBride (2022 and Chapter 2) argue for a positive shift in emphasis to consider what people subjected to hostility need to thrive, which they identify as 'a positive discourse of recognition' that centres on people's need for 'respect, esteem and love in order to flourish' (James and McBride, 2022: 104). Many of the authors in this collection demonstrate the complexities and perhaps impossibilities of isolating out hate and hostility from other aspects, experiences and emotions of everyday life that are in various ways exclusionary, yet are also the basis for solidarity and progress (see Bowler and Razak, Chapter 11). Fear, hostility, and violence speak not only to an acceptance of the complexities of social harm, and the continuum of experiences of violence, but also the co-existence with other affective states and experiences, including 'love' (James and McBride, 2022); and, for example, the fun and excitement of being at university, despite 'atmospheres' that convey a contingent sense of danger (Durey et al, Chapter 5).

We become accustomed to the everyday contexts we live in and know, and arguably we therefore get used to the hate that is manifest, either not seeing it or not being surprised when it emerges. The notion of landscape encourages us to examine more closely the stretched fabrics – social, political, cultural, institutional – of the spaces we inhabit, how they shape the lives of individuals and communities, and what can be done to not simply suppress or push hate back but properly recognize the wider and deeper violent contexts and relations it is embedded in and the circumstances and moments within which it emerges.

Organization of the collection

Importantly, the book is not organized as many texts on hate crime are, in sections examining the different 'protected characteristics'; indeed, as Hopkins draws out in the Afterword (Chapter 13), we acknowledge the intersectionalities of everyday experiences of hate. Instead, the chapters address different aspects of landscapes of hate. The first three chapters examine and critique the concept of 'hate' (James and McBride; Vera-Gray and Fileborn; Butler-Warke), including a critical hate studies approach, the potential extension of hate crime legislation to cover misogyny and the representational sense of hate as applied to a specific place. The following five chapters (Durey et al; Clayton et al; Daly and Smith; Wilkin; Goerisch) explore experiences of hate in a range of contexts and everyday spaces, including university campuses, public transport, leisure spaces, places of religious worship and neighbourhoods. The final three chapters (Browne and Nash; Bowler and Razak; Hall) consider different responses to hate, from attempts to challenge its meaning and usage, to emphasizing agency over victimization and to rethinking hate crime policy and practice. While the genesis of the book was a session at the Royal Geographical Society (with the Institute of British Geographers) Annual Conference 2018, the authors are not all geographers, a reflection of a broader emerging appreciation of the potential of applying a spatial lens to the study of hate.

The perspectives and foci of the authors are diverse. It should be noted that not all authors wholly align with or explicitly emphasize the perspective we outline in this introductory chapter. However they all, in different ways, connect with a geographically sensitive take on hate that speaks in different ways to a set of themes: first, the spatial and structural conditions (at a range of scales) under which and through which hate is experienced, which is broader than the interpersonal; second, the limitations of the criminal justice system as a response to the complexity and contextualized nature of hate; third, an appreciation of the diversity of experiences of hate and the spectrum of harm from extreme physically violent acts to everyday hostility; fourth, and relatedly, the fact that there is a continuum both of harm and motivations for hate requires a continuum of responses from criminal justice to community and individual interventions; and fifth, many of the chapters emphasize agency, or at least a recognition of how those victimized actively deal with and respond to or navigate hate. Importantly, all of the authors go further than describing experiences of hate – all are searching for answers. For example, the chapters in the final part of the collection speak to this need to respond and to do better, in ways which look beyond the criminal justice system, and harness the needs and will of those communities subjected to hate and wider spectrums of harm and violence.

Considering and critiquing hate

Zoë James and Katie McBride (Chapter 2) use a critical hate studies perspective to emphasize the 'harms' of hate. Using evidence from case-studies of Gypsies and Travellers, and trans people, they examine how although people negotiate harassment in social spaces in a bid to avoid harm, they continue to experience ontological insecurity, such is the pervasiveness of neoliberalist socio-cultural and policy norms. In their chapter, Fiona Vera-Gray and Bianca Fileborn (Chapter 3) critique the move towards including gender or misogyny in hate crime legislation and practice. They argue that classifying the harassment and violence that women and girls experience as hate distracts attention from the multiple and complex experiences of hostility and exclusion women experience in society. In the final chapter in this section, Alice Butler-Warke (Chapter 4) considers how a place is constructed and represented through a lens of hate and its longitudinal impacts for residents. Toxteth in Liverpool, England, is hated through its labelling and stigmatization as a problematic 'inner city' in the political and media discourses of the 1980s.

Experiences of hate

In their chapter, Matthew Durey, Nicola Roberts and Catherine Donovan (Chapter 5) use the notion of 'atmosphere' to explore how women recognize, experience and negotiate the hostile yet 'ambivalent' and potentially shifting emotional and material environment of university life. They further argue that these atmospheres are shaped by broader processes of neoliberalism. John Clayton, Catherine Donovan and Stephen J. Macdonald (Chapter 6), consider the socio-materiality of space in producing hate directed at minoritized communities, through the material and symbolic association of particular sites with these groups (using as examples the mosque, the gay scene, and the home/neighbourhood), and how use of these physical locations render these groups 'hyper visible'. The following two chapters both address the experiences of hate for disabled people and the role of specific spatial contexts. Ellen Daly and Olivia Smith (Chapter 7) examine the 'disablist' harassment and violence that disabled people experience, particularly the 'low-level' fear that forces people to navigate and avoid certain spaces and sites. They draw on and apply feminist theoretical ideas from the field of 'street harassment' to make sense of disablist violence and harassment but also to tender suggestions for resistance. In his chapter, David Wilkin (Chapter 8) focuses on hostility and experiences of hate for disabled people on public transport and, in particular, buses. In theory such spaces would seem to provide opportunities for contesting isolation through mobility and social participation, but the chapter demonstrates how these spaces are commonly experienced as sites of verbal abuse and physical harassment.

Responding to hate

One practice-based response to incidents or fear of hate is to designate 'safe spaces' for people from affected groups to claim as their own. Denise Goerisch (Chapter 9) discusses a study of a population of ethnic minority students at a university in the US Midwest, and the role of safe spaces in how they navigate their presence within a Predominantly White Institution. Another response to hate has been to challenge the application of the term to certain discriminatory views, as part of a broader contestation of equality policy and legislation. Kath Browne and Catherine Jean Nash (Chapter 10) cite evidence from Ireland to examine how 'heteroactivists' try to challenge references to hate in accounts of their activities by casting it as supporting moral values and a sign of their faith-inspired love. In their chapter, Rick Bowler and Amina Razak (Chapter 11) focus on the range of everyday encounters of racism that people from racialized communities experience, its impact and the opportunities to challenge this hostility. The authors, from a community and youth-work perspective, reflect on their own experiences of racism to illustrate how these lived experiences shape and are shaped by their research. In the final chapter in this section, Edward Hall (Chapter 12) adopts a socio-ecological model to both understand the production of hate and, further, to develop a framework for not only better responding to incidents of hate but also by seeing hate as a public health issue and so shift policy attention to prevention.

In the Afterword (Chapter 13), Peter Hopkins provides a reflection on the collection and draws out three key themes from the chapters which he sees as essential to the study of landscapes of hate: intersectionality, relationality and emotions.

Conclusion

We hope this is a timely and thought-provoking collection, gathering authors from different disciplines, covering diverse aspects of this critical topic, and together tracing the spaces and relations of, and responses to, landscapes of hate. We are grateful for all of the authors' contributions, and hope this collection drives forward debate and change to critique and address hate, within the UK and beyond.

Notes

[1] A hate incident is 'an incident that is perceived by the victim or any other person to be motivated by hostility or prejudice based on a person's "race", religion, sexual orientation, disability or transgender status'. A hate crime is a 'criminal offence that is perceived by the victim or any other person to be motivated by a hostility or prejudice based on the same characteristics'. A Court of Appeal judgement in 2021 has led to revised guidelines to police officers (in England and Wales) that state that while 'responses to allegations of hate crime are unaffected', for 'allegations of hate incidents, police need to apply their judgement in establishing whether there is hostility towards a protected characteristic group' in context of not 'infring[ing] freedom of expression' (College of Policing, 2021).

[2] The UK Law Commission has recently undertaken a review of hate crime legislation (2021), which recommended that 'sex or gender should not be added as a protected characteristic for the purposes of aggravated offences and enhanced sentencing' (204) and 'government undertake a review of the need for a specific offence of public sexual harassment, and what form any such offence should take' (208).

References

Ahmed, S. (2001) 'The "organisation of hate"', *Law and Critique*, 12: 345–65.

Allen, G. and Zayed Y. (2021) Hate Crime Statistics, Commons Library Research Briefing, Number 8357, 26 November 2021.

BBC News (2018) 'Misogyny hate crime in Nottinghamshire gives "shocking" results', Available from: https://www.bbc.co.uk/news/uk-engl and-nottinghamshire-44740362 [Accessed 25 February 2022].

BBC News (2021a) 'Bukayo Saka "knew instantly of hate" he would receive after England defeat', Available from: https://www.bbc.co.uk/sport/footb all/57855251 [Accessed 23 August 2021].

BBC News (2021b) 'Online racists face football ban of up to 10 years, vows Boris Johnson', Available from: https://www.bbc.co.uk/news/uk-polit ics-57837003 [Accessed 24 August 2021].

BBC News (2021c) 'Euro 2020 racist abuse: 11 people arrested', Available from: https://www.bbc.co.uk/news/uk-58094408 [Accessed 21 February 2022].

BBC News (2021d) 'England's Tyrone Mings criticises Patel over racism response', Available from: https://www.bbc.co.uk/news/uk-politics-57778 668 [Accessed 24 August 2021].

BBC News (2021e) 'MSPs approve Scotland's controversial hate crime law', Available from: https://www.bbc.co.uk/news/uk-scotland-scotland-politics-56364821 [Accessed 8 July 2022].

BBC News (2021f) 'Police to record crimes motivated by sex or gender on "experimental basis"', Available from: https://www.bbc.co.uk/news/ uk-politics-56435550 [Accessed 24 August 2021].

BBC News (2022) 'LGBT tolerance "going backwards" as hate crimes up', Available from: https://www.bbc.co.uk/news/uk-wales-60257602 [Accessed 25 February 2022].

BBC Sport (2021) 'Racist abuse of England players Marcus Rashford, Jadon Sancho and Bukayo Saka "unforgivable"', Available from: https://www.bbc.co.uk/sport/football/57800431 [Accessed 24 August 2021].

Beckett, A. (2018) 'The death of consensus: how conflict came back to politics', Available from: https://www.theguardian.com/politics/2018/sep/20/the-death-of-consensus-how-conflict-came-back-to-politics [Accessed 23 February 2022].

Burch, L. (2018) '"You are a parasite on the productive classes": online disablist hate speech in austere times', *Disability & Society*, 33(3): 392–415.

Chakraborti, N. (2010) 'Future developments for hate crime thinking: who, what and why?', in Chakraborti, N. (ed) *Hate Crime: Concepts, Policy and Future Directions*, Cullompton, UK: Willan Publishing, pp 1–16.

Chakraborti, N. and Garland, J. (2015) *Hate Crime: Impact, Causes and Responses*, London: Sage.

Chakraborti, N., Hardy, S.J. and Evans, H. (2014) *The Harms of Hate*, Leicester: Centre for Hate Studies.

Clayton, J., Donovan, C. and Macdonald, S. (2016) 'A critical portrait of hate crime/incident reporting in North East England: the value of statistical data and the politics of recording in an age of austerity', *Geoforum*, 75: 64–74.

Colliver, B. (2021) *Re-imagining Hate Crime*, London: Palgrave Macmillan.

College of Policing (2021) 'Court of Appeal hate crime guidance ruling', Available from: https://www.college.police.uk/article/court-appeal-hate-crime-guidance-ruling [Accessed 25 February 2022].

Committee on Race and Ethnic Disparities (2021) *Commission on Race and Ethnic Disparities: The Report*, London: Committee on Race and Ethnic Disparities.

Donovan, C. and Hester, M. (2011) 'Seeking help from the enemy: help-seeking strategies of those in same-sex relationships who have experienced domestic abuse', *Child and Family Law Quarterly*, 23(1): 26–40.

Donovan, C., Clayton, J. and Macdonald, S. (2019) 'New directions in hate reporting research: agency, heterogeneity and relationality', *Sociological Research Online*, 24(2): 185–202.

Duffy, B., Hewlett, K.A., McCrae, J. and Hall, J. (2019) *Divided Britain? Polarisation and Fragmentation Trends in the UK*, Available from: www.kcl.ac.uk/policy-institute/assets/divided-britain.pdf [Accessed 25 February 2022].

Edwards, C. and Maxwell, N. (2021) 'Disability, hostility and everyday geographies of un/safety', *Social & Cultural Geography*, DOI: 10.1080/14649365.2021.1950823

European Commission Against Racism and Intolerance (2020) *Annual Report on ECRI's Activities*, Strasbourg: ECRI.

Flint, C. (2004) *Spaces of Hate: Geographies of Discrimination and Intolerance in the US*, London: Routledge.

Garland, J. (2010) '"It's a mosher just been banged for no reason": assessing targeted violence against goths and the parameters of hate crime', *International Review of Victimology*, 17(2): 159–77.

Gerstenfield, P. (2013) *Hate Crimes: Causes, Controls and Controversies*, London: Sage.

Guardian, The (2009) 'Incident diary reveals ordeal of mother who killed herself and daughter', Available from: https://www.theguardian.com/uk/2009/sep/24/fiona-pilkington-incident-diary [Accessed 25 February 2022].

Guardian, The (2021) 'Hate crimes in US rise to highest level in 12 years, says FBI report', Available from: https://www.theguardian.com/us-news/2021/aug/31/us-hate-crimes-2020-fbi-report [Accessed 31 August 2021].

Guardian, The (2022) 'Government strategy sidesteps Sewell race report's most criticised conclusions', Available from: https://www.theguardian.com/world/2022/mar/16/ministers-government-strategy-sewell-race-report [Accessed 6 June 2022].

Hall, E. (2019) 'A critical geography of disability hate crime', *Area*, 51(2): 249–56.

Hall, E. and Bates, E. (2019) 'Hatescape? A relational geography of disability hate crime, exclusion and belonging in the city', *Geoforum*, 101: 100–10.

Hall, N. (2013) *Hate Crime*, London: Routledge.

Hardy, S.J. (2017) *Everyday Multiculturalism and Hidden Hate*, Basingstoke: Palgrave Macmillan.

Hardy, S.J. and Chakraborti, N. (2020) *Blood, Threat and Fears: The Hidden Worlds of Hate Crime Victims*, London: Palgrave Macmillan.

Haslam, N. and Murphy, S. (2020) 'Hate, dehumanization, and "hate"', in R.J. Sternberg (ed) *Perspectives on Hate: How I Originates, Develops, Manifests, and Spreads*, Washington, DC: American Psychological Association, pp 27–41.

Healy, J. (2020) '"It spreads like a creeping disease": experiences of victims of disability hate crimes in austerity Britain', *Disability & Society*, 35(2): 176–200.

Hollomotz, A. (2013) 'Disability and the continuum of violence', in A. Roulstone and H. Mason-Bish (eds) *Disability, Hate Crime and Violence*, London: Routledge, pp 52–63.

Home Office (2016) *Action Against Hate: The UK Government's Plan for Tackling Hate Crime*, London: Home Office.

Home Office (2020) *Hate Crime, England and Wales, 2019 to 2020*, London: Home Office.

Hopkins, P. (2016) 'Gendering Islamophobia, racism and white supremacy: gendered violence against those who look Muslim', *Dialogues in Human Geography*, 6(2): 186–89.

Iganski, P. (2008) *Hate Crime and the City*, Bristol: Policy Press.

Jacobs, J. and Potter, K. (1998) *Hate Crimes: Criminal Law and Identity Politics*, New York: Oxford University Press.

James, Z. and McBride, K. (2022) 'Critical hate studies: a new perspective', *International Review of Victimology*, 28(1): 92–108.

Kelly, L. (1988) *Surviving Sexual Violence*, Cambridge: Polity.

Law Commission (2021) *Hate Crime: Final Report*, London: Law Commission.

Legg, S. and Nottingham Citizens (2021) '"No place for hate": community-led research and the geographies of Nottingham citizens' hate crime commission', *Social & Cultural Geography*, 22(8): 1164–86.

Listerborn, C. (2014) 'Geographies of the veil: violent encounters in urban public spaces in Malmö', *Social & Cultural Geography*, 16(1): 95–115.

Luger, J. (2022) 'Celebrations, exaltations and alpha lands: everyday geographies of the far-right', *Political Geography*, 96, DOI:10.1016/j.polgeo.2022.102604

Macpherson, W. (1999) *The Stephen Lawrence Inquiry: Report of an Inquiry*, London: The Stationary Office.

Milligan, C. and Wiles, J. (2010) 'Landscapes of care', *Progress in Human Geography*, 34(6): 736–54.

Mitchell, D. (2000) *Cultural Geography: A Critical Introduction*, Malden, MA: Blackwell.

Mitchell, D. (2003) 'Cultural landscapes: just landscapes or landscapes of justice', *Progress in Human Geography*, 27(6): 787–96.

Mullany, L. and Trickett, L. (2018) *Misogyny Hate Crime Evaluation Report*, Nottingham, UK: University of Nottingham and Nottingham Trent University.

National Police Chief's Council (NPCC) (2016) 'Hate crime undermines the diversity and tolerance we should instead be celebrating', Available from: http://news.npcc.police.uk/releases/hate-crime-undermines-the-diversity-and-tolerance-we-should-instead-be-celebrating-1 [Accessed 28 February 2017].

Pain, R. (1997) 'Social geographies of women's fear of crime', *Transactions of the Institute of British Geographers*, 22(2): 231–44.

Perry, B. (2001) *In the Name of Hate*, New York: Routledge.

Perry, B. (2003) 'Anti-Muslim retaliatory action following the 9/11 terrorist attacks', in B. Perry (ed) *Hate and Bias Crime: A Reader*, London: Routledge, pp 183–202.

Power, A. and Bartlett, R. (2018) '"I shouldn't be living there because I am a sponger": negotiating everyday geographies by people with learning disabilities', *Disability & Society* 33(4): 562–78.

Roulstone, A. and Mason-Bish, H. (eds) (2013) *Disability, Hate Crime and Violence*, Routledge: London.

Scottish Government (2021) *Independent Review of Hate Crime Legislation in Scotland: Final Report*, Edinburgh: Scottish Government.

Shakespeare, T. (1994) 'Cultural representation of disabled people: dustbins for disavowal?', *Disability & Society*, 9(3): 283–99.

Sherry, M. (2011) *Disability Hate Crimes: Does Anyone Really Hate Disabled People?*, Farnham: Ashgate.

Sternberg, R. (ed) (2020) *Perspectives on Hate: How It Originates, Develops, Manifests, and Spreads*, Washington, DC: American Psychological Association.

Tyler, I. (2013) *Revolting Subjects: Social Abjection and Resistance in Neoliberal Britain*, London: Bloomsbury.

Valentine, G. (1989) 'The geography of women's fear', *Area*, 21(4): 385–390.

Webber, F. (2019) 'On the creation of the UK's "hostile environment"', *Race and Class*, 60(4): 76–87.

2

Examining the Contours of Hate: A Critical Hate Studies Analysis

Zoë James and Katie McBride

Introduction

In order to appreciate the landscape of hate in contemporary late modern society, this chapter argues that a theoretically critical approach is required that specifically considers how neoliberal capitalist space frames and articulates how we live, how our structures of governance function and how our everyday lived experiences are played out. It is only from taking this broad view that we can really see the multiple and complex harms of hate that manifest as significant crimes, incidents, speech and micro-aggressions against people on the basis of their identity or perceptions thereof. Hate studies have increasingly noted the breadth of hateful experiences people have in society (Iganski, 2008), and hate agendas have oriented around identifying who is victimized, how mechanisms can be devised to facilitate reporting of such behaviours, prevention measures identified and punishment for offenders delivered (Chakraborti and Garland, 2015). However, despite collegiate and extensive work in this area, a tension within hate studies has remained wherein explanations for hate crimes, incidents and speech are considered apart from explanations for micro-aggressions in everyday life (see, for example, Iganski, 2008; Walters, 2011). By taking a critical hate studies (James and McBride, 2022) approach to bias-motivated behaviours this chapter redresses that tension through an analysis of hate that acknowledges how neoliberal capitalist space galvanizes hate.

Theorists (Harvey, 2005; Davies, 2017) have identified the growth of neoliberal capitalism within burgeoning and established democracies in the post-Second World War era. The political, economic and social norms of neoliberal capitalism are typified by allegiance to market principles, individualism and competition within all aspects of social life. As such, there has been a shift away from bounded ideas of, and aspirations for, community and equality, towards communitarian responsibilization (Hughes, 2007) that has, in turn, augmented social hierarchies. Within this environment, individuals are answerable for their own actions, strengths, weaknesses and experiences. As neoliberal capitalism has taken hold as a global political project, so the power of nation states has diminished and international businesses have attained primacy in dictating and determining our lived experience as individual consumers, rather than as communal citizens. The logic of neoliberal capitalism implies a trickle-down effect of wealth as financial barriers to growth and legitimacy have been diminished and state provision of resources have retracted. In real terms, however, this has meant an increasing divide between those with resources and/or access to them and those without (Greitemeyer and Sagioglou, 2017).

This chapter will initially identify the ways in which a critical hate studies approach to understanding hate in contemporary society explains how hate manifests within the neoliberal capitalist landscape in multiple ways. In order to do so it proposes that hate can be best understood through an analysis of hate harms, rather than within the confines of hate crimes. Taking a social harm approach to hate allows the authors to traverse the multiple and complex manifestations of hate that impact all aspects of peoples' lives: physically, socially, psychologically and interpersonally. The critical hate studies perspective presents a psycho-social approach to subjectivity that acknowledges how our personal and social identities (Moran, 2015) are effected by neoliberal capitalist norms. Further, this approach applies its tenets to hate perpetration as well as hate victimization, allowing analysis that acknowledges the interplay between identity and social structure in a way that recognizes the intersectional nature of experience and thus how hate can occur within multiple settings, spaces and contexts. It is worth noting here, however, that a critical hate studies approach particularly focuses on the spaces of society where hate behaviours are felt most: within the precariat (Standing, 2014) wherein people's lives are defined by precarity and insecurity. It is within this space that largely non-white, non-heterosexual, non-cis-gender, disabled, non-Christian, poorer people have been pushed according to the biologically determinist organizing principles of colonial capitalism and wherein it serves neoliberal capitalism's interests for the majority of those people to remain.

Having established the broad parameters of the critical hate studies perspective the chapter will then move on to elaborate on the harms of hate experienced by two specific sets of peoples, using evidence gathered by the authors' research. By providing substantive examples of the hate harms experienced by Gypsies and Travellers and transgender people, the chapter is able to elucidate the impacts of hate in contemporary society on marginalized peoples. Further, by utilizing an analytic framework that specifically explores how hate harms constitute a failure of recognition of the human need to flourish (Yar, 2012) the chapter is able to propose a positive discourse for change.

Critical hate studies

A critical hate studies approach acknowledges the hate harms that marginalized communities' experience that are constituted by subjective, systemic and symbolic violence (Žižek, 2008). Traditionally hate studies has focused its attention on the spaces and places in which subjective violence occurs in order to map, record and respond (Iganski, 2008) to the hate crimes and incidents that we can easily see in relation to ourselves. Looking at distinct places of hatefulness associated with communities (Chakraborti and Garland, 2015) has been important in defining bias-motivated behaviours in the contemporary legal and policy environment. Further, research has evidenced the 'messiness' of hateful interactions that occur within localized neighbourhoods and the role of restorative justice as an effective tool for resolution (Walters, 2014). Within critical hate studies there is also consideration of the harms of hate that occur as systemic violence that is inherent within processes and structures of governance: discrimination, social and economic exclusion, and criminalization that are partially recognized by policy and practice but often negated. In addition, the critical hate studies perspective allows for broader awareness of hate harms that are symbolically violent. Late modern neoliberal capitalism frames the lived experience through its 'language and forms' (Žižek 2008: 1). Within this context, neoliberal capitalist norms augment and facilitate systemic hate harms. As noted elsewhere, 'In order to represent the cyclic continuum of harm ... it is necessary to discuss subjective violence, but we should not be distracted by it as it is representative of systemic violence that is articulated via symbolic violence' (James, 2020: 40).

Having established that critical hate studies conceives harm as occurring within spaces of interaction, governance and discourse, it is then possible to see that the perspective is able to theorize on the genesis, development and scope of hate behaviours that range from serious crimes to micro-aggressions (Sue, 2010). In order to extrapolate it is necessary to identify two specific underlying approaches that critical hate studies uses, in order to carry out analysis of the harms of hate. The first of these, as identified earlier, is acknowledgement of the role of neoliberal capitalism in informing all aspects of power, place and space in western democratic societies (Brown, 2015), as well as increasingly those outside the realms of 'democracy'. The structures of colonial power and industrialization that have oriented social life according to class, gender, race and sexuality over centuries have been eroded by neoliberal capitalism and/or co-opted to its needs (McBride, 2019). Thus, white straight men have retained their primacy in contemporary society, but only so long as the needs of capital are met through commitment to neoliberal norms, so a Black woman can become vice-president of the US. It is important to note here that critical hate studies explicitly acknowledges the harms of classism, homophobia, misogyny and racism, and does not suggest that structures of class, gender, race and sexuality have disappeared within neoliberal capitalism. Rather, we would argue that, to use neoliberal capitalist language, they are under new management.

The second approach used by critical hate studies explains how subjectivity develops within neoliberal capitalist society. Using a transcendental materialist (Žižek, 2006; developed by Johnston, 2008) approach to human psychology, based on the work of Lacan (1977), we argue that it is possible to appreciate how the human subject is hateful on the basis of the failure of neoliberal capitalism to provide them with any sort of symbolic order in their lives that might constitute a cohesive moral code. As the human subject develops as a social being, so we are defined and define ourselves according to the interactions we have with others. Neoliberal capitalism relies on flexibility and fluidity of individuals to meet the needs of markets and thus the developing human psyche has little to order its complex innate and experiential emotions and desires within. Whichever way we may critique other systems of governance (that are entirely valid) the structures provided by them gave the human psyche a mechanism through which to make sense of our lives. Neoliberalism does not require people to have a sense of place, space or meaning; it requires a flexible workforce for the accumulation of capital. However, the sense of lack engendered within people in this environment means that they are searching for fulfilment that is expected to be met by consumerism, which serves to pacify and mollify the ontological insecurity of everyday life (Raymen, 2019). The capacity of consumerism to fill the sense of lack within the self is limited by its requirement for flexibility, for individuals to serve their own needs rather than those that are shared in communal space. The rampant individualism of neoliberal capitalism drives people apart, rather than together, as each person strives to reach the top of a hierarchy of consumption that places people in competition with each other. But, of course, consumerism functions to assure individual appetites are never fully met, and thus the desire for consumption is sustained (Bauman, 2005). The human psyche, which relies on shared learning to develop a cohesive appreciation of personal and social identity (Moran, 2015), is thus unfulfilled and left searching for ways to assuage the angst of something lacking in life. The consequences of living within neoliberal capitalist norms that generate hateful subjectivities are twofold; as we shall go on to demonstrate.

As discussed previously, hate scholars have acknowledged the breadth of hateful experiences in everyday life. Indeed, the normalcy of hate victimization has caused scholars to question the capacity of critical criminological approaches to explain why hate happens (Iganski, 2008; Walters, 2011). The rationale for the critique of critical approaches to hate is that microaggressions, hate speech and hate incidents occur as such everyday occurrences that they cannot be fully explained by existing critical theory that argues that hate emanates from people upholding structural norms that challenges those that 'do difference' (Perry, 2001). We would suggest, however, that by acknowledging the role of neoliberal capitalist governance in generating a hyper-competitive, individualist society, we are able to see how such apparently banal hateful behaviours manifest. The symbolic violence (Žižek, 2008) of neoliberal capitalism's discourse imbues interpersonal relationships with antipathy: hatefulness of the other – competition within and between peoples is inherent to neoliberal capitalism's success and the human psyche has no effective moral code upon which to draw in contemporary space to disengage from or resist such forces. Again, as discussed previously, the structural pre-conditions of neoliberal capitalism have placed those living within the precariat at the front of the firing line of hate, but no one is immune to its vagaries.

For some people the sense of lack in their everyday lives leads them to search out a moral code to ameliorate their cognitive discord. In such cases, people alight on doctrine that provides them with a symbolic order that appeases their sense of lack and provides the communal learning and engagement they naturally desire (James, 2020). Such doctrines that embrace colonial norms negate the responsibilizing discourse of neoliberal capitalism by identifying scapegoats for contemporary insecurities (Winlow et al, 2017). Therefore, hate of others is rationalized within the psyche as a reasonable response to the ontological insecurity of everyday life. Hate studies has focused its attention on extreme forms of hate enacted by individuals and groups such as the alt-right (Scrivens and Perry, 2017). We would argue that such work is essential to challenging hate and hateful discourse, but to negate the role of neoliberal capitalism in framing the psychological need for such dogma is to fail to acknowledge the enormity of the challenge before us. Indeed, dogma comes in many forms and it is arguable that the polarizing capacity of doctrine (of all types) in late modernity augments the projection of hate on to others outside the parameters of any aligned doctrine. This results in a failure of recognition of people's capacity to flourish as social beings as will be elaborated in due course.

Thus, the consequences of living within neoliberal capitalism are significant as despite the erosion of aspects of colonial industrialism and some of the lessons learned through reflection on oppression, that oppression continues and is augmented as hateful subjectivities produce hateful behaviours that are part of everyday survival in a hyper-competitive individualist space, whether they manifest as microaggressions, hate incidents or crimes, and whether they are rationalized as expressions of alignment to a particular dogma or simply an expression of neoliberal capitalist norms. We will now go on to outline the research drawn on to illuminate the harms of hate in late modernity.

Methodology

This chapter draws on evidence gathered as part of two distinct research projects that identified common facets of hate harms. The first was a small study of Gypsies' and Travellers' experiences of hate in the South West of England in 2015 that was part of a wider examination of the accommodation needs of Gypsies and Travellers (Southern et al, 2015; James and Southern, 2019). Supported and funded by a local authority, the researcher attained permission to append a series of qualitative and quantitative questions on hate crimes, incidents and wider harms to the accommodation needs assessment survey in the research area. The research asked Gypsies and Travellers whether and how hate had manifested in their lived experiences and on associated levels of reporting said experiences. As such, it was possible to quantify a range of data and open questions provided qualitative data. In total 79 people responded to the hate crime survey. Given there is no appropriate sampling frame for Gypsy and Traveller populations, the survey was carried out by accessing as many Gypsies and Travellers as possible known to the research team and the third sector Gypsy and Traveller support organization that carried out the research fieldwork. In addition, to follow up on issues raised by the survey, three in-depth interviews with Gypsies and Travellers were completed. This chapter largely draws on the qualitative data from that research as well as a review of the literature in Gypsy and Traveller studies.

The second study referred to here was completed as doctoral research that explored harms experienced by transgender individuals (McBride, 2019). This extensive qualitative research used an in-depth ethnographic method to carry out interviews with trans people over a period of approximately two years. The sample of interviewees gathered across England and Wales used snowball sampling within which people self-identified as within the broad umbrella of transgender peoples. The research asked participants about their lived experience of identity and harm across their life-course. The resultant multiple interviews with 12 participants produced qualitative data as thick descriptions (Ponterotto, 2006), which were supplemented by participatory life-story narratives (Baum et al, 2006; Singh et al, 2013). This data is drawn on here alongside a reading of the literature in trans studies (Feinberg, 1996; Wilchins, 1997; Whittle, 2002). Each of the studies discussed here attained full ethical approval from the University of Plymouth ethics committee for empirical research.

Spaces and places of hate harms

Traditionally hate studies have considered space and place in terms of mapping hate crimes and incidents (Iganski, 2008), and understanding places of hatefulness associated with communities (Chakraborti and Garland,

2015). Further, research has evidenced the role of neighbour engagement in hate behaviours and effective resolutions (Walters, 2014). Influenced by the literature on mobilities in human geography (Merriman, 2015), this chapter proposes that space and place are important to marginalized communities, whose use of place is often transitory. Spaces are used via a fluid consideration of safety and community (Halfacree, 1996) in the formation of the self through processes of recognition.

Having established previously that a critical hate studies approach allows us to explore the harms of hate in late modernity through an appreciation of the role of neoliberal capitalism as creating the conditions within which hate thrives, the chapter will move on to elucidate those harms using the theory of recognition (Yar, 2001a, 2012; based on Honneth, 1996). The theory of recognition posits that for humans to flourish they must achieve recognition in society within three realms. Those realms are the space within which we attain *respect* via provision of legal and political rights; the space within which we attain *esteem* through solidarity with others in society; and the space within which we attain *love* via acknowledgement of our unique selves. As discussed previously, the human subject is not independent, but rather is dependent on social interaction to attain self-identity, so we must consider how that inter-subjectivity occurs effectively. In order for an individual to achieve a positive sense of self-esteem, others must recognize them as valuable and those others, in turn, must be valued in order that their act of recognition is itself valuable. Any denial of recognition within these realms constitutes a harm to the fundamental formation of the self: what we might refer to as harmful subjectivity. While the theory of recognition has been questioned to some extent as to its capacity to fully address the intersectional nature of lived experience (Fraser, 2003; Toniolatti, 2015), we have found it a useful tool to explore the harms of hate as it provides for an acknowledgement of the role of neoliberal capitalism in preventing humans from flourishing. It does this specifically through an appreciation of negation. Critical race theory (Bell, 1980; Warmington, 2020) has highlighted the importance of scrutinizing absences in policy, legislative and narrative discourses. By taking a critical hate studies approach and using the theory of recognition, it is possible to highlight how the negation of peoples' essential needs impacts on their lived experience and manifests as harm.

Respect

The first aspect of Yar's (2012) theory of recognition to be considered here is the denial of recognition of the need for respect. Human subjects desire cognitive recognition that provides a form of self-respect as an equal citizen enjoying parity with others that is afforded through legal recognition of rights. Provision of governance that enshrines a coherent symbolic order would effectively recognize the human need for respect. In this sense, the contemporary hate agenda in the UK and other similar states (Schweppe and Walters, 2016) has been most successful. However, the absence of recognition of people within legal structures constitutes a denial of recognition. This manifests through reductive systems of categorization of people that fail to acknowledge their diversity as we will now go on to illustrate.

Gypsies and Travellers in the UK have attained some recognition of their identities via race relations legislation. Indeed, Romany Gypsies, Irish Travellers, Scottish Travellers and Welsh Kale are recognized within the law as ethnic groups. However, other members of the Gypsy and Traveller communities, including New Travellers,[1] Show People and Boaters, do not have legally protected identities, despite their cultural, historic and lifestyle similarities to those groups. Thus, they are denied recognition. Further, the law is complex and paradoxical in relation to Gypsy and Traveller identities, with planning legislation directly contradicting race relations legislation by defining Gypsy and Traveller identity according to mobility rather than ethnicity. Gypsies and Travellers who are mobile and defined as Gypsies or Travellers according to planning law are more likely to be allocated spaces of accommodation to stop and stay on (which are scarce), but those Gypsies and Travellers who have settled are at risk of losing their homes due to their failure to conform to the planning legislation definition of who is or is not a Gypsy or Traveller, even though they are a recognized ethnic group within race relations legislation. This ridiculous state of affairs is only one aspect of the legislative failure to recognize all Gypsies and Travellers as in need of respect. Its impact is significant, however, as Gypsies and Travellers are placed within a hierarchy of legitimate identity (James, 2022) that is situationally contingent and that places them in competition with each other over whose rights are prioritized. Further, the failure of law and policy to comprehensively acknowledge their identities means that the law fails in its symbolic value and Gypsies and Travellers experience hateful treatment that manifests as discrimination and prejudice against them. For example, one Romany Gypsy interviewee said: 'Told by a policeman that people like us should be put against a wall and shot as there was no place for people like us in society' (Res 4.5, interviewed about experiences of hate, discussing discrimination).

For trans people a similar paradox occurs within the law. Within equalities legislation those people who have medically and/or surgically reassigned their gender are acknowledged as having rights in the workplace and wider social spaces. This acknowledgement should provide trans people with the respect they require to flourish and does so for those trans people who have transitioned within a binary framework from one gender to another according to the medical profession's requirements. However, the respect is negated for the majority of trans people who do not conform to, or do not want to conform to, the ways in which 'gender reassignment' is determined within a medical model of binary identity that perceives reassignment of gender within such finite terms. The pressure to conform to the medical model for trans people is substantial. As one participant within the research said: 'Right from the get-go I said I want the surgery because that's what you have to say ... you had to go the whole way or not at all' (Trans woman discussing experiences of interacting with a gender-identity clinic).

Thus, trans people are placed within a hierarchy of legitimacy within the law and policy that harms their daily lived experience as, in the pursuit of presenting their essential self to the world, they are constricted and constrained from access to rights by a medicalized appropriation of their identities.

For both trans people and Gypsies and Travellers, the hate crime agenda has been inclusive. But that inclusivity is subject to the vagaries of other legislative environments that limit legitimacy and/or are hierarchical. The harms of hate therefore are not addressed effectively as trans people and Gypsies and Travellers only have partial recognition of their need for respect as a result of hierarchies of provision within and between those deemed legitimate.

Esteem

Following on from the failure of provision of respect to Gypsies and Travellers and trans peoples via identity defining structures, it is necessary to consider the ways in which this feeds in to how they are limited in their capacity to build solidarity between their own communities and with other excluded peoples and wider society. Human subjects desire 'self-esteem' that is found in relationships and interactions with others regarded as 'capable and worthy of granting recognition' (Yar, 2001a: 294). In this sense, subjects actively engage in interactions designed to produce reciprocal solidarity. Solidarity is achieved through the establishment of a set of 'shared cultural characteristics and social identities' (Yar, 2001b: 67) deemed as of value and worth in society which further bestows those individuals with the relevant 'affirmatory power' (Yar, 2001a: 294) to recognize others with whom they share those characteristics or identities.

Solidarity can be gained through community recognition of intersectionality and this occurs to some degree and has been evidenced within emerging coalitions within and between Gypsies, Travellers and Roma, and lesbian, gay, bisexual and transgender communities. Also, Stonewall UK acknowledged and apologized for harms caused by the omission of trans people within its work over time, and many Gypsy and Traveller support groups and communities have acknowledged and embraced the intersectional diversity of their own communities through celebrations of Pride, for example. However, despite some gains made, the hierarchies of legitimacy problematized by legislative and policy environments are emboldened by cultural constructions of 'good citizens', who are those people who are perceived to conform to these hierarchies and indeed who embrace them to further their power within neoliberal spaces of provision. As such hierarchies are *reproduced within* Gypsy, Traveller and Roma communities and trans communities and horizontal discrimination (Howard and Vajda, 2017) occurs wherein notions of, for example, the mythical Romany Gypsy (Kenrick and Puxon, 1972; Okely, 1983), and the passing trans person (Carroll, Gilroy and Ryan, 2002) are held up as idyllic representations of those communities that by no means personify the reality of Gypsy and Traveller or trans peoples identities or lives.

The embracing of hierarchies of identity and the need to be successful in their adherence to others' determination of legitimacy was evidenced by one trans person interviewed in the research presented here. In her endeavour to socially pass, the interviewee noted that she had become involved with a media channel in order to get speedier access to gender reassignment surgery and be offered the opportunity to receive facial reconstructive surgery that is otherwise unavailable to trans people via the National Health Service and which is prohibitively expensive to most as a privately funded option. While others approached by the media channel expressed concerns about the exploitative potential of the programme, the research participant proclaimed to the TV show producers, '*Please exploit me*' (Trans woman interviewee). Thus, the nature of neoliberal norms are not necessarily unknown to those people who are subject to their pressures. Gypsies and Travellers often hide their identities in order to traverse the vagaries of prejudice and discrimination that manifest when their identities are known, and similarly the very notion of passing in one's physical representation of gender is a form of hiding. And yet, when needs-must the interviewee here shows that she is willing to engage with and collude with the capitalization of her identity in order that she might achieve the recognition she desires through her fulfilment of the expectations of a 'good' trans woman as one who can effectively represent the heteronormative ideals of femininity.

Neoliberal capitalism relies on our collusion with its norms in order to succeed. Within an environment that places the self above and beyond others, despite the ontological insecurity this elicits, those living marginalized lives are most likely to be pacified by small gains that assuage the sense of lack in their lives. Solidarity between and within groups is difficult to attain in a system of governance that limits access to resources and makes such access a competitive process. That sense of competition between identity groups is typically stated by one person in the Gypsy and Traveller research study: '[There was] a petition in a shop near my transit site. Racist in my view but, apparently not in the eyes of the police. I'm sure if it had been against Black/Asian minorities action would have been taken' (Res 2.3, interviewed about experiences of hate, discussing discrimination).

Other authors have likewise noted the competitive nature of Gypsy and Traveller relations (Greenfields, 2006; Bhopal and Myers, 2008), with specific references to the problematization of New Travellers as illegitimate, despite having lived culturally nomadic lifestyles for generations (Clark, 1997).

Evidencing the lack of solidarity between excluded peoples and wider society, hate speech functions as a divisive tool in all aspects of social life used by politicians and neighbours alike, and perpetuates hateful conceptions of others. This scapegoating serves the needs of neoliberal capitalism within wider society, wherein the ills of disintegrating communities (Cresswell, 2010) that the political economy has created are rationalized as the fault of those 'others' within the system rather than the system itself (Winlow et al, 2017). In the competitive individualist culture of contemporary society, those with the sharpest elbows are the most successful. Even within the precariat, the lack of solidarity between communities, whether Gypsies and Travellers, trans peoples or other excluded communities, manifests as what Hall and Winlow (2015: 120) refer to as 'special liberty', wherein 'one is entitled to do whatever it takes to participate in profitable market activity and achieve economic security and social status, even if it risks the infliction of harm on others and their social and physical environments'. Meritocratically driven personal evaluation frameworks of what holds value and worth in society, and which characteristics and social identities these traits are associated with, are informed by the aforementioned provision of legally defined respect, and thus drive a perpetuation of this exclusionary structure.

Love

The final realm within which subjects assemble a basic self-confidence is through a need for emotional support. This support is found in primary relationships with parents, siblings, intimate partners, children and other family members, as well as close friends. Recognition in this realm is founded on the ability to express oneself, including fundamental needs and desires, and one's particularity without fear of judgement or rejection by others. Achievement of such recognition equates to an overall sense of receiving unconditional 'love'. The gains made in attaining respect and esteem for, within and between excluded communities, as discussed previously, have potentially facilitated increased communication and acceptance within some primary relationships. However, these are most likely to have occurred for those who have greater social and fiscal capital, which can serve to insulate some individuals from othering processes. However, the lack of respect and esteem also discussed previously, and the subsequent hierarchies and tensions that occur from their negation mean that the harms of abjection occur within the realm of love.

As previously noted, Gypsies and Travellers and trans peoples are commonly placed in positions wherein they feel they must hide their identity in some sense. Gypsies and Travellers and trans people traverse and negotiate where they feel safe (Halfacree, 1996) in both public and private spheres of their lives and sometimes in collusion with those whom they trust and rely on as part of their close relationships and community. However, psychological harms result from the suppression or concealment of particularities of identity that lie counter to hegemonic norms, even though they are often engendered as protective behaviours. For example, parental regulation of expressions of gendered identity occurs in an effort to prevent a child from being bullied, and parental concealment of Gypsy, Traveller or Roma status within schools, health and welfare services occurs to prevent discrimination against children. Such attempts at protection, however, can result in adverse childhood experiences of harm that become embedded within individuals' psyche in the form of internalized phobias and that instruct later relationships in a problematic way.

One trans interviewee identified how early experiences denied recognition of her particularity and resulted in the development of a harmful subjectivity: 'I just lacked so much confidence in myself, that I just … I didn't have the self-confidence. … I just think I just grew up feeling pretty worthless' (Trans woman reflecting on her experiences of childhood).

The parental urge to protect their children from the subjective harms of malignant social attitudes can place families and communities in a space of siege mentality. The lack of places for Gypsies and Travellers to live in has meant that they are perceived as 'invaders' in the public imagination (Kabachnik, 2010). This can cause Gypsy and Traveller parents to go to extreme measure to protect their children, as detailed in notes from an interview in the Gypsy and Traveller research: 'The Travellers were so fearful that they had arranged escape routes from the site and hiding places for the children in case the farmers should return. This involved placing sheepskin rugs over barbed-wire fences and placing duvets, torches and food in secluded hiding spots nearby' (Notes from interview with New Travellers who were trying to find a safe place to live).

Denial of respect and esteem can mean that familial love intended as protective measures is actually potentially harmful. The cognitive dissonance borne of a tension between one's social and personal identity (Moran, 2015) means that a coherent sense of self is denied. The trauma that derives from rejection and abjection in the realm of recognition that is love, informs the increased significance of the need to achieve recognition through self-esteem with others who share characteristics and social identity. Set against the neoliberal norms of individualism and competition within contemporary society, critical hate studies explains the complicit role that some individuals of minority communities can play in the perpetuation of harmful reductive closed systems of recognition in the realms of esteem and respect.

Conclusion

In this chapter we have identified an approach to understanding hate in late modernity that appreciates its multiple and complex harms. In order to do so we have utilized a critical hate studies approach that acknowledges the impact of neoliberal capitalism on human relations and in turn on human subjectivity. In order to fully explicate the harms of hate we have used Yar's (2012) theory of recognition as an effective tool to frame how hate manifests in the lived experience of excluded communities, and specifically we have drawn on evidence gathered with research participants from trans and Gypsy and Traveller communities (see also, McBride, 2019, and James, 2021 for elaborated discussion). The harms of hate occur as human self-realization is negated by failure of recognition in the realms of respect, esteem and love.

The focus of attention in hate studies on interpersonal subjective violence and on aspects of systemic violence means that there is a lack of acknowledgement of the symbolic violence that is caused by the negation of recognition. Gypsies, Travellers and Roma, and trans people share common lived experiences of an ultimate dilemma that is whether to conceal their identity or to freely express themselves and risk the consequences of doing so. This is due to their navigation and negotiation of these spaces of recognition, which are disrupted by capitalist neoliberal values. The failure to achieve recognition under the terms set by this hegemony results in a form of 'social death' (Cacho, 2012: 145), 'a desperate space, overwrought with and overdetermined by the ideological contradictions of ineligible personhood'. It is our aim here to have evidenced the need to recognize the role of neoliberal capitalism in disrupting spaces of recognition and thus to identify that human flourishing cannot be attained solely through legislative and policy means, but rather it is necessary to consider the spaces of human interaction, governance and discourse within which hateful subjectivities emerge and hate harms manifest.

Note

[1] New Travellers are the most recent people to take up a nomadic style of living in the UK, having come in to being in the late 1970s and early 1980s. The New Travellers, or 'New Age' Travellers as they were originally known, were borne of the music festival culture of the 1970s, inspired by traditional Gypsy and Traveller lifestyles.

References

Baum, F., MacDougall, C. and Smith, D. (2006) 'Participatory action research', *Journal of Epidemiology & Community Health*, 60(10): 854–7.

Bauman, Z. (2005) *Liquid Life*, Cambridge: Polity Press.

Bell, D.A. (1980) 'Brown v. Board of Education and the interest-convergence dilemma', *Harvard Law Review*, 93(3): 518–33.

Bhopal, K. and Myers, M. (2008) *Insiders, Outsiders and Others: Gypsies and Identity*, Hatfield, UK: University of Hertfordshire Press.

Brown, W. (2015) *Undoing the Demos: Neoliberalism's Stealth Revolution*, New York: Zone Books.

Cacho, L.M. (2012) *Social Death: Racialized Rightlessness and the Criminalization of the Unprotected*, New York: New York University Press.

Carroll, L., Gilroy, P.J. and Ryan, J. (2002) 'Counseling transgendered, transsexual, and gender-variant clients', *Journal of Counseling & Development*, 80(2): 131–9.

Chakraborti, N. and Garland, J. (2015) *Hate Crime: Impact, Causes and Responses* (2nd edn), London: Sage.

Clark, C. (1997) ' "New Age" Travellers: identity, sedentarism and social security', in T. Acton (ed) *Gypsy Politics and Traveller Identity*, Hatfield: University of Hertfordshire Press, pp 125–41.

Cresswell, T. (2010) 'Towards a politics of mobility', *Environment and Planning D: Society and Space*, 28: 17–31.

Davies, W. (2017) *The Limits of Neoliberalism*, London: Sage.

Feinberg, L. (1996) *Transgender Warriors: Making History from Joan of Arc to Dennis Rodman*, Boston: Beacon Press.

Fraser, N. (2003) 'Rethinking recognition: overcoming displacement and reification in cultural politics', in B. Hobson (ed) *Recognition Struggles and Social Movements: Contested Identities, Agency and Power*, Cambridge: Cambridge University Press, pp 21–33.

Greenfields, M. (2006) 'Gypsies, Travellers and legal matters', in C. Clark and M. Greenfields (eds) *Here to Stay: The Gypsies and Travellers of Britain*, Hatfield, UK: University of Hertfordshire Press, pp 133–182.

Greitemeyer, T. and Sagioglou, C. (2017) 'Increasing wealth inequality may increase interpersonal hostility: the relationship between personal relative deprivation and aggression', *The Journal of Social Psychology*, 157(6): 766–76.

Hall, S. and Winlow, S. (2015) *Revitalizing Criminological Theory: Towards a New Ultra-Realism*, London: Routledge.

Halfacree, K. (1996) 'Out of place in the country: Travellers and the "rural idyll"', *Antipode*, 28(1): 42–72.

Harvey, D. (2005) *A Brief History of Neoliberalism*, Oxford: Oxford University Press.

Honneth, A. (1996) *The Struggle for Recognition*, Cambridge: Polity Press.

Howard, J. and Vajda, V. (2017) *Navigating Power and Intersectionality to Address Inequality*, IDS Working Paper: 504.

Hughes, G. (2007) *The Politics of Crime and Community*, Basingstoke: Palgrave Macmillan.

Iganski, P. (2008) *Hate Crime and the City*, Bristol: Policy Press.

James, Z. (2020) *The Harms of Hate for Gypsies and Travellers: A Critical Hate Studies Perspective*, London: Palgrave Macmillan.

James, Z. (2022) 'Roma, Gypsies and Travellers as a community of difference: challenging inclusivity as an anti-racist approach', *Critical Romani Studies*, forthcoming.

James, Z. and McBride, K. (2022) 'Critical Hate Studies: a new perspective', *International Review of Victimology*, 28(1): 92–108.

James, Z. and Southern, R. (2019) 'Accommodating nomadism and mobility: challenging the application of a sedentarist binary approach to provision for Gypsies, Travellers and Roma', *International Journal of Sociology and Social Policy*, 39(3/4): 324–36.

Johnston, A. (2008) *Žižek's Ontology: A Transcendental Materialist Theory of Subjectivity*, Evanston, IL: Northwestern University Press.

Kabachnik, P. (2010) 'Place invaders: constructing the nomadic threat in England', *The Geographical Review*, 100(1): 90–108.

Kenrick, D. and Puxon, G. (1972) *The Destiny of Europe's Gypsies*, London: Chatto-Heinemann.

Lacan, J. (1977) *Écrits*, Tavistock: Tavistock Publications.

Merriman, P. (2015) 'Mobilities I: departures', *Progress in Human Geography*, 39(1): 87–95.

McBride, K. (2019) *A Critical Analysis of Harms Experienced by Transgender Individuals*, Unpublished PhD thesis, University of Plymouth.

Moran, M. (2015) *Identity and Capitalism*, London: Sage.

Okely, J. (1983) *The Traveller-Gypsies*, Cambridge: Cambridge University Press.

Perry, B. (2001) *In the Name of Hate: Understanding Hate Crimes*, New York: Routledge.

Ponterotto, J.G. (2006) 'Brief note on the origins, evolution, and meaning of the qualitative research concept thick description', *The Qualitative Report*, 11(3): 538–49.

Raymen, T. (2019) 'The enigma of social harm and the barrier of liberalism: why Zemiology needs a theory of the good', *Justice, Power and Resistance*, 3(1): 133–162.

Schweppe, J. and Walters, M. (eds) (2016) *The Globalization of Hate: Internationalizing Hate Crime?* Oxford: Oxford University Press.

Scrivens, R. and Perry, B. (2017) 'Resisting the Right: countering Right-Wing extremism in Canada', *Canadian Journal of Criminology and Criminal Justice*, 59(4): 534–58.

Singh, A.A., Richmond, K. and Burnes, T.R. (2013) 'Feminist participatory action research with transgender communities: fostering the practice of ethical and empowering research designs', *International Journal of Transgenderism*, 14(3): 93–104.

Southern, R., James, Z. and Buckman, E. (2015) 'Supporting an assessment of the accommodation needs of Gypsies and Travellers in Cornwall 2015', Southern Horizons with Plymouth University and Buckman Associates Report, Available from: https://www.cornwall.gov.uk/media/16179632/cornwall-gypsies-travellers-needs-assessment-final-draft-for-cornwallcouncil-251115.pdf [Accessed 2 December 2015).

Standing, G. (2014) *A Precariat Charter: From Denizens to Citizens*, London and New York: Bloomsbury Academic.

Sue, D.W. (2010) *Microaggressions in Everyday Life: Race, Gender, and Sexual Orientation*, Hoboken, NJ: Wiley.

Toniolatti, E. (2015) 'From critique to reconstruction: on Axel Honneth's theory of recognition and its critical potential', *Critical Horizons*, 10(3): 371–90.

Walters, M.A. (2011) 'A general theories of hate crime? Strain, doing difference and self control', *Critical Criminology*, 19(4): 313–30.

Walters, M.A. (2014) *Hate Crime and Restorative Justice: Exploring Causes, Repairing Harms*, Oxford: Oxford University Press.

Warmington, P. (2020) 'Critical race theory in England: impact and opposition', *Identities: Global Studies in Culture and Power*, 27(1): 20–37.

Whittle, S. (2002) *Respect and Equality: Transsexual and Transgender Rights*, Abingdon: Routledge Cavendish.

Wilchins, R. (1997) *Read My Lips: Sexual Subversion and the End of Gender*, Riverdale, NY: Magnus Books.

Winlow, S., Hall, S. and Treadwell, J. (2017) *The Rise of the Right: English Nationalism and the Transformation of Working-Class Politics*, Bristol: Policy Press.

Yar, M. (2001a) 'Recognition and the Politics of Human (e) Desire', *Theory, Culture and Society*, 18(2–3): 57–76.

Yar, M. (2001b) 'Beyond Nancy Fraser's 'perspectival dualism'', *Economy and Society*, 30(3): 288–303.

Yar, M. (2012) 'Critical criminology, critical theory and social harm', in S. Hall and S. Winlow (eds) *New Directions in Criminological Theory*, London: Routledge.

Žižek, S. (2006) *The Parallax View*, London: MIT Press.

Žižek, S. (2008) *Violence: Six Sideways Reflections*, New York: Picador.

3

Hiding the Harm? An Argument against Misogyny Hate Crime

Fiona Vera-Gray and Bianca Fileborn[1]

This chapter is dedicated to the activist Emma Ritch, the kind of feminist we all want to be. The world was made better because you were in it.

Introduction

This chapter focuses on the current debate about the inclusion of misogyny[2] as a hate crime category in England and Wales. We write as feminist academics and activists working across hemispheres who have both foregrounded the study of public sexual harassment in our research, writing and campaigning. Our work focuses on public spaces, both physical and online, and has drawn on feminist geographers such as Gill Valentine (1993) and Rachel Pain (Pain, 1991, 2000; Koskela and Pain, 2000) to suggest that such harassment can be understood as a spatial expression of patriarchy, functioning to reinforce and reproduce the exclusion of women, and more broadly of trans, non-binary, and gender non-conforming people and communities, from public life (Fileborn, 2013; Fileborn and Vera-Gray, 2017; Vera-Gray and Fileborn, 2018; Vera-Gray and Kelly, 2020).

Reflecting on our own and others' research, as well as existing evidence on the operation of both hate crime policy broadly and 'misogyny hate crime' specifically, here we set out an argument against the introduction of the category of misogyny hate crime. We do so not to undermine the activism and passion of our sister campaigners who support such a move. We hold up the work of Nottingham Women's Centre and its then manager, Melanie Jeffs, in advocating for this new policy in Nottingham (English Midlands, UK), as an example of feminist activism at its best: channelling the experiences of women to change the mechanisms of the state. The result has been to grow the evidence base on whether, how and to what ends, hate crime policy works to prevent and provide recourse for men's violence against women and girls (VAWG). Instead of a challenge or criticism of the work that has come before us, we are motivated by a shared desire to end violence against women. We believe that the evidence shows that not only will the introduction of misogyny as a hate crime category not achieve the ends that are attributed to it, but that it may work against them.

To speak directly to the current Law Commission's review into hate crime,[3] we will be focusing on England and Wales only. We have organized the chapter to respond to the key claims we have identified in feminist campaigns supporting the change. Though these six claims are interrelated and may overlap in practice, we separate them here to ensure we reply to each in detail. The claims are not exhaustive and may not be shared across campaigning groups, but we found them to be the reasons most appealed to in publicly available documents advocating for misogyny hate crime. The first three relate primarily to the substantive benefits of misogyny hate crime, namely that it: (1) provides women with greater protection against violence and harassment; (2) supports the collection of better data on non-criminal forms of VAWG; and (3) responds to widespread support from victim–survivors. There are, however, an additional set of reasons that argue for its more conceptual or symbolic function, that is that misogyny hate crime (4) acknowledges the root causes of VAWG; (5) connects women's experiences across the continuum of sexual violence; and (6) helps change attitudes and supports prevention. We believe that both sets of arguments, the practical and the principled, do not justify the introduction of misogyny hate crime. Before addressing these in detail, we first set out the basics of hate crime policy in England and Wales.

Gender and hate crime: the current context

The need to separately address crimes motivated by hostility or prejudice gained prominence in the UK after the murder of Stephen Lawrence, an 18-year-old Black British student who was stabbed to death by a group of white racists while he was waiting for a London bus (Yuval-Davis, 1999). Stephen's murder, and the subsequent mishandling of the case by police, fuelled the introduction of the Crime and Disorder Act 1998, which is generally accepted as the first piece of 'hate crime' legislation in England and Wales (Mason-Bish and Duggan, 2020). As the idea of crimes motivated by hate or prejudice as worthy of unique attention grew, other nationally recognized strands of hate crime were introduced: religion (2001); disability and sexual orientation (2003); and transgender identity (2012). This means that there are now five nationally monitored strands.

Notably, 'gender' was not excluded from this development merely by omission. The debate about whether gender-based crimes should be considered hate crimes is not new, with a history of feminists in the UK and internationally arguing both for its usefulness (for example, Gill and Mason-Bish, 2013) and against (for example, Horvath and Kelly, 2007). Our intention here is to both reference and build on this ongoing discussion, using the evidence we now have from how misogyny hate crime has operated in Nottingham.

Misogyny hate crime sits within the broader problematic framework of hate crime in the UK outlined in Chapter 1 and noted by others (for example, Walters et al, 2016; HMICFRS, 2018). Using the ability of police to monitor and record local strands of hate crime, Nottingham was the first policing district in England and Wales to introduce misogyny hate crime in May 2016 (Nottingham Police, 2018). The change followed a locally organized hate crime commission run by the charity Nottingham Citizens during 2014 (for more detail see Legg and Nottingham Citizens, 2021). The commission found a significant proportion of hate crime against women was experienced as being motivated by their gender and that the majority of this would be best understood as forms of public sexual harassment, something that was felt to have less attention in policy terms than other forms of VAWG (Nottingham Women's Centre, 2018). As a result, Nottingham Women's Centre – whose then CEO was a commissioner on the inquiry – put forward a successful case to local police that misogyny should be included in hate crime definitions (Nottingham Women's Centre, 2018).

At the time of its introduction the policy generated extensive media interest, furthered two years later when an evaluation of the policy heralded it a success (Mullany and Trickett, 2018). The report authors recommended that the policy be implemented nationally (albeit with some changes, such as moving away from the term 'misogyny' and introducing efforts to improve public awareness of the policy). At the time of writing, local rollouts of both misogyny hate crime (for example, in North Yorkshire) or gender hate crime (for example, in Bristol) have fuelled the push for the category to be adopted nationally, including a tabled amendment to the Domestic Abuse Bill. This groundswell of support led to the government seeking a review from the Law Commission into hate crime, including whether it should include a category designed to capture VAWG (see Law Commission, 2020). While the review has been broadly welcomed, Parliament's Women and Equalities Select Committee has made clear the need to consider whether introducing what will ostensibly be a hate crime category for VAWG 'would bring *substantive advantages to victims* and *achieve a reduction in the incidence* of such harassment' (Women and Equalities Select Committee, 2019, para 86, emphasis added). The evidence that we present here suggests, unfortunately, that it won't.

Providing greater protection to women

A 2019 joint letter from campaigning groups supporting the inclusion of misogyny as a hate crime category, puts forward an equalities-based argument centred on protecting women and girls:

> At present if someone is abused because they are disabled, from an ethnic minority group, because they are LGBT, or because of their faith, that is recognised as a hate crime ... however because misogyny – acts that are targeted at women, because they are women – is not included within the law, women are left unprotected. (Fawcett, Citizens UK, Women's Aid, 2019)

Increasing protection is one of the most visible claims in feminist campaigns for the introduction of misogyny hate crime. However, it rests on confusion as to what 'protections' are actually offered by the hate crime provisions. The campaigns for misogyny hate crime in England and Wales are not broadly campaigns for misogyny to become a standalone aggravated offence[4]. This is contrary to the position in Scotland, where leading women's groups were strongly opposed to the introduction of misogyny hate crime. As such, gender has not been included as a hate crime category in Scottish legislation and instead a standalone offence of serious misogynistic harassment is being discussed as part of a governmental working group on criminal justice and misogyny (Scottish Government, 2021). In short, misogyny hate crime as campaigned for in England and Wales provides women with the same forms of legal recourse against men's violence and harassment that already exist. Women will receive *the same legal protection* after the reforms, which, given the extent of violence against women in England and Wales (and indeed worldwide), has little, if any, preventative effect.

Given that campaigners are aware that misogyny hate crime creates no new offences, what they may be referring to is sentence enhancement. The substantive argument here is that women will gain increased protection by offenders being incarcerated for longer. We believe this argument rests on a fundamental mistake about how successful the criminal justice system currently is in convicting offenders of VAWG. The enhanced sentencing provisions require proof to be established of the crime being motivated by hostility *after* guilt for the offence has already been established. Leaving to one side the evidential difficulties in attempting to prove that the forms of violence against women most intended to be picked up as hate crimes (such as forms of public sexual harassment) are motivated by hostility, there is a clear problem here for any feminist who has knowledge or experience of how the criminal justice system responds to violence against women.

Drawing on decades of practice-based knowledge from frontline service providers, we know that most forms of VAWG are simply not reported or processed through the criminal justice system at all. This is heightened for women from minoritized communities, with evidence from specialist Black and minoritized ethnic women services that reporting violence to the police can result in their feeling criminalized themselves (Imkaan, 2018). Indeed, at present in England and Wales, feminist campaigning groups the End Violence Against Women Coalition and the Centre for Women's Justice have launched a legal challenge against the Crown Prosecution Service for their failures in prosecuting rape (Hymas, 2020).

These failures are in many ways amplified in relation to sexual harassment in public and semi-public spaces, such as the street, public transport, licensed venues and so forth. International research shows that women and girls routinely experience harassment and intrusion from men, ranging from verbal comments and uninvited conversation, staring/leering, wolf-whistling, following, catcalling and so forth (Livingston, 2015). There are practical policing difficulties directly connected to public sexual harassment such as the fleetingness of the encounter and the anonymity of the perpetrator that combine with the broader failures of policing and prosecution in relation to all forms of VAWG (Fileborn and Vera-Gray, 2017). These issues may be amplified for the most common forms of harassment, such as verbal comments and staring, which can be ambiguous in nature and typically leave little tangible evidence. These issues have been acknowledged by Nottingham Police as real limitations of the misogyny hate crime provisions (Nottingham Police, 2018), meaning that low rates of arrests and prosecutions are inevitable.

Further, the evaluation of the Nottingham provisions found that over the two years since its introduction (April 2016 – March 2018), 174 women had reported misogyny hate crimes, with 101 of these classified as incidents, that is, recorded but not constituting a crime (Mullany and Trickett, 2018). Importantly, only one perpetrator was convicted during this period where misogyny hate crime featured as a flag on their record. Thus, existing evidence shows that most reports of misogyny hate crime do not and would not progress to the point of prosecution and conviction, meaning that the aggravated sentencing provisions will have no real impact in terms of offering women additional protection.

Providing better measurement of non-criminal forms of VAWG

Connected to the protective claim, is the argument that misogyny hate crime gives women a substantive basis from which to report incidents of misogynistic harassment to the police, even where these are not criminal offences. Protection is seen in its widest sense; women are able to 'walk taller' (Fish, 2020) because they can report manifestations of men's violence and harassment that do not meet criminal thresholds of harm – as is often the case with public sexual harassment (Fileborn, 2017). Here the benefit of the hate crime provisions orients around not hate crimes but 'hate incidents'. Advocates of misogyny hate crime often point to the mechanism it provides for reporting hate incidents, arguing that this recognizes the seriousness of non-criminal forms of VAWG, enabling their better measurement, and helping police to divert resources to prevent crimes before they occur (for examples see Hooper, 2018; Fawcett, Citizens UK, Women's Aid, 2019; Oppenheim, 2020).

This argument rests on a fundamental problem: namely that reports of hate crimes generally, including incidents of misogyny hate crime, have been publicly acknowledged by police as 'the tip of the iceberg' (Bates, 2016). Put simply, instead of recognizing the harms of such behaviours and supporting better management and resourcing, using hate crime provisions as a mechanism to collect data on non-criminal forms of VAWG has real potential to undermine the extent of the problem.

As researchers working on public sexual harassment, we routinely encounter the limits of the existing evidence base about the prevalence of the most mundane forms of the harassment and intrusion many women experience from men in public. There is clearly an urgent need for reliable, national data in this area. The introduction of misogyny hate crime will not do this. One of the consistently acknowledged operational problems with the existing hate crime provisions is low reporting (Walters et al, 2016; HMCIFRS, 2018). This is echoed in the existing evidence on misogyny hate crime. After two years of the policy being in place the Nottingham evaluation showed *no change* in reporting levels. Just 6.6 per cent of survey respondents who had experienced behaviours identified by Nottinghamshire Police as Misogyny Hate Crime had reported these to the police (Mullany and Trickett, 2018: 12), and close to 85 per cent of respondents said that the change in policy *did not influence* their decision to report.[5] The report concludes that 'under-reporting is a significant issue and remains so, despite the introduction of the policy' (Mullany and Trickett, 2018: 12).

Under-reporting is not unique to public sexual harassment: it plagues virtually all forms of police data on VAWG. However, we believe that the argument for misogyny hate crime as a data collection mechanism risks shoring up a system that sees police reports as the only legitimate form of knowledge on women's experiences. This in turn provides fuel for the myth that if a woman does not report criminal forms of violence, then they either were not harmed or it did not really happen. Given that we know that both police data on VAWG in general, and police data on hate crime in general, gives a wholly unreliable picture about what is happening on the ground, the combination of the two is most likely to severely distort the real prevalence of VAWG as it will inevitably be under-reported through this mechanism. This could have serious consequences, including the potential for local commissioners to reroute funding (for specialist women's services as well as other resource allocation such as policing) based on 'low levels' of VAWG in their area.

Responding to widespread support from victim–survivors

The third substantive argument we see made in campaigns for a national rollout of misogyny hate crime is that the policy change is widely supported by victim–survivors, namely women. Here we are happy to agree that this may be the case. We draw only on academic research and acknowledge the practice-based knowledge of frontline support providers may paint a different picture.

Saying that, our discussion of this argument begins from the premise that hate crime should be understood as a criminal justice system response in that it uses the police as the mechanism to report, whether or not what is being reported 'counts' as criminal. There is an ever-growing research basis pointing to the limitations of this system in meeting the justice needs of victim–survivors of sexual, domestic and 'honour'-based violence (McGlynn and Westmarland, 2019; Gangoli et al, 2020; McCulloch et al, 2020). Our own work on victim-centred responses to public sexual harassment supports this, finding that many victim–survivors prefer non-criminal justice responses (Fileborn and Vera-Gray, 2017). Here our participants highlighted how the harms of public sexual harassment were experienced as cumulative, lived as an ongoing process, rather than a one-off event. This meant that many wanted a community-based response, outside of a criminal justice system that is designed for discrete incidents connected to individual perpetrators. In this they are not alone, for example Donovan et al's (2018) conceptualization of 'hate relationships' also challenges a purely episodic understanding of what constitutes harassment and thus how we can measure harm.

In connection with this, we argue that the evaluation from Nottingham cannot be said to accurately reflect the voices and experiences of the women who had used the ability to report misogyny hate crime. Here we want to focus on the evaluation in a little more detail. The claim that the policy in Nottingham is supported by victim–survivors is based on both qualitative and quantitative data. However, victim–survivors who had used the ability to report in Nottingham are not properly represented in the qualitative data: of the 174 reported victims of misogyny hate crime, only four came forward to talk to researchers (Mullany and Trickett, 2018: 3). There is limited exploration in the report as to why there was such a low-level of engagement with the research if the policy was so supported by those who had used it.

There are also clear limitations with the quantitative data. For example, findings that suggest that just over a third of survey respondents supported treating the behaviours that comprise misogyny hate crime as criminal (Mullany and Trickett, 2018: 7) should also be viewed with caution. There is a methodological point here about providing a list of behaviours to respondents – some of which are criminal and would be broadly supported by most people to be criminal (for example, sexual assault), and some of which are not criminal and would be broadly understood as impossible/ undesirable to criminalize (that is, whistling) – and then asking respondents their opinions on criminalization based on that broad list. This makes the data unreliable. Respondents may have strongly supported criminalization for already criminal acts, such as sexual assault, but this does not necessarily mean that, on their own, they would similarly support criminalizing wolf-whistling. With the list combined in this way, it is not possible to establish whether respondents were in favour of criminalizing non-criminal acts. This point about confusion is also applicable to broader public opinion polls showing support for the policy. As we have explored previously, hate crime is notoriously misunderstood both regarding what it is supposed to do, and what it actually does, which means that opinion polling data is fairly unreliable as it does not provide a space to question understandings or definitions. A YouGov (2017) poll, for example, often used as evidence of support for the policy, explained misogyny hate crime as meaning 'longer sentences for ... perpetrators found to have acted out of a hatred for women'. It is likely that respondents to this question did not understand that crimes such as rape or domestic violence were excluded from misogyny hate crime, nor that sentence enhancement provisions do not actually allow for any longer sentences than the maximum sentences already set for offences. As such we would urge caution in using opinion polls as a measure of public support for what the changes actually mean in practice.

There is also not enough engagement with the limited representation of the experiences of minoritized women in the Nottingham evaluation. Survey respondents were overwhelmingly white (only 2 per cent of respondents were Black, and just 0.7 per cent were Asian), a key limitation acknowledged in the report. We contrast this with evidence from Australia on the ways in which hate crime provisions can perpetuate inequality by disproportionately processing minoritized perpetrators of hate crime through the criminal justice system (Mason, 2014). There is an ethical imperative for feminists engaged in any form of police or criminal justice advocacy for women to seriously contend with its implications for racial injustice – something brought into sharp focus through the global Black Lives Matter movement.

Taken together all of this suggests considerably more work is needed to understand the views of women who have used misogyny hate crime, centring the experiences of women from minoritized ethnic groups, before any such measures should be claimed as widely supported by victim–survivors.

Defining motivation and acknowledging the root causes

The problems we have outlined so far regarding misogyny hate crime are largely operational. Now, we move to address the more conceptual arguments for the change, the most visible of which is the claim that '(a)cknowledging the misogyny that drives ... crimes against women makes plain its roots' (Creasy, 2020). We suggest that on closer examination the hate crime framing obscures what motivates most perpetrators of violence against women and, in doing so, makes it harder for us to work towards prevention.

Our concern orients around the need for hate crimes to be perceived by the victim as motivated by hostility or prejudice – something that has again been identified as a problem with hate crime provisions in general. It is far from clear that hate crimes are always or only driven by hostility (Chakraborti, 2018; Hall, 2013). Though 'hate crime' may resonate with some victim–survivors, there is evidence to suggest that many, including those who have experienced what would be counted as misogyny hate crime, do not perceive perpetrator motivations in this way. Bianca Fileborn's research with people who have experienced street harassment in Australia (Hindes and Fileborn, 2022) has found that participants most commonly believe that men engage in street harassment for the purpose of homosocial bonding (see also Quinn, 2002), a sense of entitlement, fear of the 'other' (particularly for harassment relating to gender diversity and sexual orientation), power, misplaced notions about appropriate sexual interaction and the absence of any meaningful community-based approaches to hold perpetrators to account. Very few participants have viewed their experiences as a result of hatred and prejudice, and none in relation to misogyny. Research from the UK has found similar results. A joint inspection report on hate crime from 2017 found that for the existing strands of monitored hate crime, the majority of victims do not perceive perpetrators to be motivated by hostility (HMCIFRS, 2018), and a 2020 study specifically on victims of gender-related victimization found that just 35 of the 85 participants labelled their experience as a hate crime (Mason-Bish and Duggan, 2020).

These findings, particularly when related to VAWG, are unsurprising. Most forms of VAWG are perpetrated by those closest to us, partners, relatives, friends – positioned in relationships of intimacy, trust and care (Horvath and Kelly, 2007). Known perpetrators are unlikely to be motivated by hostility or prejudice, and even if they are, it is even more unlikely that they would be perceived to be either by ourselves or by society at large. The motivation of hostility then is more likely to be applied to stranger perpetrators, and here we see the hate crime frame as propping up harmful myths about VAWG. This is acknowledged in the recently published consultation paper from the Law Commission (2020: 258), which found evidence that 'implementing laws concerning sex or gender-based hate crime in the context of sexual offences might have the unintended consequence of contributing to damaging myths about "real rape"'.

Too often, men's violence is positioned as an 'isolated incident' perpetrated either by 'deviant' individuals or by normal men 'made deviant' by extremes of emotion generally caused by women, whether that be sexual arousal, anger, or jealousy. Though there may of course be perpetrators who are driven by thrill and fear, if not outright prejudice and hatred, this focus hides the extent to which many forms of men's violence are normalized as legitimate sexual interaction (Gavey, 2018); ways of doing masculinity. This 'public story' (Donovan and Hester, 2010) about VAWG as driven by individual pathology or emotion will only be further embedded by locating some forms as worthy of enhanced sentencing (thus positioned as more serious) when a motivation of hostility or prejudice is proven. Far from revealing the root causes of VAWG then, we find that misogyny hate crime conceals them: perpetuating damaging myths about perpetrators and supporting a hierarchy of harm.

Connecting women's experiences and positions

The argument about root causes is in many ways an argument about connection being made for misogyny hate crime in two respects: the first about connecting women's experiences across the continuum of sexual violence and the second about intersectionality.

The claim that hate crime provides a needed means to link the different forms of VAWG through the common framing of misogyny applies predominantly to the legal framing of VAWG, which positions it as a series of distinct offences ordered hierarchically in terms of their harm or seriousness. In contrast, policy frameworks in the UK already recognize the interconnections between all forms of VAWG, with the more recent strategy refresh specifically addressing sexual harassment (Home Office, 2019). As with the claim about root causes, we find the opposite of this argument to be true. Rather than drawing connections, the inclusion of misogyny as a hate crime in practice *separates* the various forms of men's violence that women experience over a lifetime. It separates these in terms of what forms are and are not included, as well as by separating out motivations and locating those as motivated by hostility only as eligible for enhanced sentencing.

While the siloed effect caused by hate crime provisions applies generally, it is particularly problematic in relation to VAWG as it runs directly counter to the widely accepted continuum model of sexual violence (Kelly, 1988). The continuum model recognizes the interconnection between *all* forms of sexual and gender-based violence and does not assume their seriousness or harm based on a presumed hierarchy of motivation. Such a model is antithetical to misogyny hate crime both conceptually, and in practice, something that has been acknowledged by campaigners.

Nottingham Women's Centre (2018) for example, have publicly stated that their intention in introducing misogyny hate crime was for the provisions to cover *some* forms of VAWG *and not others*. The Fawcett Society have similarly argued against applying a hate crime aggravation in the context of sexual offences and domestic abuse as 'to do so may forge an artificial distinction between "misogynistic" and "non-misogynistic" sexual offences or domestic abuse against women' (Law Commission, 2020: 257). As such, misogyny hate crime is simply not intended to be applicable to all forms of VAWG. In fact, it works to separate out forms that are mostly perpetrated by strangers and, through its enhanced sentencing provisions, imply these are more serious and/or more harmful than the other forms on the continuum. In this we see it advancing problematic narratives of 'stranger danger', narratives that are subtly classed (see Meyer, 2014) and raced (see Burke, 2019).

In addition to missing the connections between different forms of violence, the hate crime framework itself runs the risk of further embedding identity-based inequality and difference. Hate crime provisions have been widely critiqued for siloing inequalities (Mason-Bish, 2011; Chakraborti, 2014), treating identity categories as homogeneous and reified (Perry, 2008) and creating hierarchies of worth and seriousness based on whose experiences of prejudice 'count' (Mason-Bish, 2011; Hall, 2013; Chakraborti, 2014; Mason-Bish and Duggan, 2020). These critiques become particularly important when discussing how misogyny hate crime interacts with an intersectional feminist perspective.

Despite the intersectional nature of harassment being recognized by some supporters of misogyny hate crime (Bates, 2016), others such as Stella Creasy MP, have advocated for the ability of misogyny hate crime to 'ensure that no woman from any background is asked to tick a box in order for the police and courts to act when she is a victim of crime' (Topping, 2020). Our concern is that this latter argument hides rather than reveals the ways in which women who are located differently in relation to social inequalities are differentially targeted by perpetrators and differentially responded to by both bystanders and criminal justice agencies (Gill and Mason-Bish, 2013). In many ways, it suggests that gender is the primary inequality for women, a position that has been critiqued by decades of thought from Black, Indigenous and post-colonial feminists (see, for example, Amos and Parmer,

1984; or more recently Suzack et al, 2011). Though victim–survivors are able to identify multiple 'motivations' (for example, reporting one incident as both misogyny hate crime and a disability hate crime), this embeds an additive rather than intersectional approach to social inequalities. They are presented as discrete boxes to be ticked and prioritized, multiplied and subtracted, instead of understanding how they co-constitute one another and often cannot be readily separated. In this way, hate crime as a framework for VAWG disconnects and ranks different forms of violence and requires victim–survivors to disconnect and rank ourselves. As such we find it irreconcilable with an intersectional feminist perspective.

Changing attitudes and preventing violence

All of which brings us to the final claim for misogyny hate crime and the central aim of all feminist anti-violence campaigns: to change attitudes and ultimately prevent the violence from happening in the first place. Melanie Jeffs who led the campaign in Nottingham, has stressed that the aim of the change is to change attitudes, challenge the normalization of misogynistic abuse and 'enable women to move freely around their city without being intimidated, abused or harassed' (Bates, 2016). Others have pointed out that we cannot 'measure the success of this by the number of calls, but by the number of women who've said they feel like they're walking taller – just to know it's there' (Bates 2016). This sentiment is also encapsulated by former CEO of Women's Aid, Polly Neate, in giving evidence on misogyny hate crime to the All-Party Parliamentary Group on Domestic Violence in 2017. Neate explained that 'while categorising misogyny as a hate crime won't stop it from occurring completely, it sends a clear message that society does not condone this behaviour – which is vital for preventing domestic abuse and VAWG in the long term' (All-Party Parliamentary Group on Domestic Violence, 2017).

Symbolic effects are important. In our research, the symbolic and communicative power of the law was the main reason some participants supported legislative regulation of street harassment, even if they viewed a criminal justice response as otherwise ineffective (Fileborn and Vera-Gray, 2017). Additionally, the work in Nottingham has had a significant impact in sparking widespread public debate about the extent of public sexual harassment and its consequences for women's safety and freedom. We recognize the importance this kind of public conversation can have in informing the general public and potentially shifting attitudes (Maher et al, 2015).

While acknowledging these potential benefits, we remain sceptical that these will actually come into fruition through changing hate crime policy. It is unfortunately not the case that the existence of the hate crime provisions in relation to race, religion, disability, sexual orientation and transgender identity have had this effect in practice. We know this is also true for criminal justice responses to VAWG more broadly where problematic attitudes and misconceptions persist (and are often perpetuated by the criminal justice system itself), even in the face of seemingly 'progressive' reforms (Burgin, 2019). It is also questionable whether impacts such as 'walking taller' or feeling more able to report will persist over the longer term if they are not met with substantive change in the operation of the criminal justice system or a reduction in perpetration.

The Nottingham evaluation even offers evidence that introducing misogyny hate crime will not change public attitudes, not least because the report found that many respondents were unaware of the policy. The high level of public support for the policy found by the report, something that has since been drawn on by campaigners to support a national rollout, was only found *after the policy was explained*. It is hard to argue for a change in attitudes if no one knows about the change in policy. It appears that shifting attitudes is much more related to public awareness campaigns about what misogyny is and why it is incompatible with a fair and just society, than about including it as a form of hate crime. This echoes wider work on the prevention of VAWG, which has found the key to prevention lies is changing social norms and reducing gender inequality (Jewkes et al, 2015; Alexander-Scott et al, 2016; Haylock et al, 2016).

Conclusion

Evaluating the arguments for misogyny hate crime in relation to the evidence has left us with the distinct feeling that we are trying to fit a square peg in a round hole. There are numerous problems with the hate crime frame, and the current campaign for misogyny hate crime has simply not engaged enough with its potential to negatively impact feminist efforts against violence against women. The policy's potential for harm has been hidden in an attempt to seek public and state recognition of the seriousness of men's violence and harassment in public space. We hope here to have made this harm visible.

We have outlined how responding to VAWG through a hate crime framework has the potential to severely distort the prevalence of VAWG; shore up a system that sees police reports as the only legitimate form of knowledge on women's experiences; reinforce damaging myths about the perpetrators, causes and victims of violence; disconnect and rank different forms and victims of violence; and undermine the integrated VAWG framework at a national level. For a possible benefit of some women feeling safer for some of the time, these risks just are not worth it. Particularly when there are alternatives.

We suggest something much simpler is needed, drawing on the lessons from public health. The World Health Organization is clear that VAWG is 'a public health problem of substantial proportions' (Krug et al, 2002: 172), yet in England and Wales a public health perspective is commonly superseded by one focused on crime. A public health approach takes a population rather than an incident-based approach. This means it is possible to gain reliable evidence on the nature and extent of VAWG without hitting the problems encountered in using the criminal justice system as a measurement tool. A key recommendation from the Women and Equalities Committee inquiry into public sexual harassment was that '(d)ata on sexual harassment in public places should be collected through the Crime Survey of England and Wales or brought together through other official data-gathering processes' (Women and Equalities Committee, 2018: 23), something the government has agreed to do (Women and Equalities Committee, 2019). Without further information on government plans here we are unable to evaluate how this would work in practice. However, given that such data-gathering will provide population level information, we believe this would deliver a more robust evidence base to inform resource allocation and preventative work. As such, both advocates for and against misogyny hate crime should come together to hold the Government to its commitment.

Likewise, there are examples of non-criminal legislation internationally that would support the symbolic and communicative function campaigners see as driving the usefulness of misogyny hate crime. A key example here is the Washington DC *Street Harassment Prevention Act of 2018*, which created a legal definition of street harassment, and an imperative for government to undertake data collection, introduce policy and develop public awareness campaigns among other actions (Vizvary, 2020). Importantly, this Act *does not* criminalize perpetrators, out of recognition that this would only work to perpetuate other forms of inequality and marginalization (Vizvary, 2020). The approach taken in DC thus represents an avenue for addressing VAWG that prioritizes prevention through education and capacity building, rather than criminalization. Importantly, this response emphasizes structural factors underpinning this violence, and maintains a firmly intersectional understanding rather than taking a siloed approach.

Both examples illustrate that it is possible to implement alternative responses to address the substantive and symbolic changes that campaigners for misogyny hate crime are fighting for. Such responses do so while avoiding the harmful consequences of trying to fit VAWG into a framework that is full of problems to begin with. After reviewing the available evidence, we are both more convinced than ever that hate crime is incompatible with feminist aims and that a national rollout of misogyny hate crime has real potential to rollback efforts to achieve greater public understanding of VAWG as well as its prevention.

Notes

[1] Bianca's contribution to this chapter is supported by funding from the Australian Research Council (DE190100404).

[2] The feminist campaigns in England and Wales have been focused on the introduction of 'misogyny' as a hate crime category, not 'gender', and so our discussion uses the term 'misogyny hate crime' as it is to these campaigners that we want to speak. We note that the current Law Commission consultation into hate crime recommends the inclusion of gender/sex as a characteristic, not misogyny. While our discussion speaks directly to misogyny hate crime, we believe that some of our arguments can be applied to the category of gender/sex particularly insofar as it is operationalized in relation to men's violence against women. Indeed, the evaluation of the Nottingham misogyny hate crime provisions found that the term misogyny was not widely understood, and that gendered hate crime may have greater resonance with victims, police, and members of the public (Mullany and Trickett, 2018). We recognize, however, that there are differences in intention and application of the two terms and highlight that Nottingham police (2018) have argued for misogyny not gender/sex as the preferred term to meet the aims of the policy. As such we believe that 'misogyny' or 'gender/sex' are not completely interchangeable and require full and detailed consideration in and of themselves, some of which can be found in Mason-Bish and Duggan (2020) and Haynes and Schweppe (2020).

[3] The Law Commission Review into hate crime was announced on 18 October 2018, with the public consultation launched on 23 September 2020. See Law Commission (2020).

[4] A key exception here is the work of the young women-led campaigning group *Our Streets Now* (Pike, 2020).

[5] Though it is unclear as to whether these incidents took place in the two-year period within which misogyny hate crime had been introduced (as well as whether this is about experiencing or witnessing).

References

All-Party Parliamentary Group on Domestic Violence (2017) *Tackling Misogyny as a Hate Crime*, Minutes of meeting, 29 March, London: House of Commons, Available from https://www.womensaid.org.uk/appg/ [Accessed 23 September 2020].

Alexander-Scott, M. Bell, E. and Holden, J. (2016) *DFID Guidance Note: Shifting Social Norms to Tackle Violence Against Women and Girls (VAWG)*, London: VAWG Helpdesk, Available from: https://www.gov.uk/government/publications/shifting-social-norms-to-tackle-violence-against-women-and-girls [Accessed 30 September 2020].

Amos, V. and Parmar, P. (1984) 'Challenging imperial feminism', *Feminist Review*, 17(1): 3–19.

Bates, L. (2016) 'Six things we've learned about misogyny hate crime', *The Guardian*, 22 September, Available from: https://www.theguardian.com/lifeandstyle/womens-blog/2016/sep/22/six-things-weve-learned-about-misogyny-as-a-hate [Accessed 28 September 2020].

Burke, M. (2019) *When Time Warps: The Lived Experience of Gender, Race, and Sexual Violence*, Minneapolis: University of Minnesota Press.

Burgin, R. (2019) 'Persistent narratives of force and resistance: affirmative consent as law reform', *British Journal of Criminology*, 59(2): 296–314.

Chakraborti, N. (2014) 'Re-thinking hate crime: fresh challenges for policy and practice', *Journal of Interpersonal Violence*, 30(10): 1738–54.

Chakraborti, N. (2018) 'Responding to hate crime: escalating problems, continued failings', *Criminology and Criminal Justice*, 18(4): 387–404.

Creasy, S. (2020) 'Why we're fighting to change the law and make misogyny a hate crime', *The Telegraph*, 11 June, Available from: https://www.telegraph.co.uk/women/politics/fighting-change-law-make-misogyny-hate-crime/ [Accessed 28 September 2020].

Donovan, C. and Hester, M. (2010) 'I hate the word "victim": an exploration of recognition of domestic violence in same sex relationships', *Social Policy and Society*, 9(2): 279–89.

Donovan, C., Clayton, J. and Macdonald, S. (2018) 'New directions in hate reporting research: agency, heterogeneity and relationality', *Sociological Research Online*, DOI: 10.1177/1360780418798848

Fawcett, Citizens UK, Women's Aid (2019) *Joint Open Letter to Cressida Dick CBE QPM, Commissioner of the Metropolitan Service and Sara Thornton CBE QPM, Chair of the National Police Chiefs' Council*, 11 January, Available from: https://www.fawcettsociety.org.uk/news/new-fawcett-data-reveals-gender-is-most-common-cause-of-hate-crime-for-women [Accessed 23 September 2020].

Fileborn, B. (2013) 'Conceptual understandings and prevalence of sexual harassment and street harassment, ACSSA Resource Sheet', Melbourne: Australian Institute of Family Studies.

Fileborn, B. (2017) 'Justice 2.0: street harassment victims' use of social media and online activism as sites of informal justice', *British Journal of Criminology*, 57(6): 1482–501.

Fileborn, B. and Vera-Gray, F. (2017) ' "I want to be able to walk the street without fear": transforming justice for street harassment', *Feminist Legal Studies*, 25: 203–27.

Fish, S. (2020) 'I made misogyny a hate crime in Nottinghamshire – and it's changed women's lives', *The Telegraph*, 10 September, Available from: https://www.telegraph.co.uk/women/life/made-misogyny-hate-crime-nottinghamshire-changed-womens-lives/ [Accessed 23 September 2020].

Gangoli, G., Bates, L. and Hester, M. (2020) 'What does justice mean to black and minority ethnic (BME) victims/survivors of gender-based violence?', *Journal of Ethnic and Migration Studies*, 46(15): 3119–35.

Gavey, N. (2018) *Just Sex? The Cultural Scaffolding of Rape* (2nd edn), London and New York: Routledge.

Gill, A. and Mason-Bish, H. (2013) 'Addressing violence against women as a form of hate crime: limitations and possibilities', *Feminist Review*, 105: 1–20.

Hall, N. (2013) *Hate Crime* (2nd edn), Oxon: Routledge.

Haylock, L., Cornelius, R., Malunga, A. and Mbandazayo, K. (2016) 'Shifting negative social norms rooted in unequal gender and power relationships to prevent violence against women and girls', *Gender and Development*, 24(2): 231–44.

Haynes, A., and Schweppe, J. (2020) 'Should hate crime legislation include misogynistic crimes?', in R.J. Sternberg (ed) *Perspectives on Hate: How It Originates, Develops, Manifests, and Spreads*, Washington, DC: American Psychological Association, pp 277–97.

Hindes, S. and Fileborn, B. (2022) '"Why did he do it? Because he's a fucking bloke": victim insights into the perpetration of street harassment', *British Journal of Criminology*, DOI: 10.1093/bjc/azac029

HMICFRS (2018) *Hate Crime: What Do Victims Tell Us? A Summary of Independent Research into Experiences of Hate Crime Victims*, Her Majesty's Inspectorate of Constabulary and Fire and Rescue Services, October, Available from: https://www.justiceinspectorates.gov.uk/hmicfrs/publicati ons/hate-crime-what-do-victims-tell-us/ [Accessed 23 September 2020].

Home Office (2019) *Ending Violence Against Women and Girls Strategy 2016–2020: Strategy Refresh*, March, Available from: https://www.gov.uk/gov ernment/publications/strategy-to-end-violence-against-women-and-girls-2016-to-2020 [Accessed 23 September 2020].

Hooper, R. (2018) 'Misogyny should be classed as a hate crime, campaigners tell police', *The Independent*, 9 July, Available from: https://www.inde pendent.co.uk/news/uk/home-news/campaign-groups-misogyny-hate-crime-police-citizens-uk-nottingham-a8437341.html [Accessed 23 September 2020].

Horvath, M. and Kelly, L. (2007) *From the Outset: Why Violence Should Be a Priority for the Commission for Equality and Human Rights*, London: London Metropolitan University.

Hymas, C. (2020) 'Crown Prosecution Service faces judicial review over policy on rapes as convictions fall to record low', *The Telegraph*, 20 July, Available from: https://www.telegraph.co.uk/news/2020/07/30/rape-prosecutions-fall-record-low-just-1439-offenders-convicted/ [Accessed 6 October 2020].

Imkaan (2018) *From the Margin to the Centre: Addressing Violence Against Women and Girls Alternative Bill*, Background Paper, October, Available from: https://www.imkaan.org.uk/resources [Accessed 28 September 2020].

Jewkes, R., Flood, M. and Lang, J. (2015) 'From work with men and boys to changes of social norms and reduction of inequities in gender relations: a conceptual shift in prevention of violence against women and girls', *The Lancet*, 385(9977): 1580–89.

Kelly, L. (1988) *Surviving Sexual Violence*, Cambridge, UK: Polity Press.

Koskela, H. and Pain, R. (2000) 'Revisiting fear and place: women's fear to attack and the built environment', *Geoforum*, 31: 269–80.

Krug, E.G., Mercy, J.A., Dahlberg, L.L. and Zwi, A.B. (2002) *The World Report on Violence and Health*, Geneva: World Health Organization.

Law Commission (2020) *Hate Crime Laws: A Consultation Paper*, Consultation paper 250, 23 September, Available from: https://www.lawcom.gov.uk/project/hate-crime/ [Accessed 28 September 2020].

Legg, S. and Nottingham Citizens (2021) '"No place for hate": community-led research and the geographies of Nottingham citizens' hate crime commission', *Social and Cultural Geography*, 22(8): 1164–86.

Livingston, B. (2015) 'Cornell international survey on street harassment', Available from: https://www.ihollaback.org/cornell-international-survey-on-street-harassment/#ar [Accessed 13 July 2021].

Maher, J.M., McCulloch, J. and Mason, G. (2015) 'Punishing gendered violence as hate crime: aggravated sentences as a means of recognising hate as motivation for violent crimes against women', *Australian Feminist Law Journal*, 41(1), 177–93.

Mason, G. (2014) 'The hate threshold: emotion, causation and difference in the construction of prejudice-motivated crime', *Social and Legal Studies*, 23(3): 293–314.

Mason-Bish, H. (2011) 'Examining the boundaries of hate crime policy: considering age and gender', *Criminal Justice Policy Review*, 24(3): 297–316.

Mason-Bish, H. and Duggan, M. (2020) '"Some men deeply hate women, and express that hatred freely": examining victims' experiences and perceptions of gendered hate crime', *International Review of Victimology*, 26(1): 112–34.

McCulloch, J., Maher, J.M., Walklate, S., McGowan, G. and Fitz-Gibbon, K. (2020) 'Justice perspectives of women with disability: an Australian story', *International Review of Victimology*, 1–15, DOI:10.1177/0269758020906270

McGlynn, C. and Westmarland, N. (2019) 'Kaleidoscopic justice: sexual violence and victim–survivors' perceptions of justice', *Social and Legal Studies*, 28(2): 179–201.

Meyer, D. (2014) 'Resisting hate crime discourse: queer and intersectional challenges to neoliberal hate crime laws', *Critical Criminology*, 22(1): 113–25.

Mullany, L. and Trickett, L. (2018) *Misogyny Hate Crime Evaluation Report*, Nottingham, UK: University of Nottingham and Nottingham Trent University, Available from: https://www.nottinghamwomenscentre.com/wp-content/uploads/2018/07/Misogyny-Hate-Crime-Evaluation-Report-June-2018.pdf. [Accessed 28 September 2020].

Nottingham Police (2018) 'Written submission from Nottingham Police (SPP0049) Misogyny as a Hate Crime to Women and Equalities Committee, Sexual harassment of women and girls in public places inquiry', February, Available from: http://data.parliament.uk/writtenevidence/committeeevidence.svc/evidencedocument/women-and-equalities-committee/sexual-harassment-of-women-and-girls-in-public-places/written/79374.html [Accessed 28 September 2020].

Nottingham Women's Centre (2018) 'Written submission from Nottingham Women's Centre (SPP0063) to Women and Equalities Committee, Sexual harassment of women and girls in public places inquiry', March, Available from: http://data.parliament.uk/writtenevidence/committeeevidence.svc/evidencedocument/women-and-equalities-committee/sexual-harassment-of-women-and-girls-in-public-places/written/79607.html [Accessed 28 September 2020].

Oppenheim, M. (2020) 'Police forces should immediately record misogyny as hate crime, says campaigner as Labour mayor backs plan', *The Independent*, 7 July, Available from: https://www.independent.co.uk/news/uk/home-news/misogyny-police-hate-crime-labour-mayors-domestic-abuse-bill-a9604491.html [Accessed 23 September 2020].

Pain, R. (1991) 'Space, sexual violence and social control: integrating geographical and feminist analyses of women's fear of crime', *Progress in Human Geography*, 15: 415–31.

Pain, R. (2000) 'Place, social relations and the fear of crime: a review', *Progress in Human Geography*, 24: 365–87.

Perry, J. (2008) 'The "perils" of an identity politics approach to the legal recognition of harm', *Liverpool Law Review*, 29: 19–36.

Pike, N. (2020) 'These sisters were sick of being catcalled. Now they're fighting to make street harassment a crime', *Vogue*, 6 September, Available from: https://www.vogue.co.uk/miss-vogue/article/our-streets-now-maya-tutton-interview [Accessed 23 September 2020].

Quinn, B.A. (2002) 'Sexual harassment and masculinity: the power and meaning of "girl watching"', *Gender and Society*, 16(3): 386–402.

Scottish Government (2021) *Misogyny and Criminal Justice in Scotland Working Group*, Available from: https://www.gov.scot/groups/misogyny-and-criminal-justice-in-scotland-working-group/ [Accessed 30 July 2021].

Suzack, C., Huhndorf, S.M., Perreault, J. and Barman, J. (eds) (2011) *Indigenous Women and Feminism: Politics, Activism, Culture*, Vancouver: UBC Press.

Topping, A. (2020) 'London bus attack victims join campaign to make misogyny a hate crime', *The Guardian*, 10 September, Available from: https://www.theguardian.com/uk-news/2020/sep/10/london-bus-attack-couple-join-campaign-to-make-misogyny-a-hate [Accessed 28 September 2020].

Vera-Gray, F. and Fileborn, B. (2018) 'Intersectional alterity and the harms of "cheer up"', *The Philosophical Journal of Conflict and Violence*, 2(1): 78–96.

Vera-Gray, F. and Kelly, L. (2020) 'Contested gendered space: public sexual harassment and women's safety work', *International Journal of Comparative and Applied Criminal Justice*, 44(4): 265–75.

Valentine, G. (1993) '(Hetero) sexing space: Lesbian perceptions and experiences of everyday spaces', *Environment and Planning D: Society and Space*, 11: 395–413.

Vizvary, M. (2020) *The State of Street Harassment in DC: A Report on the First Year of Implementing the Street Harassment Prevention Act*, Washington, DC: Office of Human Rights.

Walters, M., Brown, R. and Wiedlitzka, S. (2016) *Causes and Motivations of Hate Crime: Equality and Human Rights Commission Research Report*, 102, Manchester: Equality and Human Rights Commission, Available from: https://www.equalityhumanrights.com/sites/default/files/resea rch-report-102-causes-and-motivations-of-hate-crime.pdf [Accessed 23 September 2020].

Women and Equalities Committee (2018) *Sixth Report of Session 2017–19, Sexual Harassment of Women and Girls in Public Places (HC 701)*, 23 October, House of Commons: London, Available from: https://publications.par liament.uk/pa/cm201719/cmselect/cmwomeq/701/701.pdf [Accessed 23 September 2020].

Women and Equalities Committee (2019) *Eighth Report of Session 2017–19, Sexual Harassment of Women and Girls in Public Places (HC 2148)*, 8 May, House of Commons: London, Available from: https://publications.par liament.uk/pa/cm201719/cmselect/cmwomeq/2148/2148.pdf [Accessed 25 May 2022]

YouGov (2017) *Treating Misogynistic Offences as Hate Crimes; Art; Which City Should Be the Capital of Israel*, Available from: https://yougov.co.uk/topics/ politics/articles-reports/2017/12/08/treating-misogynistic-offences-hare-crimes-art-whi [Accessed 29 September 2020]

Yuval-Davis, N. (1999) 'Institutional racism, cultural diversity and citizenship: some reflections on reading the Stephen Lawrence Inquiry Report', *Sociological Research Online*, 4(1): 115–23.

4

Constructing Britain's Hated Landscapes: The Linguistic and Ideological Construction of Toxteth

Alice Butler-Warke

Introduction: hated landscapes

The concept of hate is well-defined by Rempel and Burris (2005: 297) as 'a motive based on devaluing the other and is associated with the goal of diminishing or destroying the other's well-being'. This frames hatred towards an 'other' as an extreme form of outgroup hostility (Allport, 1954). In their account of the functional perspective of hate, Fischer et al (2018) suggest that hate stems from who people/groups are, rather than what they do (Fischer et al, 2018: 309). Furthermore, they argue that when engaging in hate, individuals imbue their hate target with 'malicious intentions and being immoral, which is accompanied by feelings of lack of control or powerlessness. Such appraisals are not the result of one specific action, but of a belief about the stable disposition of the hated person or group' (Fischer et al, 2018: 310).

Recent discussions of hate in relation to space and place tend to focus on 'hatescapes' where, for example, a coalescence of 'social discrimination and spatial exclusion' experienced by disabled people leads to a lived experience of space defined by fear and ableist structures (Hall and Bates, 2019: 100). However, we can extend the notion of spatial hate or hostility and link it to experiences and processes of place-based stigmatization. The growing literature on territorial stigma (Wacquant, 2008; Kirkness and Tijé-Dra, 2017; Slater, 2017; Butler-Warke, 2020a; Butler-Warke, 2020b) underscores the centrality of perceptions (Garbin and Millington, 2012) of 'the stable disposition' (Fischer et al, 2018: 310) of particular districts.

These stigmatized landscapes are subjected to 'hate and national abjection' (Nayak, 2019: 929) as they are transformed into spatial others (Pinkster et al, 2020) that are relegated to outcast status (Wacquant, 2008) and rendered mythical (Byrne and Chonaill, 2014: 2). Once entered into the social imagination, this reputation and hostility is difficult to remove (Butler-Warke, 2020b; Pinkster et al, 2020) being based like human objects of hatred on the perceived 'stable disposition' of the area (Fischer et al, 2018: 310). If we consider, then, hating as a means of devaluing (Rempel and Burris, 2005), we see that landscapes come to be hated and stigmatized through widely held perceptions (Garbin and Millington, 2012) for economic or political ends (Slater, 2017) or as part of a broader socio-cultural performance of abjection (Butler et al, 2018). Stigmatization and hatred of place are embedded within a broader neoliberal framing (Scambler, 2018), exemplified through a form of 'symbolic, diffuse, slow and indirect' violence (Tyler, 2020) that erodes the reputation, symbolic capital, and value of the area and its residents as a mechanism of power (Link and Phelan, 2014).

Recent discourse analytic approaches to othered and stigmatized spaces has considered the use of specific terminology and discursive framings that perpetuate the negative perceptions of certain spaces. The term 'shithole' is used at multiple geographic scales (Butler et al, 2018) and 'sink estate' is a 'semantic battering ram' that flows freely in journalism and policy (Slater, 2018: 877) and contributes to the maintenance of hostility and stigma towards certain geographies. This chapter takes another semantic framing – 'the inner city' – and examines how the inner city 'poster child' of the 1980s – Toxteth, Liverpool – was similarly discursively constructed.

Study design

Data come from three sources: British press; policy and financial texts, and declassified government documents from the Thatcher prime ministership; and interviews with journalists and politicians active in the 1980s. Ethical approval was granted for both the discourse analysis of texts and for the interviews.

News articles about Toxteth were selected from the *Times*, the *Guardian*, the *Mirror*, the *Express* and the *Financial Times* following the selection criteria detailed in Butler (2019). An inductive content analysis to identify frequency of descriptors, taglines and co-occurrences of phrases, and a critical discourse analysis to interrogate deeper social and politico-economic meaning (van Dijk, 1996) were undertaken. Thus, a two-stage analysis considered both semantics and features *within* the texts and contextual meaning that allowed the linking of 'intra-textual elements with broader ideology and political discourse' (Butler, 2019: 4).

Relevant policy and financial documents selected mostly from the Margaret Thatcher Archives following an open search for 'Toxteth', were subjected to detailed critical analysis to consider their ideological underpinnings and the broader framing of Toxteth specifically and 'the inner cities' more generally both during the 1980s and beyond. Documents from the Thatcher Archives include now-declassified speeches, memos, notes, and briefings. Together they reveal the Conservative concern about the 'the inner cities' in the 1980s. Additional documents were drawn on for context including investment and property development websites.

Ten interviews with key journalists and two former politicians and policymakers provided further context and allowed the developing themes to be situated in relation to political and media narratives. Data from these interviews shape this chapter's analysis.

The policy positioning of the 'inner city problem'

The symbolism of the phrase 'inner city' refers to race, class and deviance (Burgess, 1985; Gilroy, 1987) and is tightly bound with a social and policy history on both sides of the Atlantic. Ngram[1] data on Google shows that the peak use of the term 'inner city' in American English occurs in 1975. Carried by what appears to be a fear of the transatlantic convergence of the 'inner city problem', the peaks in British English[2] occur first in 1981 and then in 1989, closely matching the leadership of Prime Minister Margaret Thatcher (1979–90). The story of the inner city began in the United States and travelled across the Atlantic in response to a fear that race riots and racial enclosure – the ghetto (Wacquant, 2000: 381) –would arrive at British shores. The term has been applied in British policy since the late 1960s and early 1970s (Imrie and Thomas, 1999: 5). This was in response to perceived 'urban decline' (Imrie and Thomas, 1999: 5) understood as being the result of individual pathology until the Community Development Programme (CDP) under Labour Prime Minister Harold Wilson (1964–70 and 1974–76). CDPs reoriented the understanding of the inner city from being solely pathological in origin to consider larger structural causes. Under Labour Prime Minister James Callaghan (1976–1979), a White Paper and a parliamentary Act reaffirmed this view and foregrounded the role of the economy. Central government dispensed funds spent at a local level, and the role of the local authority was paramount (HMSO, 1977 in Lawless, 2008: 40).

This local authority-level focus changed when Margaret Thatcher became prime minister in 1979. Her government bypassed local government and embraced a central, managerial approach to the questions of the inner city. Michael Heseltine, serving as Secretary of State for the Environment, further changed the tone of British inner city policy as he introduced pump-priming initiatives and public–private partnerships, reflecting the Conservative government's belief that the private sector could 'fix' the inner cities (Lawless, 2008: 60–76). This necessarily resulted in a 'value for money' approach (Imrie and Thomas, 1999: 25), with the Thatcher government reformulating the inner city question as one of marketizing of lives and spaces.

Symbolic meaning and the 'inner city'

As well as its policy and political history, the term 'inner city' also has a symbolic story that connects the term with ideas of race, class and otherness. The term is 'the geographical euphemism used by normal US social science to designate the black ghetto, precisely to avoid *naming* it' (Wacquant, 2008: 10, emphasis in original; and see also Parisi and Holcomb, 1994). Gilroy explains that 'Britain's "race" politics are quite inconceivable away from the context of the inner-city which provides such firm foundations for the imagery of black criminality and lawlessness' (Gilroy, 1987: 311), implying that the inner city is intricately bound up with notions of race and criminality. The idea of the inner city is based on a myth of 'an alien place, separate and isolated, located outside white, middle-class values and environments' (Burgess, 1985: 193). This idea is, in part, aided by the grammatical construction that refers to 'the inner city' using the definite article '*the*', through which a discourse is produced of a shared knowledge (Lyons, 1980) of a unique location with specific socially constructed deviant attributes.

Toxteth: *l'enfant terrible* of British inner cities

In her study of the 1981 uprisings (including Toxteth, Brixton and Moss Side), Burgess (1985) notes that the idea of the inner city was used in the press to connote a mythologized notion of a substandard physical environment, white working class, Black and street cultures (1985: 206). She argues that the press functions hegemonically to maintain 'existing social conditions' (Burgess, 1985: 222), underscoring the fact that areas experiencing 'riots' should be feared. According to Teun van Dijk's approach, this is achieved by the press providing 'carefully selected facts' that direct the reader to produce the 'preferred models of the elites' (1996: 16), whose interests are 'largely supported by the mainstream press' (1996: 22). In this case, the dominant view of the elites is that inner cities are to be feared, avoided, and contained in line with the Conservative policies of the 1980s. Crucially, any suggestion of a structural cause of the disturbances is removed and, instead, the ideology that 'inner cities' are deviant is normalized in the press.

In examining press use of the term 'inner city' in relation to Toxteth over the entirety of the 20th century, only the *Guardian* uses the term 'inner city' in relation to the district prior to 1981 and this usage is minimal (a total of 6 articles from 1974 to 1980). All newspapers see a sudden increase in the use of the terms 'Toxteth' and 'inner city' co-occurring in 1981 in three articles in the *Express*, five in the *Mirror*, 37 in the *Times*, 2 in the *Financial Times*, and 36 in the *Guardian*.[3] The usage in the press then decreases and peaks again in 1985 with roughly half the level of usage compared to 1981, coinciding with the proliferation of inner city policies under Thatcher's Conservative government during this period; particularly reflecting the advent of the Urban Development Corporations (UDCs) in 1981 (Lawless, 2008).

In these co-occurrences of 'Toxteth' and 'inner city', the press employs the term 'inner city' in ways that are connected to notions of scalar governance and that reflect government discourse. The first use of the term 'inner city' works at a regional scale and spatially ties Toxteth to the city of Liverpool or the region of Merseyside and represents the archetypal 'inner city' of the wider area. Through this use, the press moves the focus away from Toxteth alone and connects it to a larger urban or regional focus that obscures the unique identity of Toxteth, making it a city-wide or regional focus. It applies symbolic and social values of the inner city to Toxteth, masking its unique contours and making it part of a national 'problem' geography. In so doing, the press creates a monolithic view of all inner-cities and generalizes Toxteth's issues and identity so that they become part of a national discourse and debate around these landscapes of hate. This discursive positioning escalates issues faced in Toxteth to a larger discourse that serves to justify a national intervention. These processes reflect the Conservative government policy of the 1980s that saw an increasing nationalization of inner city policy (Fraser, 1996: 57) or, termed otherwise, a nationalization of the local.

Connecting 'inner city' Toxteth to a national landscape of hate

The labelling of Toxteth through this first use of the term 'inner city' connects closely to the second use of the term, which generalizes and changes the scale of Toxteth, connecting it to a larger national – as opposed to regionally defined – discourse. This second use of the term builds up a monolithic and national-scale vision of an imagined geography of British inner-urban areas.

In the *Express* in 1981, journalist Max Hastings generalizes all inner urban areas when discussing the uprisings, writing that 'The essential, unstated demand of the principal riot areas of the inner cities is that local black communities should be allowed to exist by their own rules and habits above all freely circulating marijuana' (Hastings, 1981: 9).

Here, Hastings creates a generalized caricature of all inner cities as places of free-flowing drugs and blackness; his assertion paints inner cities as hotbeds of deviance. His reference to 'the inner cities' – using the definite article 'the' – highlights his treatment of all inner urban areas as monolithic in terms of character and difficulties. Similarly, an article entitled 'Holidays of Hope' discusses an initiative that will see 'twenty teenagers from Brixton and Toxteth' go on holiday with policemen to 'ease tension in the inner-city troublespots' (*The Express*, 1982: 13). Here too, the inner city is made general and monolithic: all areas have the same problems that can be remedied in the same way, through external intervention and through government and private sector presence.

This generalizing trend is apparent especially in articles relating to Heseltine's involvement in Liverpool as Minister for Merseyside. In an article about his time in Liverpool and being pelted with eggs by demonstrators, careful juxtaposition highlights the implicit use of the inner-cityization of Toxteth by the press. The reporter quotes Heseltine speaking with determination about continuing his efforts stating that he 'will be back in Toxteth in a few weeks' (Heseltine in Kent, 1982: 5). The next paragraph transitions from this mention of Toxteth to a discussion of inner cities: 'Mr Heseltine said he was very dismayed about the state of the inner cities and how they had decayed over the past 70 years' (Kent, 1982: 5). This juxtaposition of Toxteth with the larger discourse of inner cities up-scales it from the local to the national, moving the discussion away from one specific inner city area (Toxteth) to a state-level observation. The reporter both implies that Toxteth is to be seen as an 'inner city' with all of the symbolic baggage that such a label connotes, and masks all of the unique nuances of Toxteth's identity by generalizing and placing it as part of a generic 'inner city problem' to be solved at a national level as opposed to a distinctive and specific set of issues related to a particular place.

A similar use of the term is seen again when referring to Heseltine's plan for a Garden Festival in the city. 'Mr Michael Heseltine, Secretary of State for the Environment, announced a £10m jobs boost for Merseyside last night. He plans to develop Europe's biggest garden exhibition amid the debris of July's clashes in Toxteth, Liverpool' (*The Times*, 1981: 2). Following a brief discussion of the garden festival movement, Heseltine is then quoted as saying that 'national garden festivals provide great opportunities for the rejuvenation of run-down inner-city areas' (Heseltine in *The Times*, 1981: 2). Here, Toxteth is sandwiched between two generalizations at different scales, both of which ignore the local character of Toxteth. By beginning the article with mention of improvement to Merseyside, the reporter regionalizes the focus, considering the plight of the region more generally rather than considering Toxteth specifically. Then, the reporter refers to the 'debris' of Toxteth, bringing the focus back to the specific area before generalizing to a national level by referring broadly to 'inner cities', connecting Toxteth to a national landscape of inner cities and hate.

Coverage of Heseltine's work in Liverpool – and, indeed, the work itself – is frequently associated with press up-scaling of Toxteth's 'inner city' status from the local to the national (Lawless, 2008). In an article in the *Guardian* about the Environment Secretary's secondment to Liverpool 'to judge inner city policies all over the country' (Aitken, 1981: 1), the reporter explains that 'the choice of Liverpool for the main inquiry underlines the belief of Ministers that the Toxteth riot contained factors which are typical in other areas' (Aitken, 1981: 1). Here the *Guardian* both produces and reproduces the inner city discourse coming from the Conservative government. It argues that Toxteth stands for a national issue and, as such, the discourse is scaled up from a local concern where it could deal with the specificities of Toxteth to a national concern that relates to and represents *the* 'inner city problem'.

An article in the *Mirror*, at first reading, appears to employ a slightly different approach to coverage of the 'inner city' and takes on a critique of 'Mrs Thatcher's Year of the Inner City' and her ' "fact-finding" tour of the inner-cities' (Wigmore, 1987: 4). The coverage suggests that the Conservative Party is doing too little and not truly engaging with the issues at play, writing that 'unlike Mrs Thatcher, the *Mirror* has followed the failing fortunes of the inner-cities for years … [which] have suffered riots during the Thatcher years … [and] have suffered heavily under Mrs Thatcher's cash cut-backs' (Wigmore, 1987: 4). However, the language used by the *Mirror* remains as stigmatizing as the other newspapers. Reporter Barry Wigmore describes the Falkner Estate in Toxteth with reference to overcrowding, giant rats and broken windows. He concludes that 'no one should have to live in a place like this. … This is Toxteth, Liverpool 8, the scene of the bloody riots in 1981, and they all started from here on the crumbling Falkner Estate. It's the sort of inner-city ghetto that breeds discontent' (Wigmore, 1987: 4).

Such coverage uses emotive and figurative language. It relies on negativity in the form of visual imagery to conjure up an image of a truly damaged place which, presumably, with the paper's left-wing bent, is meant to elicit horror in the readers that the government has failed Toxteth residents. Instead, what is conveyed is a stigmatizing view of Toxteth and, in addition to the damning description of the area, it is ultimately then generalized as part of a larger inner city problem. The *Mirror's* coverage style is reminiscent of the work of Victorian reformers such as Charles Dickens, Charles Booth and Friedrich Engels who sought to draw attention to the poor and the appalling conditions that they endured in the early modern city but, in so doing, further stigmatized the very group they were trying to assist (Deverell, 2007: 36). While the *Mirror* highlights the plight of those living in the inner cities and suggests that the political elite are doing too little to help, through language use and discursive structuring, it continues to reaffirm the stigma of inner city living.[4]

Thatcher and the inner city

The Thatcher government's labelling of Toxteth as the 'inner city' further justified its fiscal policies as interventions to address social disorder within a wider urban agenda. The labelling relied on the core stigma (Butler-Warke, 2020b) and race- and class-based stereotypes of the idea of the inner city – Parisi and Holcomb's 'geographical periphrasis ... [to] describe urban problems' (1994: 385).

Only months after taking office, a letter was sent from Thatcher's private secretary to the Department of the Environment detailing Thatcher's opinions on the inner city. She did not favour 'a major review' of policies but rather preferred 'a simplification of the existing bureaucratic processes and much greater emphasis on the private sector and voluntary effort, with the public sector concentrating on creating the right climate and conditions for enterprise to flourish' (Pattison, 1979: 1). Thatcher was concerned with privatizing solutions to the constructed inner city and to a centralization of policy rather than having local authority involvement.

However, while the term 'inner city' has clear symbolic connotations and value, finding a cohesive, coherent and consistent definition of what the Thatcher government meant and understood by the term is more difficult. Thatcher, Howe and Joseph were opposed to Heseltine's more ambitious plans for inner city 'revival'. In a personal interview for this study, Lord Heseltine explained his understanding of the term 'inner city' as being "like an elephant, difficult to define but you recognize it when you see it. And so, first thing to do is to look for derelict sites and empty buildings or whatever" (Personal interview with Heseltine for this study, 2017). This suggests that dereliction is the key feature he used to delineate the inner city. His pamphlet, 'Reviving the Inner Cities', published in 1983, opens with the following:

> The inner city problem is about concentrations of relatively poor people, inadequately educated and trained, living in badly maintained housing in areas of declining economic activity, rising unemployment and increasing crime and vandalism. It is not necessarily a problem of physical location. Many inner cities are relatively prosperous. Many outer housing estates meet the conditions I have set out. The inner city label is about concentrations of social deprivation and economic decline. We know what we mean by the inner city problem. (Heseltine, 1983: 3)

Thus, the inner city, as defined by Heseltine, stems from economic decline, increasing deviance, dereliction, and poverty. However, what the definition does *not* depend on is geographical location. Reference to the inner city being a byword for 'concentrations of social deprivation and economic decline' that may even be in 'outer housing estates' (Heseltine, 1983: 3) is revelatory: with this structuring, we can understand why policy attention on the 'inner city' was, in fact, regional or national in focus, in accordance with the press up-scaling of Toxteth. The Urban Programme, the Urban Development Grants, the Garden Festival, the Land Registry, the Enterprise Zones, and the Merseyside Development Corporation did not focus on the inner-cityized Toxteth but on the *rest* of the city of Liverpool, the region, or even the whole country. The Conservative inner city policies did not have to focus on inner urban areas at all but on anywhere that met the vague criteria that 'you recognize it when you see it' (Personal interview with Heseltine for this study, 2017). Thus re-scaling from the local to the national – the nationalizing of the local – was largely inevitable. The stigma of the 'inner city' was used by the Conservative Party as a label or shorthand to signify economic decline, dereliction, and deviance. The term was largely symbolic, suitably vague, and served to label areas – regardless of their geographical location – in order to justify privatized intervention.

The Thatcher government's views on Liverpool

The Thatcher government labelling of Toxteth as the 'inner city' further justified its fiscal policies as part of a wider urban agenda. Press coverage of the notion of the inner city closely follows the political discourse of the time, which treated Toxteth as the *enfant terrible* of the perceived inner city problem of the 1980s and justified the development of punitive urban policies that enacted symbolic violence upon the very communities suffering. However, despite press and political discourse upscaling the focus from the local to the national, this story is not complete without consideration of Thatcher's wariness towards and opposition to the city of Liverpool specifically.

Using the Margaret Thatcher Archives, official documents point to her government's suspicion about the city of Liverpool and the county of Merseyside. In Geoffrey Howe's (Chancellor of the Exchequer, 1979–83) 'The right approach to the economy' speech in which he outlined the proposed actions of the future Conservative government, he notes Merseyside alongside areas of Scotland, Wales, the North East and Northern Ireland, as being one of the 'worst discouragements to enterprise' – enterprise being one of the future Conservative government's priorities (Howe, 1977): Merseyside is shown to be at odds with the party's aims. In December 1978, only months before Thatcher became prime minister, her advisor Keith Joseph wrote a letter in support of Geoffrey Howe's suggestion of establishing a Merseyside Task Force. In the top right corner of the letter, Margaret Thatcher hand-writes, 'I am very much against the idea' (Joseph, 1978: 1). She further annotates the letter to mark her agreement with John Hoskyns, policy advisor, who 'thinks it [a Merseyside Task Force] will be a distraction from our main purposes' (Joseph, 1978: 1). Joseph's letter continues that 'the other objection is that Merseyside is notorious for obstruction and our ideas have least chance of flowering in that particular soil' (Joseph, 1978: 1). The tone of this letter and Thatcher's comments imply that aiding Merseyside falls outside the aims of her main economic objectives, and that Conservative ideals are not likely to take hold in Merseyside. In this way, Liverpool is structured as being separate from the rest of the country and is positioned as a challenge to, and outwith, government economic policy.

Once the disturbances had commenced, the party rhetoric towards Liverpool moved from exasperation at its 'obstruction' to an antipathy that was apparent in the desired withholding of funds from the city and the county. In a private letter from Howe to Thatcher in August 1981 entitled 'Liverpool', he writes of Heseltine's plans for the city and advises 'of the need to be careful not to over-commit scarce resources to Liverpool ... and having nothing left for more promising areas' (Howe, 1981). Here, Howe not only hierarchizes urban areas, placing the less 'promising' Liverpool at the bottom, but he directly advises against investing money in a city in need, in favour of waiting for 'brighter ideas for renewing economic activity' elsewhere (Howe, 1981). This spatial hierarchization exemplifies the processes by which hate and abjection come to be applied to place; elite discourse relegates places and their populations to the symbolic dumping ground, which has consequent tangible effects for place and population. The feelings of abjection or hatred surrounding a place often rely on the 'presence of an abject population and the state's response to this population' (Butler et al, 2018: 506). An abject population – the 'wretched' (Tyler, 2013) – is created through an elite construction of society whereby sections of the population become residual, surplus to requirements, simultaneously repelled yet with an enduring allure. The creation of an abject population is the ultimate mark of sovereign power (Tyler, 2013): the power to name, to distinguish whose life has value and who can be left behind. An abject place can, then, simply be home to such a population or its very spatiality may become abject (Butler et al, 2018) as sovereign power withdraws from or, conversely, inserts itself into the geography of an area as a mark of domination.

Howe's hierarchization is shown to be based on predicted value-for-money and economic gains, and he ranks Liverpool as low on this scale. In the now-infamous letter, Howe concludes with his opinion on the benefits of a managed decline for the city: 'I cannot help feeling that the option of managed decline, which the CPRS [Central Policy Review Staff] rejected in its study of Merseyside, is one which we should not forget altogether. We must not expend all our resources in trying to make water flow uphill' (Howe, 1981).

Howe's comments about the overt and visible allocation of funds reflect the Conservative government's foregrounding of privately organized economic solutions to social and structural problems. A similar focus can be seen in John Hoskyns' note to Thatcher on 10 July 1981, days after the disturbances broke out in Toxteth. Here, unlike Howe, Hoskyns prioritizes the role of money in solving Toxteth's disturbances. He states that any minister sent to the area 'must be seen to spend money' but adds that 'this money is likely to be money wasted' (Hoskyns, 1981). Financial solutions are constructed as the Conservative government's main response to structural problems, even when it is acknowledged that spending money will not ameliorate the situation. This focus on money underscores the Conservative government emphasis on – often misdirected – pecuniary solutions as part of a wider urban policy agenda. Imrie and Thomas frame this as the Thatcher government's foregrounding of 'market goals over social and community objectives' (Imrie and Thomas, 1999: 28), and Howe's letter shows a prioritization of fiscal returns over the social conditions of Liverpool. While uneven concentration of capital underpins economic and social disadvantage, the Conservative government here demonstrates a focus on overt spending even when a solution cannot be bought; ill-thought financial expenditure in this instance represents a top-down sticking plaster that fails to adequately address deeper structural concerns.

Toxteth and Thatcher's urban agenda

While Heseltine and Thatcher were at odds over the ways to tackle it, Toxteth came to typify the constructed inner city problem and the testing ground for the proposed solutions to the problem: direct central government intervention, private sector involvement, private investment, and bypassing local authority decision-making. In his report entitled *It Took a Riot*, which was leaked to the press, Heseltine notes 'Merseyside has been suffering from long term decline at least since the Great War. … Nor are prospects good' (Heseltine, 1981: 1). He refers to industrial decline across the city and notes that despite city-wide problems, 'of course, the headlines have concentrated on Liverpool 8 or Toxteth and here the problem is most acute' (Heseltine, 1981: 4). This justifies using Toxteth as the poster child of problems while upscaling the solution to the rest of the city.

It was to Toxteth that Michael Heseltine rushed in the aftermath of the uprisings of summer 1981, where he served as Minister for Merseyside for 12 months. In a personal interview, he explained that Liverpool was the target of 30 regeneration projects in the wake of the uprisings (Personal interview with Heseltine for this study, 2017). In *It Took a Riot*, Heseltine emphasizes that he was quick to gather support from 'some 30 representatives of the Financial Institutions … to join the Government in a comprehensive examination of the role of the private sector in financing urban development and in the revival of the older urban areas' (Heseltine, 1981: 9), thereby highlighting the urban privatization agenda of Thatcher's government. A letter from Tom King (Minister of State for Local Government, 1979–83) on 16 July 1981 – less than two weeks after the disturbances in Toxteth broke out – suggests 'private sector involvement' to 'tackle economic and employment problems in the inner cities' (King, 1981). That the press echoed this construction and stigma of Toxteth as the example of the inner city problem highlights the close interplay between press and politics, reflecting Herman and Chomsky's propaganda model that sees 'mutual interests' (1988: xi) and elite and unquestioned sources as determining press coverage (1988: 112).

Unhating Toxteth

One of the effects of the government's response to Toxteth was a tide of gentrifying forces. Territorial stigma and gentrification 'form two sides of the same conceptual and policy coin' (Kallin and Slater, 2014: 1351) and, in the case of Toxteth, the correlation between private sector regional involvement and the stigma surrounding the inner city is evidenced in the *Guardian* in 1988. Martyn Halsall highlights an example of the uprisings in Toxteth and attendant government policy enabling gentrification and investment *outside* Toxteth, and not where it was most needed. He writes that 'luxury apartments along the Liverpool waterfront are probably the most curious by-products of the anger which fuelled the Toxteth riots in 1981' (1988: A30). These new apartments in the renovated Albert Dock – not in Toxteth – re-developed through the Merseyside Development Corporation (MDC), attracted a waiting listing of 1,700 names and 'new owners include an inevitable lubrication of yuppies; barristers, accountants and business persons' (Halsall, 1988: A30): a far cry from facilitating change for those living in the discursively constructed 'inner city'. This highlights the urban and regional focus of the MDC that sought to make area changes that, it was asserted, would trickle down into the deprived urban cores.

Having already been enacted to justify intervention, the government and press label of the 'inner city' now facilitated the arrival of gentrifiers, as its discursive meaning was changed to imply economic potential and an authentic urban experience. Nearly 20 years after the uprisings, the *Express* reports on the 'invasion of the yumbies' or 'Young Upwardly Mobile Bohemians' who 'are educated and creative, but also crave a sense of reality by living in Britain's gritty inner cities' (Minton, 1998: 24). Describing a group that appears similar to the current hipster subcultural movement, reporter Anna Minton, writes that in addition to craving a creative career, purchasing fair-trade and ethical products, and enjoying the outdoors, a Yumbie 'Lives in inner-city areas around the country and particularly favours places once tarred with the urban front-line tag, such as Brixton in London, Hulme in Manchester or Liverpool's Toxteth' (Minton, 1998: 24).

This suggests a process of intense stigmatization followed by a move to gentrify is common with 'symbolic defamation [providing] the groundwork and ideological justification for a thorough class transformation of urban space' (Slater, 2017: 118). An article in the *Guardian* in 1999, further reflects the media's role in shaping external public perceptions that are opposed to internal or insider views of an area. Linda Grant explains, 'say Toxteth in London, and people think, "Riots". Say Toxteth in Liverpool, and they think, "Yuppie gentrification". Toxteth is now Liverpool's Islington' (Grant, 1999: C8). Here Grant explains that Toxteth has seen an influx of gentrifiers in recent years, echoing Kallin and Slater's assertion that 'stigmatisation lays the foundations for state-sponsored gentrification. ... The "blemish of place" was not only *constructed* by the state, but also the target for *demolition* by the state' (2014: 1353, emphasis in original). While it is oversimplified to state that the arrival of private capital and middle-class white residents brought an end to the constructed hatred of the inner city, I argue that the hatred was no longer of ideological benefit. The focus of demonized and marginalized spaces was shifting from the hated inner city to the afeared 'Muslim enclave' (Tissot 2007: 366) representing a shift in hegemonic discourse (Butler-Warke, 2020b) and, thus, a symbolic unbridling of hatred and the 'inner city'.

State-sponsored gentrification peaked in the years after the dawn of the 21st century with the Housing Market Renewal (HMR) Pathfinders scheme initiated in 2002 by the Labour government under PM Tony Blair (1997–2007). A response to housing market failure, defined by 'high vacancy rates, increasing population turnover, low sales values and, in some cases, neighbourhood abandonment' (Allen, 2007: 123), the HMR scheme – which was itself ultimately abandoned – was a scheme of mass demolition that would have used Granby, Toxteth, as one of its sites. The 'housing failure' it noted had, in Toxteth's case, been the result of decades of disinvestment, retrenchment of social services and public resources laid bare particularly in the aftermath of the 1981 uprisings and the subsequent 'inner cityization' of the area. The HMR scheme would have required:

> The mass demolition of approximately 50,000 'unwanted' dwellings in Merseyside ... with at least 11,000 of these being located in the inner-urban ring of the city of Liverpool. ... The purpose of this mass demolition programme is to provide large parcels of land to developers, who will be charged with the task of creating an inner-urban dwellingscape that is attractive to middle-class house purchasers. (Allen, 2007: 123)

This quote highlights the linchpin in the HMR vision, which can be understood as the desire to attract capital and the middle class to previously deprived areas: a formalized continuation of the discursive yumbie-ism of the 1980s and 1990s. The HMR scheme demonstrates the overt state-led gentrification that arose in parts of Liverpool – including Granby – immediately following a period of government and media stigmatization of Toxteth.

Today, the debate over housing regeneration in Toxteth continues with the movements such as the Granby 4 Streets Community Land Trust (CLT), which has successfully implemented an independent and community-led redevelopment project (see Figure 4.1). This has occurred at the same time that private developer Placefirst, teamed with Liverpool City Council, have, after several years of failed trials, submitted a plan for the Welsh Streets – once the focus of the HMR Pathfinder initiative – to be redesigned to make 'aspirational' properties that will appeal to a variety of renters (Houghton, 2018; see also Figure 4.2).

Toxteth is being blatantly marketed and gentrified by the state and private investors; a webpage on property developer Aspen Woolf Ltd.'s website draws on the label and idea of the inner city problem as it explains that:

> For many people, Liverpool's Toxteth area is synonymous with the 1981 riots where a civil disturbance broke out between police and local youths. However, despite the negative image this portrayed, its repercussions only highlighted the greater need for social stability and increased investment across Liverpool's inner-city areas. ... Today, Toxteth is a hotbed of investment, buoyed by relatively inexpensive housing and attractive rental yields ... meaning that regenerated Toxteth is now a great place to invest. (Pooley, 2016)

This example of investment-oriented discourse highlights the private sector's attempts to transform a hated landscape to an unhated landscape as Toxteth is defined, first, in relation to the 'riots' and, second, in purely economic terms as it is shown to have risen, phoenix-like from the ashes, thanks to external private investment. Of course, to pit earlier 'hated Toxteth' against later 'unhated Toxteth' in a strictly lateral temporal sense masks the complexity and textures of the complex, scalar and multiple versions of place that exist for residents and non-residents alike at every moment, and in the multiplicity of experiences that make each moment (Stephenson, 2010). But, looking at the imposed top-down narrative surrounding Toxteth, we see that the discourse has shifted from one of strife and urban disorder signalling fear and panic, to one of grittiness and authentic urban experiences that yield investment potential and profit. The grassroots initiative of the Granby 4 Streets CLT sits in

Figure 4.1: Site of Granby Street Market in Granby 4 Streets

Source: Author's own image

opposition to the private developments, showing the grassroots potential to overcome creeping privatization. The Placefirst and Aspen Woolf stories highlight, however, the tenacious attempts of state-led and state-initiated gentrifying forces.

Figure 4.2: The 'Welsh Streets' in Toxteth prior to redevelopment by Placefirst

Source: Author's own image

Conclusion

The press and political discursive positioning of Toxteth during the last decades of the 20th century and into the 21st century highlight three key issues. First, and perhaps most evident, we see the interplay between press and central government policy. This mutual reinforcement allows key state ideologies to be transmitted at scale. Second, we see that semantic and discursive tropes such as 'inner city' are not benign; they can be used to pave the way for gentrifiers to demolish and destroy. Third, we see that intense stigmatization followed by gentrification is not a coincidence; framing areas as 'inner cities' is a deliberate choice that is usually part of a broader political and economic story and effort.

The creation of a landscape of hate through discursive framing and positioning, then, can be seen as intentional. In the case of Toxteth, structural inequality led to the uprisings (Butler, 2019) which, combined with government urban policy that benefitted the wider area rather than Toxteth itself, led to the framing of Toxteth as a landscape of hate to be feared: the *enfant terrible* of Britain's urban inner areas. But this cycle of denigration, disinvestment and dereliction led to gentrification as Wacquant aptly summarizes:

Once a place is publicly labelled as a 'lawless zone' or 'outlaw estate', outside the common norm, it is easy for the authorities to justify special measures, deviating from both law and custom, which can have the effect – if not the intention – of destabilizing and further marginalizing their occupants, subjecting them to the dictates of the deregulated labour market, and rendering them invisible or driving them out of a coveted space. (Wacquant, 2007: 69)

Toxteth saw the labelling that set it outside the 'common norm' and special measures abounded in the months following the uprisings of 1981. The special measures being linked to Toxteth but being enacted at a wider urban and regional scale had the effect of 'further marginalizing' residents while simultaneously reinforcing the district's position as the troubled area of the city, thereby beginning the process through which private investment arrived and gentrifying forces took hold to gradually 'unhate' the area. Toxteth's unhating, of course, as with most stories of gentrification, came in the form of private capital and an influx of white middle-class residents seeking both a lucrative investment opportunity and a chance to enjoy an edginess and cheaper housing that the 'inner city' offers.

We must, when thinking about hated and unhated landscapes, ask who constructs these narratives of hate and who stands to benefit from their unhating. Returning to Rempel and Burris' understanding of hate as a means of 'devaluing the other' (2005: 300), we see that in the stigmatization–gentrification cycle, this 'devaluing' is not merely symbolic but economic. Until the unhating process yields a removal of the structural barriers and generates positive outcomes for the area's residents, the pernicious stigmatization–gentrification cycle will continue, discursively building landscapes of hate ripe for gentrification. We can hold on to hope; however, grassroots initiatives such as the Granby 4 Streets CLT show that communities can confront this stigmatization–gentrification cycle and, along with a more nuanced discourse of place in media and policy, we can begin to discuss systematic neglect without constructing a landscape of hate.

Notes

[1] The Google Ngram Viewer is a computer linguistics programme that traces the use of a words in a corpus of scanned books.

[2] The contested use of the term 'British' is acknowledged and the author recognizes that Britishness is not monolithic. In this chapter 'British English' is used to differentiate between American forms of English, for example. 'British press' is used to reflect that the newspapers in question are national rather than regional in focus. 'British' when applied to policy in this chapter refers to non-devolved policies and narratives.

[3] It is notable the *Guardian* – once a left-leaning 'broadsheet' – has such a high level of use of the term 'inner city' and I suggest that, like the left-leaning *Mirror*, some of this coverage constitutes a well-intentioned awareness-building among a concerned readership. However, that such stigmatizing language was used uncritically without consideration for the perpetuation of symbolic violence highlights the Chomskyan interpretation that 'the media system is entangled in an unconscious system in which it is part of a structure that enables powerful voices and views of society to dominate' (Butler, 2019: 554). Thus, such uncritical use of the term reflects the practices of the media industry as a whole, bound as it is in complex relationships of power.

[4] This coverage presents a striking conundrum regarding how we can talk about stigmatized areas or geographies of neglect without perpetuating this stigma. This argument is discussed further in Butler-Warke (2020b).

References

Aitken, I. (1981) 'Heseltine on mission to Liverpool', *The Guardian*, 17 July, p 1.

Allen, C. (2007) *Housing Market Renewal and Social Class*, London: Routledge.

Allport, G.W. (1955) *The Nature of Prejudice*, Cambridge, MA: Addison-Wesley.

Burgess, J. (1985) 'News from nowhere: the press, the riots and the myth of the inner city', in J. Burgess and J. Gold (eds) *Geography, the Media and Popular Culture*, London: Croom Helm, pp 192–228.

Butler, A. (2019) 'Toxic Toxteth: understanding press stigmatization of Toxteth during the 1981 uprising', *Journalism*, 21(4): 541–56.

Butler, A., Schafran, A. and Carpenter, G. (2018) 'What does it mean when people call a place a shithole? Understanding a discourse of denigration in the United Kingdom and the Republic of Ireland', *Transactions of the Institute of British Geographers*, 43(3): 496–510.

Butler-Warke, A. (2020a) 'Foundational stigma: place-based stigma in the age before advanced marginality', *The British Journal of Sociology*, 71(1): 140–52.

Butler-Warke, A. (2020b) 'There's a time and a place: temporal aspects of place-based stigma', *Community Development Journal*, 56(2): 203–19.

Byrne, M. and Chonaill, B.N. (2014) '"Ghettos of the mind": realities and myths in the construction of the social identity of a Dublin suburb', *Sociological Research Online*, 19(3): 15–29.

Deverell, C. (2007) 'Looked after children, their parents, disadvantage and stigma', in P. Burke and J. Parker (eds) *Social Work and Disadvantage: Addressing the Roots of Stigma through Association*, London: Jessica Kingsley Publishers, pp 27–44.

Express, The (1982) 'Holidays of hope', 3 August, p 13.

Fischer, A., Halperin, E., Canetti, D. and Jasini, A. (2018) 'Why we hate', *Emotion Review*, 10(4): 309–20.

Fraser, P. (1996) 'Social and spatial relationships and the "problem" inner city', *Critical Social Policy*, 49: 43–65.

Garbin, D. and Millington, G. (2012) 'Territorial stigma and the politics of resistance in a Parisian banlieue: La Courneuve and beyond', *Urban Studies*, 49(10): 2067–83.

Gilroy, P. (1987) *There Ain't No Black in the Union Jack*, London: Routledge.

Grant, L. (1999) 'Calm down yourself', *The Guardian*, 10 July, p C8.

Halsall, M. (1988) 'Life on the waterfront', *The Guardian*, 17 December, p A30.

Hall, E. and Bates, E. (2019) 'Hatescape? A relational geography of disability hate crime, exclusion and belonging in the city', *Geoforum*, 101: 100–10.

Hastings, M. (1981) 'Save us from all these excuses', *The Express*, 10 July, p 9.

Herman, E.S. and Chomsky, N. (1988) *Manufacturing Consent: The Political Economy of the Mass Media*, New York: Pantheon Books.

Heseltine, M. (1981) *Heseltine Minute to MT ("It Took a Riot")* [Report], Margaret Thatcher Foundation, Margaret Thatcher Archives.

Heseltine, M. (1983) *Reviving the Inner Cities*, London: Conservative Political Centre.

Hoskyns, J. (1981) *Hoskyns Minute to MT ("A Minister for Urban Renewal Etc")*. [Letter], Margaret Thatcher Foundation, Margaret Thatcher Archives.

Houghton, A. (2018) 'Who will live in the new-look Welsh Streets?' *Liverpool Echo*, 13 August, Available from: https://www.liverpoolecho.co.uk/news/liverpool-news/who-live-new-look-welsh-13468875 [Accessed 30 May 2018].

Howe, G. (1977) *The Right Approach to the Economy (Conservative Policy Statement)* [Statement], Margaret Thatcher Foundation, Margaret Thatcher Archives.

Howe, G. (1981) *Chancellor of the Exchequer Minute to MT ("Liverpool")* [Minute], Margaret Thatcher Foundation, Margaret Thatcher Archives.

Imrie, R. and Thomas, H. (1999) 'Assessing urban policy and the urban development corporations', in R. Imrie and H. Thomas (eds) *British Urban Policy* (2nd edn), London: Sage, pp 3–42.

Joseph, K. (1978) *Sir Keith Joseph to MT (Howe Suggests I Chair a Merseyside 'Task Force')* [Letter], Margaret Thatcher Foundation, Margaret Thatcher Archives.

Kallin, H. and Slater, T. (2014) 'Activating territorial stigma: gentrifying marginality on Edinburgh's periphery', *Environment and Planning A*, 46(6): 1351–68.

Kent, P. (1982) 'I'll be back says Minister', *The Express*, 4 August, pp 4–5.

King, T. (1981) *Tom King Minute to MT (Business in the Community Unit to Help Deal with Inner City Problems)* [Letter], Margaret Thatcher Foundation, Margaret Thatcher Archives.

Kirkness, P. and Tijé-Dra, A. (eds) (2017) *Negative Neighbourhood Reputation and Place Attachment: The Production and Contestation of Territorial Stigma*, Abingdon: Routledge.

Lawless, P. (2008) *Britain's Inner Cities* (2nd edn), London: Paul Chapman Publishing Ltd.

Link, B.G. and Phelan, J. (2014) 'Stigma power', *Social Science and Medicine*, 103: 24–32.

Lyons, C.G. (1980) 'The meaning of the English definite article', in J. van der Auwera (ed) *The Semantics of Determiners,* London: Croom Helm, pp 81–95.

Minton, A. (1998) 'Invasion of the yumbies', *The Express*, 10 November, pp 24–5.

Nayak, A. (2019) 'Re-scripting place: managing social class stigma in a former steel-making region', *Antipode*, 51(3): 927–48.

Parisi, P. and Holcomb, B. (1994) 'Symbolizing place: journalistic narratives of the city', *Urban Geography*, 15(4): 376–94.

Pattison, M. (1979) *No. 10 Letter to Department of Environment ("Inner Cities")* [Letter], Margaret Thatcher Foundation, Margaret Thatcher Archives.

Pinkster, F.M., Ferier, M.S. and Hoekstra, M.S. (2020) 'On the stickiness of territorial stigma: diverging experiences in Amsterdam's most notorious neighbourhood', *Antipode*, 52(2): 522–41.

Pooley, A. (2016) 'Toxteth regenerated: now a great place to invest', *Aspen Woolf*, Available from: https://aspenwoolf.co.uk/from-an-interesting-hist ory-to-works-of-art- regenerated-toxteth-is-now-a-great-place-to-invest/ [Accessed 30 May 2018].

Rempel, J.K. and Burris, C.T. (2005) 'Let me count the ways: an integrative theory of love and hate', *Personal Relationships*, 12(2): 297–313.

Scambler, G. (2018) 'Heaping blame on shame: "weaponising stigma" for neoliberal times', *The Sociological Review*, 66(4): 766–82.

Slater, T. (2017) 'Territorial stigmatization: symbolic defamation and the contemporary metropolis', in J. Hannigan and G. Richards (eds) *The Handbook of New Urban Studies*, London: Sage, pp 111–25.

Slater, T. (2018) 'The invention of the "sink estate": consequential categorisation and the UK housing crisis', *The Sociological Review*, 66(4): 877–97.

Stephenson, J. (2010) 'People and place', *Planning Theory and Practice*, 11(1): 9–21.

Times, The (1981) 'Merseyside gets 4,000 more jobs', 16 September, p 2.

Tissot, S. (2007) 'The role of race and class in urban marginality: discussing Loïc Wacquant's comparison between the USA and France', *City*, 11(3): 364–69.

Tyler, I. (2013) *Revolting Subjects: Social Abjection and Resistance in Neoliberal Britain*, London: Zed Books Ltd.

Tyler, I. (2020) *Stigma: The Machinery of Inequality*, London: Zed Books Ltd.

van Dijk, T. (1996) 'Power and the news media', in D. Paletz (ed) *Political Communication in Action*, Cresskill, NJ: Hampton Press, pp 9–36.

Wacquant, L. (2000) 'The new "peculiar institution": on the prison as surrogate ghetto', *Theoretical Criminology*, 4(3): 377–89.

Wacquant, L. (2007) 'Territorial stigmatization in the age of advanced marginality', *Thesis Eleven*, 91(1): 66–77.

Wacquant, L. (2008) *Urban Outcasts: A Comparative Sociology of Advanced Marginality*, Cambridge: Polity Press.

Wigmore, B. (1987) 'Inner cities', *Mirror*, 21 September, pp 4–5.

5

Negotiating Landscapes of (Un)safety: Atmospheres and Ambivalence in Female Students' Everyday Geographies

Matthew Durey, Nicola Roberts and Catherine Donovan

Introduction

The connection between university life and interpersonal – and especially sexual – abuse and violence has come under scrutiny in recent years. High-profile sexual assault cases in the US and the UK, and the media furore around, for instance, the #MeToo movement, have drawn attention to the scale and pervasiveness of sexual harassment, abuse and violence directed at women, and there has been a rise in attention paid to student experiences of hate, violence and abuse, and questions of student safety over the past decade (see, for example, NUS, 2010, 2011/2012; UUK, 2016; Fedina et al, 2018; Bartos, 2020; Bovill and White, 2020). Consequently, experiences of and possible responses to interpersonal violence and abuse in higher education have risen high on universities' agendas, and the geographies of hate and violence in students' experiences of university, the environments of university campuses and their surroundings have become particularly topical issues.

This comes at a time in which discourses of hate – within and without the academy – have become critical battlegrounds for myriad, and often conflicting, social and political projects; particularly concerning hate-crime legislation and the social groups protected under it. The England and Wales Crown Prosecution Service's definition of hate crime is based on criminal behaviour 'motivated by hostility or prejudice'. While the presence of hate (or some form of prejudice) as a motivating factor may qualitatively distinguish such behaviours from more prosaic offences, such understandings are constrained. Placing emphasis on the individual psychology of a perpetrator and focusing on hate as an (individual) motivator can downplay the significance of the structural conditions through which individuals and groups come to be (perceived as) 'hated' in the first place. For many, the most significant factor of hate crimes is that they constitute attacks on the 'identity' of the target: as a (perceived) member of a particular group, rather than as an individual (Gerstenfeld, 2017; Garland and Chakraborti, 2012); more broadly as attacks on the idea of 'difference' itself (Chakraborti and Garland, 2012). Consequently, they are seen to 'transmit a message not just to the immediate victim but also to the victim's wider community that their behaviour, cultural norms or presence will not be tolerated' (Garland and Chakraborti, 2012: 40). Hate as a motivating factor can therefore be seen to reflect prevailing, or even dominant attitudes within society (Perry, 2009), and hate-crime legislation, rather than being primarily a legal tool, can be better understood symbolically (Mason, 2014), as an act of atonement by the state for institutionalized discriminatory behaviours against the protected characteristics (see Donovan et al, 2019). As such, even if hate crime is mired in definitional and procedural obstacles on a practical level for criminal justice, it can nevertheless play a significant boundary maintenance role: asserting the social value of difference and diversity in general, and of particular social groups specifically.

The question of the inclusion of misogyny – hate directed at women as a sex class – within hate-crime legislation is complex (Mason-Bish, 2012; Gill and Mason-Bish, 2013; Mason-Bish and Duggan, 2020; Chapter 3) and compounded among other things by difficulties of definition and conceptualization (Garland, 2011; Garland and Chakraborti, 2012), problematic notions of 'vulnerability' (Chakraborti and Garland, 2012) and the 'politics of reporting' of hate incidents (Clayton et al, 2016). Nevertheless, the omission of women as a protected category under hate-crime legislation arguably indicates the lowly position of women within the hierarchy of victimhood and the pervasive and deep-rooted nature of misogyny within society. This casts light on the significance of the (albeit contested) intersection between hate and violence and abuse against women that forms a background of everyday misogyny, often explicitly sexual in character, which is a fundamental part of female students' everyday experiences.

Reflecting on data from an online survey exploring students' experiences of interpersonal violence on and off-campus while attending Northfacing University[1] in the North of England, this chapter considers how landscapes of (un)safety feature in female students' experiences of, and strategies to avoid – predominantly sexual – harassment, abuse and violence. While there are certain places and features within the urban landscape regularly regarded as either 'safe' or, more pertinently, 'unsafe', their identification as such is contingent; indicating a complex, and often ambivalent relationship between the experience of, and responses to, urban landscapes. It is argued that urban landscapes are experienced not only in relation to the material characteristics of certain features of the urban environments but also to the ways in which these material aspects are brought together with social, emotional, and affective aspects – including understandings of everyday misogyny – and coalesce to form 'atmospheres', which are implicated in female students' everyday experiences and negotiations of their urban landscapes.

These issues speak to broader concerns regarding changes in urban landscapes associated with neoliberal urbanism, and the significance of the creation, or staging, of atmospheres (Bille et al, 2015) as part of the production of experiential spaces of consumption in postindustrial capitalism. These in turn have important implications for (especially young women's) experiences of urban landscapes, and how fear, safety, hatred and violence become implicated in everyday negotiations of urban spaces.

The chapter begins with a discussion about urban spaces as hostile and/ or safe spaces, as material as well as emotional and affective spaces, and as conducive of atmospheres of safety and risk. This is followed by a brief account of the study from which the data are drawn before developing a discussion using snippets of insight from students' accounts to argue that atmosphere is a crucial lens through which to understand female students' experiences of their urban environments, and that their negotiations in responding to these atmospheres underscores the ambivalence of urban landscapes and the ways in which they are experienced. The final section reflects on how female students' accounts of their urban landscapes cast light upon the ways in which hate, fear and safety relate to the atmospheres of urban landscapes and the changes to these landscapes brought about by postindustrial capitalism and neoliberal urbanism.

Encounter, atmosphere and urban landscapes

Intensity and diversity of experience have always been central to the urban. The idealized image of cities as sites of potential, experience and freedom deriving from the heterogeneity of social interactions has long influenced the popular imagination. In quite fundamental ways, cities are sites of *encounter* (Watson, 2006; Valentine, 2008, 2013) where differences are thrown together and negotiated, and it is through everyday encounters and negotiations that urban life is carried out.

While the significance of the size, heterogeneity and density of urban populations for the nature of the associations between people within cities has been recognized since Aristotle, it was with the rise of modern industrial cities that the character of the urban came under particular scrutiny. Early urban theorists quickly made the connection between the characteristics of the urban environment and the emotional sphere, or *Lebenswelt*, of city-dwellers. For Simmel (1971: 325), it was the 'intensification of emotional life due to the swift and continuous shift of external and internal stimuli' that characterized the modern city. This intensity and saturation of encounter and its emotional content was captured in Benjamin's vertiginous exploration of urban life (Benjamin, 1999), wherein the fleeting experience of urban landscapes and their material components provided a revealing glimpse into the conditions and consequences of modernity. It was characteristic of what Wirth (1938) called the urban 'way of life' that urban encounters 'may indeed be face to face, but they are nevertheless impersonal, superficial, transitory, and segmental' (Wirth, 1938: 12). Simmel (1971) argued that in order to protect against the 'onslaught' of myriad urban encounters, it was necessary that urbanites treat city life with indifference by developing a 'blasé attitude'. This was essentially an 'intellectualistic quality'; a response to the rationalization of urban life and the 'relentless matter-of-factness and its rationally calculated economic egoism' (1971: 326) that characterized urban encounters. Understood in this sense, the city is not simply a place, but 'a particular form of human association', 'mode of life' (Wirth, 1938: 4–5), or 'way of seeing' (Miles, 2010: 24) and ordering human relations and interactions. The arrangement of landscapes, like the production of maps, thereby becomes an ordering principle that gives meaning to spatial and social relations by setting spatial agendas that become fixed in place.

Sennett (2000) has suggested that 21st century postindustrial cities are characterized by 'mutual indifference', and urban life underpinned by a bleak, uncaring form of civility. But civility, especially in this sense, often serves as a mask for hostility (Valentine, 2008); and deep resentment and prejudice can underlie the indifference of everyday encounters. Moreover, for many, particularly those – like women – who are clearly recognizable as members of typically vulnerable or disadvantaged groups, urban landscapes are not sites of 'mutual indifference', but are often characterized by everyday acts of hostility, hatred, and violence.

Thrift (2005: 140) has spoken of 'a misanthropic thread [that] runs through the modern city'. Far from existing together harmoniously, the manifold combinations of material, social, cultural and psychological factors that make up cities, produce conflict and contradiction, and 'urban experiences,' that as Thrift (2005: 140) has it, 'are the result of juxtapositions which are, in some sense, dysfunctional, which jar and scrape and rend'. Feminist geography particularly has long recognized these contradictions and juxtapositions in establishing the link between urban landscapes and experiences of hate and fear – especially of interpersonal and sexual abuse and violence. A wealth of research has demonstrated how the fear of violence and abuse – especially sexual violence and abuse perpetrated by male strangers – has a powerful influence on women's access to and use of public urban spaces in general (Koskela, 1999; Bondi and Rose, 2003; Beebeejaun, 2017; Fluri and Piedalue, 2017; Vera-Gray, 2018), and university campuses in particular (Day, 1999; King, 2009). Women's movements through urban landscapes are not a free choice determined by unhindered preference, but 'the product of social power relations' (Koskela, 1999: 112). 'Women's decisions concerning the route they choose and places they go to' as Koskela (1999: 112) put it, 'are modified by the threat of violence' in complex and nuanced everyday practices by which women trade freedom for safety (Vera-Gray, 2018) against a background of misogynistic language, verbal harassment and the 'lower-level' sexual victimization described by Mason-Bish and Duggan (2020: 128ff). Such everyday hostility, rather than being events or behaviours experienced *within* urban landscapes, become, albeit in varied forms and to varying extents, ubiquitous features of those landscapes themselves; intertwined with female students' everyday experiences and spatial negotiations. Datta (2016: 179) has drawn attention to the geography of this everyday misanthropy by identifying what she calls 'genderscapes of hate', in which hate and violence against women become 'an integral factor in the process of place making, creating a lived space where such violence is itself normalized'. Emphasizing the relationality of such geographies of hate, Hall and Bates (2019: 101) have crucially argued that 'hatescapes' such as those created by the role of gendered hate and violence in urban placemaking 'can be understood not as individual and isolated, nor as inevitable features of particular sites and spaces, but rather as the ongoing outcome of relations and contexts'.

Recent years have seen increased appreciation of the importance of emotional or affective dimensions to urban encounters. It is recognized that the 'intangible feelings that can overlay particular spaces at particular times' (Lucherini and Hanks, 2020: 100) play a key role in how landscapes are experienced, and that the 'thickness' of emotional or affective geographies has significant implications for enabling or constraining human agency (Thibaud, 2011; de Backer and Pavoni, 2018). In particular, the idea of 'atmosphere' has been deployed as a way of conceptualizing the combination of the material, social, emotional and affective character of places (Anderson, 2009; Edensor, 2012; Bille et al, 2015; Edensor and Sumartojo, 2015; Sørensen, 2014). Böhme (1993) has explored the idea of atmosphere in terms of aesthetics, arguing that atmosphere is that quality that lies 'in-between' the qualities of material objects and environments and the 'human states' of consciousness and emotion – including hate and fear – through which those environments are known and judged, and by which they are related. The importance of atmosphere for the changing landscapes of postindustrial cities has been noted in recent work (for example, Gandy, 2017; Jones et al, 2017; Adams et al, 2020), which has highlighted how urban atmospheres 'appear from an interplay between different human and non–human elements, including buildings, sites, landmarks, landscapes and so on', which 'shape individuals' feelings, behaviours and perceptions as they interact with their surroundings' (Adams et al, 2020: 309). Urban atmospheres, as Gandy (2017: 357) has described, 'are both experienced and created: they encompass extant features of emotional and material life as well as its staging or manipulation', which, as Bille et al (2015) have pointed out, are often associated with neoliberal urban redevelopment projects seeking to create not only material environments but also atmospheres of individualism and consumption.

Understood in this way, the concept of atmosphere acknowledges the importance of the emotional and affective aspects of the experience of places, while remaining anchored to material actuality, and offers potential insight into how the changing and contested urban landscapes contribute to the encounters and experiences which comprise female students' everyday geographies.

Researching students' geographies

In 2016 an online survey was sent to all undergraduate and postgraduate students studying on campus at the post-92 civic-style Northfacing University in 'Northtown', a formerly industrial city in the north of England. The university is spread over two campuses across the city. Student accommodation is located around the city in four university-operated and three private sites, all separate to campus locations and intermingled with either residential or commercial properties. Most students attending the university come from the surrounding region (although there are significant populations of international students), and many do not live in student accommodation but either elsewhere in the city or within commuting distance.

The survey aimed to capture the prevalence and the nature of interpersonal violence and abuse (hereafter IVA) (measured across general categories of verbal abuse and bullying, physical abuse and violence, sexual abuse and violence, and stalking and online harassment and abuse) experienced by students on and off campus during their time as students. The survey was carried out in consultation with a steering group of university community stakeholders and students studying a third-year gender and violence module who acted as critical friends. The research was approved by the University Research Ethics Committee.

The survey received 1,034 usable responses from undergraduate and postgraduate students across all faculties of the university (approximately 10 per cent of the total student population). The proportions of female and male students (67 and 33 per cent respectively) were broadly consistent with the wider student population (59 per cent female and 41 per cent male), although male students were slightly underrepresented.

The principal findings of this research are reported elsewhere (Roberts et al, 2022), but were consonant with previous research (for instance, Barberet et al, 2004; Kavanaugh, 2013; ONS, 2018) indicating that young female students were more likely to report having experienced verbal sexual harassment and physical sexual assault than male students, and to believe that they were targeted because of their sex. Verbal sexual harassment was the most common form of abuse and experienced everywhere but most frequently on campus. The most prevalent form of physical sexual abuse was unwanted sexual contact – typically opportunistic assaults in public places, especially clubs and bars (see also Fedina et al, 2018) – although rarer instances of sustained and violent assaults on campus and in private spaces were reported. Female students were significantly more likely to report feeling unsafe both on campus and in the broader urban environment than their male counterparts, and the influence of spatial and temporal context exerted a stronger influence on these feelings of (un)safety for female students. Much smaller numbers of both male and female students from Black, Asian and Arab backgrounds reported experiences of verbal racial abuse.

In addition to exploring prevalence and patterns of IVA, the survey contained a range of open questions exploring students' experiences of IVA and perceptions of safety on campus and in the broader urban environment. In their responses to these questions, a number of respondents provided information about the impact of their experiences and perceptions of IVA on their attitudes and behaviours while navigating their urban environments, which cast light on complex and ambivalent processes of everyday negotiations concerning the atmospheres of urban landscapes.

While overall engagement with the survey broadly reflected the demographics of the university population, the accounts regarding experiences and perceptions of IVA that emerged from this research were of a type. While accounts from Black and Asian female students, lesbian, gay and bisexual students, as well as those reporting some form of disability were represented, the accounts belonged primarily to young, white, heterosexual female students. While ethnicity, sexual orientation and disability are implicated here, and suggest a complex relationship regarding marginality (for a discussion of which see Roberts et al, 2019), and will likely generate important variations in experience and response to IVA, the most significant predictor of experiencing IVA – and sexual violence and abuse in particular – was being female, and the focus of the present discussion reflects this.

Students' everyday negotiations of urban landscapes

Encounters with, and the perceived threat of, hate, fear and violence feature frequently in female students' experiences of urban landscapes. These 'landscapes of (un)safety' result from their everyday (re)assessment of urban environments but are also shaped by broader discourses informed by media portrayals, shared accounts of experiences of hate, abuse and violence, and previous experiences of (un)safe landscapes and encounters (Roberts et al, 2022). 'Every social space,' Lefebvre argued, 'is the outcome of a process with many aspects and many contributing currents, signifying and non-signifying, perceived and directly experienced, practical and theoretical' (1991: 110). Navigating the landscape of such spaces involves making practical sense of these contributing currents, and experiences and perceptions of (un)safety are notable contributors to this process of sense-making, particularly for female students. This is not a straightforward matter of identifying certain spaces or features as either 'safe' or 'unsafe'; rather, it involves the (re)assessment of a range of varying and interacting features contributing to the perception of 'unsafe' landscapes (Nasar and Fisher, 1992) as they are encountered.

While there are noticeable patterns in female students' constructions of these landscapes, the locations and conditions they typically feature, and their responses to these (un)safe landscapes (Roberts et al, 2022), on a deeper level, there is also considerable ambivalence and contradiction (Karner and Parker, 2010). Rather than undermining the regularities in these constructions, however, the argument made here is that these ambivalences speak to more fundamental aspects of how hate, fear and safety feature in female students' experiences of their urban environments by drawing attention to the role of atmospheres in the experience of urban landscapes, and of everyday spatial negotiations in their (re)production.

Ambivalent atmospheres of (un)safety

'Hotspots' of unsafety – such as underpasses, public transport, 24-hour access buildings, and bars and clubs – featured frequently in students' accounts but were identified as 'unsafe' under particular circumstances (typically during darkness, in the presence of potentially dangerous others or when female students were themselves alone); which is to say, when such locations were experienced as possessing a particular atmosphere. As one student described: 'I feel unsafe in the underpass where [the public transport link] is, on the way to [riverbank] campus, during the day but especially at night when there's not a lot of people around' (20, White British, heterosexual). Or, as another neatly summarized, the city is unsafe: 'where it is dark and empty' (23, Bangladeshi, heterosexual).

This was not a question of fixed or static conditions, however, but of contingency. Places that were sometimes feared and avoided – such as spaces between university buildings or the spaces where public transport is accessed – were at other times viewed as safe, or safely negotiated by travelling in groups, or, in yet other circumstances became key features in safety strategies.

The ambivalence between crowded and desolate spaces is especially striking in this regard. Empty spaces are associated with vulnerability and exposure (Nasar and Fisher, 1992; Fileborn, 2016). However, unsurprisingly, crowded public and leisure spaces such as bars and clubs – commonly acknowledged sites of the unwanted sexual harassment that comprises the majority of everyday low-level sexual abuses to which women are subjected (Fedina et al, 2018; Fileborn, 2016) – are also frequently cited as 'unsafe' locations, even as they were simultaneously locations of enjoyment and sociability. While isolation was commonly reported as a significant contributing factor to unsafe atmospheres, for other students, such perceptions were the result of the presence of (generally unfamiliar and potentially threatening) others. As one student remarked: 'At times when I have felt unsafe, it is usually due to large groups of people who are passing through the area rather than the area itself' (23, White British, heterosexual).

This is even the case, as the following student made clear, on dedicated 'student nights', which, despite crowds of fellow students, and the safety of friendship groups, are often identified as unsafe environments: 'I feel safe when I am with a group of friends. I feel safe in the city centre during student nights, because there are policemen' (23, other White background, heterosexual).

For many female students, therefore, the presence or absence of these atmospheres can be alleviated by the presence of friends or others: 'I feel unsafe when I am alone but if I'm with friends, then I know I have a fighting chance of not being put in much danger that night' (18, White British, sexuality not reported).

Such ambivalence was also found in relation to university buildings and campus sites, where safety is contingent on time of day, darkness and isolation, and can be both refuge and a site of exposure, depending on whether other students are present, or whether the buildings are (or are seen to be) secure: "I generally feel safe inside the buildings and on site, but walking home or to [public transport] stations especially in the late afternoon/evenings, I feel particularly unsafe around … campus" (22, White British, lesbian); "I feel safer in university buildings that are familiar to me … however in the evening or out of term time the absence of undergraduate students and staff members taking leave makes the building empty and intimidating" (28, White British, heterosexual).

Temporality is a key dimension to the experience of urban atmospheres. While the predictable variations of daylight are a well-documented and common element in female students' experience of urban atmospheres, it is frequently the 'unpredictability' of specific places, especially at night, that contributes to their (un)safe atmospheres: 'I feel incredibly safe within the university grounds, ie in the library or language lab and will happily stay here till late at night; however, I will never walk home in the dark or late at night, just because you never know what will happen' (23, White British, heterosexual).

This unpredictability typically relates to unfamiliar people (often 'drunks') whose presence significantly alters the atmosphere of places, rendering the otherwise familiar unknowable and risky: 'I feel particularly unsafe while using the trains at night as they are always filled with drunken people that are unpredictable' (21, White British, heterosexual).

The wider urban environment, of course, is subject to a greater variety of change, and the 'unpredictable' character of urban environments became a notable feature in their atmospheres:

'I find that it's a bit unsafe when there's a [football] match and everyone is going to town to have a drink. Usually I will avoid these areas or not go out at all. Same goes every Friday and Saturday night, and Wednesday night when it's the student's night out.' (23, Asian, heterosexual)

The ambivalences contained in these 'differential notions of safety' (England and Simon, 2010: 203) are not at all novel or exceptional; rather, they reinforce, but go beyond, the accepted understanding that spaces are differently constructed during day and night-time, or when busy or 'desolate' (Nasar and Fisher, 1992). This suggests a more complex, active and ambivalent process of experiencing urban landscapes of safety, hate and fear, in which clear distinctions between 'safe' and 'unsafe' spaces are less relevant. Instead, atmosphere plays a key role in female students' assessment of the blurring of boundaries that is characteristic of postindustrial society and its spatial expression (Läpple et al, 2010). Yet atmospheres, by virtue of their position 'in-between' the material and the emotional, subject and object, absences and presences, are in their very nature ambivalent, ambiguous and contradictory (Böhme, 1993; Anderson, 2009; Bille et al, 2015), which means that, for female students, urban landscapes are, in a certain sense, forever uncertain and contingent.

Everyday negotiations of ambivalent landscapes

The ambivalence of atmospheres affects the ways in which urban landscapes are experienced and understood by female students; however, they are not passive in their reception of such atmospheres but play an active role in their construction. It is in the embodied act of movement – the spatial negotiations that make up much of what Vera-Grey and Kelly (2020) call 'safety work' – that the effects of urban atmospheres on female students' geographies is evident. For many female students, experiences of urban atmospheres are incorporated into their everyday routines, becoming spatial material for the practice of agency in which they respond to and 'modify and co-create' these atmospheres (Edensor and Sumartojo, 2015: 253).

Students respond to their experiences of unsafety in a variety of ways; typically, either avoiding urban spaces entirely, or making more specific renegotiations in their everyday routines: 'I have been stalked by men, especially older men especially during my first year as I did not know people so I often walked alone … it was traumatic to the point that I restricted myself from going out' (21, Black/Black British, heterosexual).

The ambivalence and contingency of these atmospheres – that is, their propensity to shift and be (re)constituted depending on the time of day, presence of others (strangers or companions) and so on – means that in many instances the actual atmosphere of a place cannot be known (at least not with certainty) in advance but only in, or close to, the moment of encounter. Previous experience and knowledge of, or presumptions about, the atmosphere of particular places is often enough to alter female students' movements to avoid such places (Nasar and Fisher, 1992; Roberts, 2019; Roberts et al, 2022), resulting in many locations being generally avoided (for instance, by not going into the city on Friday or Saturday evenings, or avoiding particular car parks and underpasses). However, the ambivalence of some atmospheres (including campus sites, university buildings and spaces in the night-time economy) mean that they can be experienced as safe, even desirable, and therefore sought intentionally. Also, these spaces and others (such as public transport) are sometimes simply unavoidable features of students' daily routines. Consequently, many landscapes and atmospheres must be negotiated in more contingent, ad hoc ways, which generate varied and nuanced everyday negotiations and contribute to equally subtle and complex geographies. For instance, as one student remarked: 'I often ensure I walk home with friends or check as I am leaving, after a night out that no 'suspicious' or drunk people are walking in the same direction' (22, White British, heterosexual).

Living with contingency and navigating urban landscapes can involve multiple reconfigurations of planned and unplanned routes: 'So there are some areas I'd rather not walk down [when it's dark] where I would in the day. I'd normally find a longer more lit way to my destination' (20, White British, bisexual).

The paths taken by female students in negotiating (un)safe landscapes, then, are spatial expressions, or 'pedestrian speech acts' (de Certeau, 1984: 97), which contribute to the 'rhetoric' of (un)safe landscapes. When female students negotiate their urban landscapes to avoid or mitigate the threat of sexual harassment and violence they interact dialectically with these landscapes, both appropriating the landscape in their own everyday strategies to negotiate the ambivalent terrain of (un)safety and 'acting out' the social relations that underpin the creation of these landscapes, atmospheres and their interpretations. By acting in response to the atmospheres of the urban environment, namely, in this case, that 'thread of misanthropy' (Thrift, 2005) that normalizes misogyny and sexual hostility toward women in public spaces, female students are editing, adding to and developing these atmospheres. By being a part of and moving through urban landscapes, female students' responses to (un)safe landscapes contribute to both the 'script' of those places and to their atmospheres: places avoided by female students can become 'male only' spaces as a consequence, while, simultaneously, the paths female students do take become those innovative spatial 'turns of phrase' (de Certeau 1984) creating spaces, and 'shortcuts' that *are* used by female students, rewriting a shifting landscape of (un)safety. This negotiation between landscape and pedestrian – plot and character – is made all the clearer when these choices are not freely made, but – as in conversations in which certain words, topics, or attitudes are 'out of bounds' – are carried out within an historical and social context of previous experience of, and discourses surrounding, the 'gender/hatescapes' (Datta, 2016; Hall and Bates, 2019) of hate and violence (Valentine, 1992; Roberts et al, 2022) that influence and censor certain movements.

Landscapes of (un)safety and neoliberal urbanism

Atmospheres, as Bille et al (2015: 34) point out, 'do not merely exist as simultaneity of human beings and material culture' but 'are susceptible to how the material environment changes, to changing human values and cultural premises'. As Edensor and Sumartojo (2015: 257) suggest, 'responses to atmospheres are contingent upon the historical and cultural contexts that condition their effects'. It follows that just as Benjamin (1999) read the consequences of modernity in his meanderings through the surrealism of the Paris Arcades, the everyday negotiations female students undertake in navigating their (unsafe) landscapes are influenced by, and cast light upon, more general elements of postindustrial urban life and the significance therein of urban atmospheres.

Simmel's prognosis for untreated modern urbanism was emotional indifference, and the depersonalization and rationalization of urban encounter. The spatial expression of modern capitalism generated a need to intellectualize the urban landscape: to treat it as a practical (and particularly economic) problem; a puzzle to be solved; a map to be negotiated. The strategies employed by female students in dealing with (un)safety are a testament to this practicality. The variety and intensity of stimuli Simmel saw as the cause of the blasé attitude, however, has only increased over the century since his analysis and is further compounded by the blurring of social and especially spatial boundaries that features so prominently in postindustrial urban configurations (Sennett, 2000; Miles, 2010).

This has significant impact on the construction of the material and atmospheric landscapes of cities with multiple consequences for female students' everyday geographies. First, urban landscapes are increasingly uncertain. Peck et al (2009: 56) have argued contemporary cities are subject to an open-ended process of 'creative destruction', which generates the need for continual redevelopment and renewal in order to realize and administrate new forms of capital. A major consequence of this is the reordering and reforming of borders and boundaries, and the (re)production of urban atmospheres (Jones et al, 2017; Adams et al, 2020). This is not only in the uses of urban space (between, for example, commercial and residential) but also between the public and the private, work and leisure, and the ways in which they manifest spatially and come to feature in people's everyday experiences and encounters with urban landscapes (Läpple et al, 2010). In a city like Northtown, this extends to the university landscape, as university spaces are typically not separated spatially from the wider urban landscapes but irregularly interspersed and intermingled with other public, private, commercial and residential spaces, with the consequence that female students are frequently required to move across, and between, different spaces and atmospheres.

These effects are exacerbated by fact that the layout, materiality and atmospheres of urban landscapes are increasingly geared to promote movement around and between sites of consumption. As Miles (2010) has remarked, places to *stop* and remain still within cities are decreasing, and urban landscapes are increasingly designed as spaces of transition, to be inhabited fleetingly and consumed *en passant*. Moreover, as Hall and Bates (2019: 106) point out, many 'havens' and 'moorings', which offer respite and defence against the enforced mobility of the city, are outside in parks and green spaces – the kinds of public places often identified by female students as 'unsafe' – or else 'part of private spaces of consumption, where lingering is not encouraged'. The consequences of the blurring of boundaries and the promotion of movement impacts female students' everyday negotiations in various ways but are particularly true of the urban commercial centres typically the epicentre of the night-time economy, which are associated with experiences of unsafety and sexual violence, as well as being, for many female students, an integral aspect of university social life.

While a regular turnover of bars and venues supports the night-time economy of Northtown city centre, it is also steadily diminishing as development moves from the centre and toward the seafront. While this may, in time, reduce the dominance of the night-time economy in city-centre public spaces, it leaves in its wake an archipelago of abandoned, unused spaces and often derelict buildings across the city-centre, which further interrupt the regularity of the landscape and introduce new pockets of unsafety. Moreover, the relocation of the bars and restaurants from the city centre, and so also the main campus area and accommodation blocks, increases the need for female students to travel across the city to participate in the night-time economy. To travel by foot from the city centre to the seafront involves crossing various uses of space, and a significant number of typically – and notoriously – unsafe features like underpasses, poorly lit and empty spaces, as well as spaces of prolonged exposure to passers-by. Public transport options are limited and, where they are available, involve exchanging one uncertain environment for another. All of which are subject to increased uncertainty at night or if travelling alone.

In addition to the increased movement between uncertain urban landscapes, the construction, or staging (Bille et al, 2015) of urban atmospheres has become a deliberate strategy in the commodification of space and place. The 'creative destruction' and reconstruction (Peck et al, 2009) by which landscapes are continually made valuable also relies on the (re)construction of emotional attachment to, or engagement with, place (Jones et al, 2017; Adams et al, 2020). Urban landscapes are designed to engage the senses and elicit an emotional response from those moving through them. Consequently, *to feel* the urban landscape becomes an economic imperative. There is a sense in which female students' encounters with the atmospheres of postindustrial urban landscapes can be seen as Simmel's blasé attitude in overdrive: where it is impossible to be *sensitive* to all aspects of the atmospheres of urban landscapes and equally impossible to be *insensitive* to them. As consumers, female students are encouraged not only to consume *in* urban spaces, but to consume those spaces, to appreciate them aesthetically, emotionally; that is, to experience their atmospheres. When this coincides with the experience of the atmospheres as unsafe, or as sites of hate or abuse, as is often the case for female students, the proliferation and staging of atmospheres, combined with their continual reconstruction, can be seen to contribute to their experience as landscapes of (un)safety.

Conclusion

Cities have always been sites and sources of encounter. For female students, urban environments are very often characterized by everyday misogyny and the experience and threat of interpersonal and especially sexual violence. Female students' everyday experiences of urban landscapes can be understood as practical negotiations of ambivalent atmospheres of (un)safety. While there is regularity and stability, these atmospheres are subject to contingent, and consequently uncertain, conditions and interpretations. These atmospheres generate correspondingly ambivalent and uncertain responses in female students' everyday negotiations, which do not simply reflect urban landscapes but are instrumental in (re)producing the atmospheres through which these landscapes are experienced.

This casts light on the utility of the concept of hate for understanding female students' everyday experiences of urban atmospheres. While landscapes cannot 'hate', and only in an extreme and strained sense could be considered 'hateful', their material construction and cultural or symbolic character can contribute to atmospheres that can be experienced and recognized by female students as threatening, (un)safe, and conducive of the background misogyny that makes the threat of sexual violence and abuse a frequent concern in urban spaces. While these experiences are anchored to particular places at particular times, they are also influenced by broader perceptions, experiences, and (often political) discourses. In this regard, the idea that any given individual encountered may be motivated by hate towards women is of less consequence than the overriding impression, which pervades the atmospheres of much urban space (and is reinforced by symbolic statements such as the omission of women from hate-crime legislation), that such atmospheres are commonplace (for some, even desirable), that women's safety in public spaces is not a concern, that they are not valued as a social group, that misogyny is acceptable. This is reflected in the lack of consideration for or consultation with women about their perceptions of safety in the continued (re)design of urban spaces.

The transformations to urban environments brought about by postindustrial society are implicated in these landscapes and atmospheres: specifically, those intended to encourage and exploit the emotional character of landscapes and their atmospheres. The staging of urban atmospheres feeds into landscapes of (un)safety by altering the material environment into increasingly private, closed-off spaces where the kinds of public and social environments that can encourage female presence, or through which female students can confidently travel, become difficult or impossible. Such landscapes exacerbate the ambivalence and uncertainty of female students' negotiations, promoting continuous movement through urban spaces, which not only increases the frequency and variety of (potentially dangerous) encounters but also, by generating a constant sense of movement, change, renewal, serves to reinforce the experience of urban landscapes as fleeting, unstable and uncertain, feeding into the unpredictability of urban atmospheres, and placing renewed demands on female students to reinterpret and renegotiate their everyday landscapes.

While much of this speaks to the general experience of women in urban spaces, female students are also a particular and heterogeneous group, and the specific context of the university and city are significant. The students at Northfacing University faced different kinds of landscapes and different atmospheres and negotiations to female students attending more wholly contained campus universities, or institutions in 'university cities' where distinctions between campus and 'city' are perhaps less stark and atmospheres less unstable. Experiences of university landscapes are also influenced by the liminality of female students' relationships to those environments. Whether a student is a native resident of the city or a newcomer; if they reside in student or private accommodation, or commute to university (particularly by public transport); as well as the added dimensions of ethnicity, disability and sexuality, can all contribute to the ways in which the landscapes are encountered, understood and negotiated. Further research could explore the relative importance of these and other dimensions in female students' experiences of and negotiations with urban atmospheres and their impacts on feelings of (un)safety and would benefit from methods that could both conceptualize and access empirically the contingencies involved in female students' practical everyday negotiations.

The ambivalence and contingency of atmospheres and their negotiation poses challenges for simple responses to addressing female students' safety concerns on and around university campuses by providing increased lighting, or more frequent transport, for instance, particularly where the boundaries of university campuses (as with Northfacing University) blur into the broader urban environment. Universities and other stakeholders (such as police, transport, venues) have a role to play, but these issues are entangled with the 'mutual indifference', 'misanthropy', and conflicts and contradictions inherent in the character of cities, and exacerbated in particular ways by their postindustrial (re)development.

Note

[1] This, like 'Northtown', is a pseudonym.

References

Adams, D., Smith, M., Larkham, P. and Abidin, J. (2020) 'Encounters with a future past: navigating the shifting urban atmospheres of place', *Journal of Urban Design*, 25(3): 308–27.

Anderson, B. (2009) 'Affective atmospheres', *Emotion, Space and Society*, 2: 77–81.

Barberet, R., Fisher, B.S. and Taylor, H. (2004) *University Student Safety in the East Midlands*, Home Office Online Report 61/04.

Bartos, A.E. (2020) 'Relational spaces and relational care: campus sexual violence, intimate geopolitics and topological polis' *Area* 52(2): 261–8.

Beebeejaun, Y. (2017) 'Gender, urban space, and the right to everyday life', *Journal of Urban Affairs*, 39(3): 323–34.

Benjamin, W. (1999) *The Arcades Project* (Trans. H. Eiland and K. McLaughlin), Cambridge, MA: Harvard University Press.

Bille, M., Bjerregaard, P. and Sørensen, T.F. (2015) 'Staging atmospheres: materiality, culture, and the texture of the in-between', *Emotion, Space and Society*, 15: 31–8.

Böhme, G. (1993) 'Atmosphere as the fundamental concept of a new aesthetics', *Thesis Eleven*, 36(1): 113–26.

Bondi, L. and Rose, D. (2003) 'Constructing gender, constructing the urban: a review of Anglo-American feminist urban geography', *Gender, Place and Culture*, 10(3): 229–45.

Bovill, H. and White, P. (2020) 'Ignorance is not bliss: a UK study of sexual and domestic abuse awareness on campus and correlations with confidence and positive action in a bystander program', *Journal of Interpersonal Violence*, DOI: 10.1177/0886260520916267

Chakraborti, N. and Garland, J. (2012) 'Reconceptualizing hate crime victimization through the lens of vulnerability and "difference"', *Theoretical Criminology*, 16(4): 499–514.

Clayton, J., Donovan, C. and Macdonald, S. (2016) 'A critical portrait of hate crime/incident reporting in North East England: the value of statistical data and the politics of recording in an age of austerity', *Geoforum*, 75: 64–74.

Datta, A. (2016) 'The genderscapes of hate: on violence against women in India', *Dialogues in Human Geography*, 6(2): 178–81.

Day, K. (1999) 'Strangers in the night: women's fear of sexual assault on urban college campuses', *Journal of Architectural and Planning Research*, 16(4): 289–312.

De Backer, M. and Pavoni, A. (2018) 'Through thick and thin: young people's affective geographies in Brussels' public space', *Emotion, Space and Society*, 27: 9–15.

De Certeau, M. (1984) *The Practice of Everyday Life*, Berkeley and Los Angeles: University of California Press.

Donovan, C., Clayton, J. and Macdonald, S.J. (2019) 'New directions in hate reporting research: agency, heterogeneity and relationality', *Sociological Research Online*, 24(2): 185–202.

Edensor, T. (2012) 'Illuminated atmospheres: anticipating and reproducing the flow of affective experience in Blackpool', *Environment and Planning D: Society and Space*, 30(6): 1103–22.

Edensor, T. and Sumartojo, S. (2015) 'Designing atmospheres: introduction to special issue', *Visual Communication*, 14(3): 251–65.

England, M.R. and Simon, S. (2010) 'Scary cities: urban geographies of fear, difference and belonging', *Social and Cultural Geography*, 11(3): 201–7.

Fedina, L., Holmes, J.L. and Backes, B.L. (2018) 'Campus sexual assault: a systematic review of prevalence research from 2000 to 2015', *Trauma, Violence and Abuse*, 19(1): 76–93.

Fileborn, B. (2016) *Reclaiming the Night-Time Economy: Unwanted Sexual Attention in Pubs and Clubs*, London: Palgrave Macmillan.

Fluri, J.L. and Piedalue, A. (2017) 'Embodying violence: critical geographies of gender, race, and culture', *Gender, Place and Culture*, 24(4): 534–44.

Gandy, M. (2017) 'Urban atmospheres', *Cultural Geographies*, 24(3): 353–74.

Garland, J. (2011) 'Difficulties in defining hate crime victimization', *International Review of Victimology*, 18(1): 25–37.

Garland, J. and Chakraborti, N. (2012) 'Divided by a common concept? Assessing the implications of different conceptualizations of hate crime in the European Union', *European Journal of Criminology*, 9(1): 38–51.

Gerstenfeld, P.B. (2017) *Hate Crimes: Causes, Controls and Controversies* (4th edn), London: Sage.

Gill, A.K. and Mason-Bish, H. (2013) 'Addressing violence against women as a form of hate crime: limitations and possibilities', *Feminist Review*, 105: 1–20.

Hall, E. and Bates, E. (2019) 'Hatescape? A relational geography of disability hate crime, exclusion and belonging in the city', *Geoforum*, 101: 100–10.

Jones, P., Isakjee, A., Jam, C., Lorne, C. and Warren, S. (2017) 'Urban landscapes and the atmosphere of place: exploring subjective experiences in the study of urban form', *Urban Morphology*, 21(1): 29–40.

Karner, C. and Parker, D. (2010) 'Conviviality and conflict: pluralism, resilience and hope in inner-city Birmingham', *Journal of Ethnic and Migration Studies*, 37(3): 355–72.

Kavanaugh, P.R. (2013) 'The continuum of sexual violence: women's accounts of victimisation in urban nightlife', *Feminist Criminology*, 8(1): 20–39.

King, R. (2009) 'Women's fear of crime on university campuses: New directions?', *Security Journal*, 22: 87–99.

Koskela, H. (1999) 'Gendered exclusions: women's fear of violence and changing relations to space', *Geografiska Annaler: Series B, Human Geography*, 81(2): 111–24.

Läpple, D., Mücklenberger, U. and Oßenbrügge, J. (eds) (2010) *Zeiten und Räume der Stadt: Theorie und Praxis*, Opladen and Farmington Hills: Barbara Budrich.

Lefebvre, H. (1991) *The Production of Space* (Trans. D. Nicholson-Smith), Oxford: Blackwell.

Lucherini, M. and Hanks, G. (2020) 'Emotional geographies' in A. Kobayashi (ed) *Encyclopedia of Human Geography* (2nd edn), Amsterdam: Elsevier, pp 97–103.

Mason, G. (2014) 'The symbolic purpose of hate crime law: ideal victims and emotion', *Theoretical Criminology*, 18(1): 75–92.

Mason-Bish, H. (2012) 'Examining the boundaries of hate crime policy: considering age and gender', *Criminal Justice Policy Review*, 24(3): 297–316.

Mason-Bish, H. and Duggan, M. (2020) '"Some men deeply hate women and express that hatred freely": Examining victims' experiences and perceptions of gendered hate crime', *International Review of Victimology*, 26(1): 112–34.

Miles, S. (2010) *Spaces for Consumption: Pleasure and Placelessness in the Post-Industrial City*, London: Sage.

Nasar, J.L. and Fisher, B. (1992) 'Design for vulnerability: cues and reaction to fear of crime', *Sociology and Social Research*, 76: 48–58.

NUS (2010) *Hidden Marks: A Study of Women Students' Experiences of Harassment, Stalking, Violence and Sexual Assault*, London: NUS.

NUS (2011/2012) *No Place for Hate: Hate Crimes and Incidents in Further and Higher Education: Disability, Sexual Orientation and Gender Identity, Race and Ethnicity, Religion and Belief*, London: NUS.

ONS (2018) *Sexual Offences in England and Wales: Year ending March 2017*, London: ONS, Available from: https://www.ons.gov.uk/peoplepopulat ionandcommunity/crimeandjustice/articles/sexualoffencesinenglandandwa les/yearendingmarch2017) [Accessed 17 June 2020].

Peck, J., Theodore, N. and Brenner, N. (2009) 'Neoliberal urbanism: models, moments, mutations', *SAIS Review* 29(1): 49–66.

Perry, B. (2009) 'The sociology of hate: theoretical approaches', in B. Perry and B. Levin (eds) *Hate Crimes vol. 1: Understanding and Defining Hate Crime*, Connecticut, NE: Praeger, pp 55–76.

Roberts, N.J. (2019) 'Gender, sexual danger and the everyday management of risks: the social control of young females', *Journal of Gender-Based Violence*, 3(1): 29–43.

Roberts, N., Donovan, C. and Durey, M. (2019) 'Agency, resistance and the non-"ideal" victim: how women deal with sexual violence', *Journal of Gender-Based Violence*, 3(3): 323–38.

Roberts, N. Donovan, C. and Durey, M. (2022) 'Gendered landscapes of safety: how women construct and navigate the urban landscape to avoid sexual violence', *Criminology and Criminal Justice*, 2(22): 287–303.

Sennett, R. (2000) 'Cities without care or connection', *New Statesman*, June, pp 25–7.

Simmel, G. (1971 [1903]) 'Metropolis and mental life', in D.N. Levine (ed) *Georg Simmel: On Individuality and Social Forms*, Chicago: University of Chicago Press, pp 324–39.

Sørensen, T.F. (2014) 'More than a feeling: towards an archaeology of atmosphere', *Emotion, Space and Society*, 15: 64–73.

Thibaud, J.-P. (2011) 'The sensory fabric of urban ambiances', *Senses and Society*, 6(2): 203–15.

Thrift, N. (2005) 'But malice aforethought: cities and the natural history of hatred', *Transactions of the Institute of British Geographers*, 30(2): 133–50.

UUK (2016) *Changing the Culture: Report of the Universities UK Taskforce Examining Violence Against Women, Harassment and Hate Crime Affecting University Students*, London: Universities UK.

Valentine, G. (1992) 'Images of danger: women's sources of information about the spatial distribution of male violence', *Area*, 24(1): 22–9.

Valentine, G. (2008) 'Living with difference: reflections on the geographies of encounter', *Progress in Human Geography*, 32(3): 323–37.

Valentine, G. (2013) 'Living with difference: proximity and encounter in urban life', *Geography* 98(1): 4–9.

Vera-Gray, F. (2018) *The Right Amount of Panic: How Women Trade Freedom for Safety*, Bristol: Policy Press.

Vera-Gray, F. and Kelly, L. (2020) 'Contested gendered space: public sexual harassment and women's safety work', *International Journal of Comparative and Applied Criminal Justice*, 44(4): 265–75.

Watson, S. (2006) *City Publics: The (Dis)enchantment of Urban Encounters*, London: Routledge.

Wirth, L. (1938) 'Urbanism as a way of life', *American Journal of Sociology*, 44(1): 1–24.

6

Becoming Visible, Becoming Vulnerable? Bodies, Material Spaces and Affective Economies of Hate

John Clayton, Catherine Donovan and Stephen J. Macdonald

Introduction

This chapter explores connections between visibility and situated vulnerability for those targeted on the basis of identities of 'race' and faith, sexuality, transgender and disability – intersecting differences historically (re)produced as threatening to prevailing social orders (Tyler, 2013; 2020). We argue that who or what becomes hyper-visible (through challenges to socio-spatial arrangements) and subject to the harms of hate (through which meaning and value becomes stuck to subjects, objects and places (Ahmed, 2001)), is constituted by more than representational visibility or markers of embodied difference. Via a lens of social materiality, we explore how hyper-visibility is produced through physical spaces implicated in wider relations of 'social discrimination and spatial exclusion' (Hall and Bates, 2019: 100) that includes circulating and violent forces of hate (Ahmed, 2004). Through attention to social materialities of the mosque, the gay scene and the home, we illustrate the ways in which material spaces stand in for, are associated with and produce hyper-visible bodies.

We begin by outlining processes of hyper-visibilization through relations between bodies, material spaces and affective economies of hate. We then draw upon three cases to exemplify the diverse ways in which hate is facilitated and distributed[1]. First, we consider attacks on mosques. Such sites act as surfaces upon which relations of hate are inscribed with an affective emanating force but also through which hate is countered. Second, we think about associations of LGBTQ+ bodies with gay scenes as a technology of targeting those moving to and from 'safe spaces'. Third, with reference primarily to disability, we consider how, over time, 'hate relationships' produce hyper-visible targets through routine spaces of the home and neighbourhood. While these spatialities are not straightforwardly implicated in experiences of easily bounded groups, there are important distinctions in the role that material spaces play in *context* and in *relation*. We conclude by stressing the potentialities of a recognition that the relation between visibility (as ascribed and claimed) and vulnerability to hate is unstable.

Producing hyper-visible bodies

Visibility is a socio-political phenomenon that is generative of forms of oppression (Smith et al, 2021). Who and what becomes subjected to public gaze and how such visibility is framed is both the product and basis of power relations that reinforce boundaries of value. Such 'threats' are produced through affective registers of economic and cultural danger, fear and disgust within specific configurations. For Tyler (2013: 23) such social abjection reveals 'less about the disgusted individual, or the thing deemed disgusting, than about the culture in which disgust is experienced and performed'. Yet, (in)visibility can be ambivalent (Simonsen et al, 2019). Visibilization can leave some 'vulnerable to erasure' (Casper and Moore, 2009: 9), with dominant representations and practices employing *both* elements of visibility and invisibility as tools of oppression. For example, Muslim communities have been constructed as visible security threats *and thus* subjected to laws on dress and restrictions on mosque construction that limit visible presence (Najib and Teeple Hopkins, 2020). Disabled people, in the context of austerity politics, are also produced as visible economic, social and moral burdens, resulting in reductions in social care and state benefits, the loss of independence (Cross, 2013: Healy, 2020) and the closure of sites and services.

There is also an ambivalence in the sense that communities produce themselves as visible through claims to recognition, contestations of subordinate positions and subtle expressions of community life including just being present. There is then a relation but also a gap between visibility produced through the circulation of hate 'between signifiers in relationships of difference and displacement' (Ahmed, 2001: 347), and visibility invested with more resistant intentions and/or outcomes. In recognition of these complex relations of (in)visibility, we consider the production and problematization of difference (as the basis for and legitimization of hate) to be a process of 'hyper-visibilization' that through material presence 'challenge[s] the spatial order ... in which any action ... is overly visible as it is excessively noted' (Cancellieri and Ostanel, 2015: 500).

As Wallengren and Mellgren (2015) explore in relation to Traveller communities, practices of concealment and negation reveal something important about the risks of being (made) visible and the boundaries of acceptance (see Chapter 2). Oppressive yet variegated hyper-visibilization produces scenarios in which it might be necessary or desirable to 'pass', thus temporarily and partially disrupting established lines of hostile distinction (Pile, 2011). Attempted performances of whiteness, straightness and/or ableness may be a means of accessing privileges ordinarily denied or avoiding unwanted attention, revealing the significance of the spatial contexts in which such passing might take place. Yet passing, while subversive, also re-produces social hierarchies – within and across minoritized groups – while placing burdens of adaptation on those required to navigate these geometries of power (Sanchez and Schlossberg, 2001).

Akiko (2008) contends that, the ability and/or desire to distance oneself from identities that are *always mis-recognized* anyway, is not so straightforward. While care may be taken to navigate everyday space-times of (not) belonging (Kitchin and Lysaght, 2003; Hall, 2005; Back and Sinha, 2016), one cannot control how and where harmful responses might manifest. Indeed, in UK hate crime legislation hate motivated offences are understood to occur as the result of *perceptions* that targeted victims belong to a protected group.[2] We develop these ideas, by thinking about how hyper-visibility is produced beyond, yet in relation to the body.

Materializing landscapes of hate

While the role of urban landscapes in constructing 'otherness' has been a key focus for critical geographers for some time (Kitchin, 1999; see Chapter 4), recent interventions have moved beyond cities as symbolic texts. From a phenomenological perspective, it is argued that social constructionist approaches have been 'inattentive to the actual, everyday materiality of the places in which people actually dwell' (Latham and McCormack, 2004: 702, citing Philo, 2000). More recently, there has also been a turn to 'new materialisms' (Forman, 2020), building on established relational ontologies of the more-than-human within social processes. A common thread to this work is attention to the capacity of the more-than-human to 'make things happen' in a way which challenges:

> any distinction between the materiality of the physical world and the social constructs of human thoughts and desires, it opens up the possibility to explore how each affects the other, and how things other than humans (for instance, a tool, a technology or a building) can be social 'agents', making things happen. (Fox and Alldred, 2018: 193)

Geographers of 'race' and racism have examined the ways 'in which the connections between [racism's] constituent components are not given but are made viscous through local attractions' (Saldanha, 2006: 18), opening up new ways of thinking through anti-racism by 'de-centering the body as the primary unit of analysis' (Hawthorne, 2019: 5). Some have attended to the materiality of state violence (Chari, 2008; Johansen, 2015; Griffiths, 2018), while others have explored mundane racializations. Swanton (2010), for example, focuses on the 'mechanic materiality' of vehicles, including taxis and 'flashy' cars, through which 'race' in a northern English town is performed. In disability studies others have emphasized the blurred boundaries of bodies and objects including consideration of how assistive technologies may be inseparable from fleshy bodies (Goodley et al, 2014) with implications that can be transformative (overcoming disabling barriers) but also 'implicated in the (re)production of the asymmetries that they seek to undo' (Moser, 2006: 373) through the creation of 'the outline of different figures or objects of hate' (Ahmed, 2001: 347).

Yet understanding why materialities are implicated in experiences of hate, also requires an acceptance of the enduring (if malleable) discursive power of what 'race', faith, sexuality, transgender and/or disability might mean within specific contexts and in relation to broader systems of oppression. Jackson (2008: 302), suggests that while there is value in exploring the materialities of 'race', this needs to be supplemented by attention to the 'longue durée' of racialized discourse. Sharp (2021) instigates a conversation between 'new materialism' and feminist geopolitics in ways that continue to hold the body as a central site of political concern in relation to both materialities *and* meaning making processes that co-constitute it. In relation to experiences of Islamophobia in France, Zouggari (2019: 278) suggests that, for example, the veil is never 'politically neutral' and that 'one must pay attention to both the social structures that make [forms of domination] possible and the materialities in which it is inscribed'. Thus, we explore here the 'social materiality' (Dale, 2005) of hate, whereby the relations between social power (as discursive and embodied) and the materiality of everyday life are mutually constitutive, intra-active and entwined (Hughes et al, 2017).

Thinking through the social materiality of hate helps us to understand how communities become targeted through forces oriented towards hyper-visible bodies/communities *in context* and *in relation*. That is, we consider vulnerability not as something that resides within individuals but that is reproduced and challenged through situated socio-spatial relations. There are two key considerations here: First, hate can be directed not just at individuals but at landscapes and collectives fixed through those landscapes. The spaces we refer to are those towards which hateful emotions and actions are directed but also those through which they are generated. As Johansen (2015: 52) suggests, emotions (including but not limited to hate) 'are not merely bodily arousals but ... bodily experiences of directedness towards something in the world'. The materiality of our surroundings mediates, and delegates hate, but in doing so we are also 'moved by those surroundings' (Johansen, 2015: 50) through 'an affective power to inspire a range of feelings and actions towards them' (Simonsen at al., 2019: 653). Material sites, therefore, in different ways 'act back' in relation to how they are seen and used by a range of actors, including their role as potential sites of safety and community (Moran et al, 2001).

Second, we suggest that such sites can be employed as a technology – a means of (mis)identification of hyper-visible bodies not seen to belong (at intersecting scales). The concern here is how bodies are subject to hyper-visibilization through judgements about the identity of victim/survivors in relation to particular spaces. The ability to 'recognize' a body as hyper-visible takes place through a spatial grammar. Being seen near a mosque (Hopkins et al, 2020), leaving a bar associated with a local gay scene (Guasp et al, 2013) or coming out of a specialist school (Wood and Orpinas, 2021) produce hyper-visibility. In other situations, such as neighbourhood-based encounters, judgements of hyper-visibility may emerge over time, particularly when markers of discernible otherness are less immediately apparent (Macdonald et al, 2021). Thinking in terms of technologies of hate, highlights the instability and ambivalence of everyday spaces that can be both safe and unsafe (see Chapter 5). In what follows we consider the social materiality of hyper-visibility through three vignettes considering the mosque, the gay scene and the home/neighbourhood.

Inscribing and resisting hate through mosques

> In the '80s we were dealing with racial discrimination and stuff like that. Being a brown person then was a sin, but being a Muslim now is a sin. (Focus Group, Newcastle [Hopkins et al, 2020])

Contemporary anti-Muslim racism, routed through discourses of 'threat', is enacted through racialization, stigmatization and direct targeting of those presumed to be Muslim at a range of scales (Hopkins et al, 2020). Nayak (2017: 298) suggests that everyday forms of physical targeting extend beyond attacks on Muslim bodies, incorporating material objects 'such as clothes, windows and cars' that 'stand in for Muslims themselves'. Our own research into experiences of Islamophobia in North East England (Hopkins et al, 2020) from which the previous excerpt is taken, identified that women are perceived as at more risk of direct anti-Muslim racism than men but also that skin colour, the wearing of headscarves, clothes associated with Islam, having a beard, and attending mosque[3] all had a bearing on the likelihood of being targeted. Allen (2017: 297) argues that mosques in particular 'function as convenient symbols against which those wishing to vent their anxieties, anger and bigotry ... can do so'. An emphasis on the social materiality of these sites entails that mosques can be 'animated' (Nayak (2017: 298), damaged and inscribed (with wider affects), but also protected and employed in ways that contest abjection.

Göle (2013) suggests that the visibilization of Islamic architecture and dress is a materialization of the post 9/11 shift in European countries of Muslims from 'invisible migrant workers' to 'visible Muslim citizenship'. Literature on new mosque construction in Europe highlights variability around localized responses to such visibility (Gale and Naylor, 2002; Gale, 2004), with Baker (2019) suggesting that rather than just representing a binary of support for or objection to, mosques are physically encountered by local residents as sites that mediate various and uneven affective responses. However, given prevailing and embedded racisms and patterns of hate directed towards already existing Islamic institutions in the UK, there is a need to understand the role of mosques as sites which variously attract, emanate and contest the harms of hate.

According to incidents reported to Tell MAMA[4] between May 2013 and June 2017 there were 167 attacks on mosques in the UK. These attacks were geographically concentrated around the North West English conurbations, London and the South East, although nearly all UK regions logged at least one incident. Across those years there was a degree of consistency in the number of attacks reported: 2013: 43, 2014: 21, 2015: 24, 2016: 45, 2017: 34,[5] but also a significant rise in the proportion of incidents reported to Tell MAMA targeting 'Muslim faith institutions and property'.

> In 2017, vandalism replaced threatening behaviour as the third most common anti-Muslim hate incident. There was a 56% increase in anti-Muslim vandalism when compared with 2016, with one in ten 'real-world' incidents being classed as vandalism. ... This demonstrated a rise in physical intimidation and actions against Muslim faith institutions and property. (Tell MAMA, 2017)

Most cases recorded between 2013 and 2017 involve the physical marking or desecration of buildings. Almost one quarter of incidents (24.6 per cent, 41 of 167) reported were categorized as 'vandalism', followed by 'criminal damage' (12.6 per cent, 21 of 167). More recently, following an attack by a far-right terrorist on two mosques in Christchurch, New Zealand on 15 March 2019, Tell MAMA recorded a spike in these types of incidents. Between February and March 2019, this increased by 433 per cent. There is then both a regularity in these attacks but also increases following geo-political 'trigger events'.

The presence of Islam as a *visibilized* element of the built environment can be seen both as the *symbolic basis* (seen through UK government Prevent policies, media associations between COVID-19 and Muslim communities and media claims of 'no-go areas' for non-Muslims) for such attacks, but also becomes the *material target*, whereby hostility is aimed at (for example, the 'mosque invasions' of far-right group Britain First) as well as inscribed onto the landscape through vandalism and graffiti. While it is the 'bricks and mortar' of these buildings that are damaged through these latter acts, harm extends to those communities running, using and otherwise associated with these sites. Muslim bodies are attacked through assaults on the built environment without perpetrators having to directly encounter those targeted (Allen, 2017). The harm caused is significant because of *what* is damaged (holy sites of religious devotion and scholarship but also sites of community, safety and belonging in often hostile environments), *how* they are damaged (insulting messages, desecration of sacred objects sometimes requiring costly and time-consuming repairs) and how this may *reinforce other experiences of exclusion and discrimination*. The broader consequences of such 'message crimes' (Perry and Alvi, 2012), reverberates not just locally but extends to a sense of (not) belonging at multiple scales (Nayak, 2017).

Recent attacks in North East England speak to such reverberations. In 2019 the Bahr Islamic Academy in Newcastle-upon-Tyne experienced two attacks in two months that involved graffiti, broken windows, flammable liquids poured on the floor and desecration of prayer books. The Academy principal explained his feelings and of those of the community: 'We feel angry, afraid and scared now. Anything could happen' (Doughty, 2020). Multiple attacks in Stockton-on-Tees in June 2020 also involved graffiti, including 'KKK' sprayed onto the exterior wall of one mosque. The impact of this act as a visible expression of racism and exclusion of the Muslim community in this town had a discernible impact upon some encountering these messages. In posting images of these attacks on Twitter local media outlet 'Tees Durham' suggested that 'The local Muslim community say they're scared to walk down the street knowing there is this hatred.'

Even if graffiti is cleaned up, such attacks have an *emanating force* that renders the division between the spaces that are, and those who are, targeted as at least porous. Hate among other affective states is not 'of the self but produced through the interaction of self and world' (Labanyi, 2010: 223). In his ethnographic study of racism in the West Midlands suburbs Nayak (2010) discusses how racist graffiti becomes a way of inscribing white territoriality thus giving affective weight to other daily encounters and experiences of racism. More permanent (or persistent) graffiti becomes a material reminder of these power relations and a means through which racialized claims to place are reinforced. But we might also think about this emanating force as a fear or threat of *potential* future acts of hate that endure, whereby this prospect (based upon previous experiences) acts as an oppressive mechanism.

However, there is an indeterminacy to these material sites that means they are never just (and often not) sites of hate (Ahmed, 2001). They exist not only in the gaze of attackers, but are established, used and valued, including as sites of safety and community. In addition to recent initiatives to improve security measures through awareness raising and protective practical modifications to mosques (Tell MAMA, 2019) that communicates a sense of defiance, other work has sought to transform attitudes and re-work the terms of visibilization. For example, by opening up mosques to broader non-Muslim publics (Hopkins et al, 2020).

The visible presence and role of the mosque is also re-framed as a tangible physical presence and source of mutual support and community in direct response to a range of contemporary social concerns including food poverty, COVID-19 responses and rising levels of anti-Muslim racism. In this focus group conducted with a group of 11 women at a mosque in Newcastle, the kinds of uses and meanings attached to the mosque space disrupt notions of the mosque as a source and target of hate but rather as an organized and supportive regional resource in the fight against discrimination:

> we have [a] congregation of 7,000 in this mosque and when people are experiencing a certain rise of hate crime, every time something happens Muslims are targets. It doesn't matter where you're living or whatever in the North East. They come and tell Imam and then we have a team of people who get allocated a family to go and speak [to] them in whatever language. We've got 37 languages in this mosque. Then we will report to the police on their behalf so that's our system here. (Focus group, Newcastle [Hopkins et al, 2020])

Through attention to the work that mosques and those tied to them do, we emphasize how challenges are made to notions of mosques as sites of problematic hyper-visibility. They are religious but also increasingly politicized sites, which attract, mediate and reproduce a range of inter-related affective orientations. This includes mosques as lively sites of community, belonging and support used, adapted and re-oriented in ways that reveal that situated vulnerability cannot and should not be challenged through reduced visibility but a *making ordinary* of these spaces and their place in trans-local lives.

Locating hyper-visibility through the scene

According to Bachmann and Gooch (2017) the overwhelming majority of LGB and/or T+ people experiencing hate are insulted, pestered, intimidated or harassed (87 per cent) while only 15 per cent involve some form of damage to property or vehicles. At first glance, this would perhaps suggest that the material environment is not as significant in our understanding of the circulation of hate as might be the case for Muslim communities discussed previously. However, we would argue that this is to miss the significance of the way in which space as a technology plays a role in locating and producing hyper-visible bodies in context and in relation to other spaces.

Our own research (Donovan et al, 2019), which examined data from a third-party reporting service in the North East of England, revealed some tentative patterns in relation to the night-time economy and spikes in homophobic hate incidents in Sunderland – a city where (at this point in time) there was very little by way of a 'gay scene' compared to its neighbour city Newcastle-upon-Tyne. Newcastle can be characterized as the regional LGBTQ+ 'hub', home to the 'Pink Triangle' – 'a section of the city that is 'triangulated' by the location of non-heterosexual bars/clubs' (Bonner-Thompson, 2017: 1613) and the pattern of reporting both temporally and spatially, suggest that these incidents are occurring in and around this city centre location but also on the journey (taken by metro)[6] back to Sunderland in the early hours of the morning. The electoral ward with highest reporting rates of any hate incident is a Newcastle city centre ward, Westgate, in which the Pink Triangle is located; and the hate incidents most often reported in this ward are homophobic hate (nearly 40 per cent compared to less than 10 per cent for both race/faith hate and disability hate [see Donovan et al, 2019]). In Sunderland, between midnight and 2am, homophobic hate is most often reported compared to race/faith and disability hate; the time when LGBTQ+ visitors to the night-time economy in Newcastle and Sunderland are travelling home (Donovan et al, 2019).

Our speculations about this are informed ones. While there has been no focused work on hate crime associated with particular 'gay spaces', research on hate crime on the grounds of sexuality and/or transgender identity suggests that being associated with gay venues can be a catalyst to hate incidents. Guasp et al (2013: 11) include participants who report hate incidents/crime in the night-time economy, for example: 'A friend of mine was assaulted. This was definitely an organised homophobic assault as it was a gang of people attacking a queue outside a gay club and several were assaulted.' In this account there is evidence of targeting and planning in the assault on those queuing outside a gay club, presumably because those in the queue are believed to be LGB and/or T. Accounts such as these are scattered throughout other pieces of research on homo-bi-trans phobic hate crime and the Leicester Hate Crime Project (2014) reports that 23 per cent of their LGBTQ+ respondents indicated that they had experienced hate crime/incidents in nightclubs.

In Britain it was the bombing of a gay bar, The Admiral Duncan, in London that was arguably a key moment in reconstructing lesbians and gay men as victims of crime rather than as potential criminals (Donovan and Hester, 2008) and which led to sexuality and later transgender identities as being protected strands in hate crime legislation. The nail bomber, David Copeland, targeted a number of venues associated with gay, Black and Asian communities in a series of hate motivated attacks. But there has also been a history of police brutality (legitimated hate) targeting gay – and trans-associated venues – bars, bookshops, nightclubs and toilets to enforce discriminatory laws. Attacks on venues as 'message crimes' (Perry, 2001) have been enacted and condoned by state institutions as well as hostile members of the public. The second largest mass shooting in the history of the US took place in a LGBT nightclub in Orlando, Florida and provides the most shocking evidence of how a venue might be understood to visibilize the 'other' – in this event, 'others' who were mainly Latino as well as LGB and/or T. Interestingly, recent evidence (Godzisz and Viggiani, 2019) has suggested that empathy for LGB and/or T+ people being victimized at Pride Marches is less than for victims in other contexts, suggesting that deliberate practices of visible community collectivism can stretch tolerance to its limits.

'Safe' gay spaces such as Manchester's Gay Village are promoted and protected from incursions of heterosexual violence through 'boundary maintenance' strategies (Moran et al, 2001). But such boundaries have an inside and an outside (that, of course, is not fixed or always easily identifiable) and the safety of spaces, whereby gay identities may be expressed with less fear of hostility, can be in marked contrast to experiences beyond those boundaries. The role of the 'gay bar' and/or 'gay scene' has been of variable importance in the lives of LGB and/or T people. Sometimes held up as the visible centre of the 'community' there have been strong critiques from within LGBTQ+ communities that they are/have been sites of misogyny, racism, ageism, transphobia, classism and body shaming, leading many 'of' the 'community' to feel excluded from and 'by' the community (see Corteen, 2002, Simpson, 2013; Formby, 2017). Nevertheless, while there has been no recent work on this specifically, we speculate here on how such identifiable LGBTQ+ spaces, whether more permanent (such as Manchester's Gay Village or the Pink Triangle in Newcastle) or more temporary (such as Pride events or 'gay', 'lesbian' or 'LGBT' night once a week or month, see Corteen, 2002) might act as a means of identifying bodies that are targeted on the basis of homo-bi-trans-phobic attitudes and play out in specific spatial contexts. While the safety of gay spaces may offer some protection (clearly this is complex and not uniformly experienced), movement to and from these sites produces situations in which some of these bodies might be seen as more 'out of place' and thus more vulnerable to hate. The venue then can be both the target of hate and method by which individuals can be identified and targeted.

Hyper-visibility and neighbourhood proximities

The history of institutional care exposes the invisible nature of victimization of disabled people within historical residential and psychiatric hospitals (Costa, 2013). Even after deinstitutionalization, recent scandals, such as Winterbourne View Hospital and Whorlton Hall Hospital,[7] have demonstrated the normalization of violence experienced by disabled people within institutional spaces (Macdonald, 2021) that has meant these experiences have only more recently been reframed through a lens of hate. Yet as recent research on hate crime notes, because of the deinstitutionalization of care services, the community has now replaced institutions as a space for disablist hate to materialize (Thorneycroft, 2017; Hall, 2019). Within the community, as Goffman notes, disabled people have to manage either 'discredited' identities, where their impairment is visible, or 'discreditable' identities, where their impairments are invisible, stigmatized identities (Goffman, 1963: 4). For disabled people with a visible or invisible impairment, their differences become visible through stigmatized physical or behavioural differences, their use of 'assistive' technologies and their relationships with stigmatized geographies, such as specialist schools, social care services and specialist living arrangements within the community (Roulstone et al, 2011; Thorneycroft, 2017; Healy, 2020).

From our own research, exploring case notes of a hate crime advocacy project in North East England, data illustrate how proximities enabled through residential neighbourhoods and the home can (over time) make visible forms of disability that might not be immediately apparent, with damaging and often enduring consequences. Within a context of austerity, disabled people have been constructed as inherently vulnerable, that is, an easy target, dangerous and a strain on local services and the economy, while also more exposed through the loss of services. Furthermore, the ongoing market-led personalization agenda, established to reduce costs of care, has resulted in the closure of shared services and consequently exacerbated isolation for many disabled people (Dickinson et al, 2020; Power et al, 2022). Thus, it is perhaps no surprise that there has been a doubling of disability hate crimes over the past six years from 4 per cent to 8 per cent of total recorded hate crimes (Macdonald, 2015; ONS, 2021).

Yet crime statistics do not present the whole picture concerning experiences of disability and victimization. Due to hierarchies of protected characteristics, many disabled people's experiences of victimization are often concealed because of other identities they are seen to occupy (Macdonald et al, 2021). For example, for a disabled person from a racially minoritized community, hate incidents are often linked with 'race' rather than as an intersectional form of discrimination underpinned by both racism and disablism as was the case in the following excerpt. The often-invisible nature of a person's disability leads to hate crime incidents being defined by a victim/survivor's visible identities (Macdonald et al, 2021):

> They were coming into her backyard with their bikes, saying 'we're going to get you', 'there's the n*****'. ... [The] client says that she feels like a prisoner in her home. She feels degraded, exhausted and very hurt. ... She has been to the doctors and takes lots of medications, [s]he has panic attacks and said she fears for her life. (Fatima:[8] Woman, aged 60-70, 'Other' ethnic group, recorded as racist hate)

Being a Black and disabled woman can reinforce hyper-visibility. Hence, as victims/survivors *become* hyper-visible within their communities, perpetrators are motivated by interconnected racist, disablist and homo/transphobic stereotypes, which reinforces alienation and 'othering' of victim/survivors at multiple scales (Donovan et al, 2019).

For disabled victims/survivors, certain locations and geographies become a focal point of hate and victimization, thus highlighting situated vulnerability (Hall, 2018). Locations in themselves often become stigmatized and are associated with disability. Examples of these relate to special needs schools, day centres, residential care homes and third sector services. Although hate crime/incidents can occur within these institutional spaces, it is often during journeys to or from these spaces where disabled people are targeted. Walking home from special needs schools, or bus journeys from services, creates a space for victimization to occur (Forster and Pearson, 2020; and Chapter 8). Due to the hyper-visible nature of disability in relation to these material spaces, disabled people's independence is significantly restricted increasing risk factors concerning social isolation and loneliness (Macdonald et al, 2018). Furthermore, journeys often connect these institutions with homes where there is a continuation of hate victimization with local perpetrators from whom there is little ability to escape. As one family reports:

> The house is situated between a park and a school. This involves verbal and physical abuse, name-calling, and taunting, mostly from children although two adults have been involved. ... The garden at the front has a low fence, and the kids call him names and throw things over the fence at him [often] stones, bottles. (Barbara: Woman, aged 40-50, White British whose son is being harassed, recorded as disablist hate)

Data from our own research speaks to what we refer to as 'hate relationships' (Donovan et al, 2019). These are cases where repeated hate incidents occur over time, sometimes escalating to more overtly violent behaviour, and involve what might be seen as a low-level incidents – such as placing rubbish or objects as obstacles on access paths and disputes over car parking. These may seem like minor anti-social behaviours but extended over a long period of time has a cumulative force, especially in the context of hate (Macdonald, 2015). In the following excerpt a brother reports experiences that he and his disabled sister have endured:

> The main issue here is that there is a long-term pattern of what may be perceived to be 'low-level' incidents in themselves. However, these incidents form a steady stream of harassment and bullying that are having an increasingly severe impact on the client's and his sister's lives. To the extent that they genuinely fear that they may be physically attacked and even killed. It is this overall pattern of harassment that is the issue. (Mustafa: Man, aged 40-50, 'Other' ethnic group, recorded as racist and religious hate)

These experiences challenge ideas of the home (and neighbourhood) as fixed spaces of security and sanctuary (Healy, 2020; Power and Bartlett, 2018). Much of our data speaks to limited mobility and social isolation, of staying in the house or flat to avoid exposing themselves to attack (Deacon et al, 2019). In this sense, individuals and families become incarcerated within their own homes (Thiara et al, 2011), which can have profound impacts for disabled people who risk losing independence (Gravell, 2011) as the following excerpt illustrates:

> [The] client can't get her mobility scooter out because it is kept in the shed in the back garden, and she is too scared to go past his gate to get to it. They don't feel safe using their own garden. They don't have a TV and keep their voices down in the house for fear of setting him off. (Layla: Women aged 30-40, 'Other' Ethnic group, recorded as racist and religious hate)

Thus, once the disabled person becomes hyper-visible within their community through encounters with neighbours who are uncomfortable and hostile to their presence, the safe space of the home can be not only targeted but colonized by acts of hate. The home, and journeys home, form networks that connect disabled institutions, to neighbourhoods, to home addresses through which disabled people become hyper-visible. Although disability and victimization are usually conceptualized through inherent vulnerabilities, the hyper-visibilization of disabled people speak to structural and situational, rather than naturalized biological vulnerability. Thus, by shifting focus from (just) disabled people's bodies to the spaces through which victimization occurs, we switch attention to the production of vulnerability through charged neighbourhood proximities, deprivation, poor housing, the disappearance of services and circulating affects that demonize and devalue disabled people.

Conclusion

Critiquing the view that those subjected to discrimination, abjection and hate are inherently vulnerable, we examine the role of material spaces in the production of hyper-visibility as part of broader contexts of social marginalization and de-valuation. We have focussed on material spaces that are more than symbolic of difference; rather they are used, lived and affected in ways that speak both to their value to communities but also to their harmful and often uncontrollable implication in affective economies of hate (Ahmed, 2004). Through attention to social materialities of the mosque, scene and home, we have illustrated some of the emergent ways in which material spaces stand in for, are associated with, and over time produce hyper-visibility as part of an accumulation of broader relations of harm. Materialities of the mosque, scene and home allow us to think through ongoing practices of hate beyond (yet including) the bodies of victims both *in context* and *in relation*.

From overtly violent attacks on property to everyday forms of 'low level' harassment, we have explored a continuum of violence for those who are marginalized because of assumptions around 'race' and religion, disability, sexuality and/or transgender identity; the effects of which linger and reinforce already established societal harms. In all examples, we note that there is never only one form of violence at work. For example, mosques have been problematized through global discourse and local tensions of fear and threat, and the violent reverberations of racist vandalism seeps into everyday life as a reminder of the range and scale of oppressions faced. Similarly, Pride events have become identifiable in different nation states as politicized contested spaces in which, temporarily, collective demands for human rights and citizenship can be made simultaneously as LGBTQ+ communities become hyper-visibilized and targeted for state and/or local violence and suppression for perceived non-conformity to heteronormative, cisgendered norms. The same can be said of the 'hate relationships' that develop in and around the spaces of the home, which can only be understood in the broader context of the ongoing dehumanization of disabled people (and intersections with other targeted identities) in contemporary Britain.

We have also briefly touched upon efforts to navigate and contest these harms – to live life beyond hate, whether through confrontation, efforts to re-work meanings associated with material environments, harnessing potentialities of sites for multiple public orientated activities or agentic efforts to problematize perpetrators through reporting. In line with arguments set out by Bregazzi and Jackson (2018) in their re-centring of 'peace within violence', we might then think through the refusal to see violence as a default reality, despite its often-overwhelming character and devasting impacts. In relation to notions of visibility, we suggest, as Colliver and Silvestri (2020: 5) argue in relation to the targeting of transgender people, that visibility (as claimed) does not and should not *have to* equate with vulnerability. Being visible by participating in communities can be an act of resistance and a way of changing public perceptions and attitudes. Addressing situated vulnerabilities should not come via a reduced presence but through sustained efforts to re-position the terms on which such presence is experienced. This applies to stigmatized bodies but also to objects, buildings and other materialities that constitute marginalized and resistant subjectivities, and allows us to think about not what these material spaces are, but what they can become.

Notes

[1] The primary research upon which these cases draw each received ethical approval from the respective Universities at which they were conducted (Newcastle University, Sunderland University and Durham University).

[2] Sections 28–32 of the Crime and Disorder Act 1998 and sections 145 and 146 of the Criminal Justice Act (2003).

[3] In total, 68.5 per cent of participants in our regional survey (North East England) indicated this put people at greater risk.

[4] Tell MAMA is a third-party reporting and support organization for those subjected to Islamophobia and Anti-Muslim attacks in the UK.

[5] For 2017 this accounts for only half the year.

[6] The Metro is an overground and underground light rail transit system serving the city of Newcastle upon Tyne, the metropolitan boroughs of Gateshead, North Tyneside, South Tyneside and the City of Sunderland.

[7] These are both relatively recent revelations regarding the violent and systemic abuse of adults with learning disabilities within UK hospital settings.

[8] All names are pseudonyms.

References

Ahmed, S. (2001) 'The organisation of hate', *Law and Critique*, 12: 345–65.

Ahmed, S. (2004) 'Affective economies', *Social Text*, 22(2): 117–39.

Akiko, S. (2008) *Lying Bodies: Survival and Subversion in the Field of Vision*, New York: Peter Lang.

Allen, C. (2017) 'Islamophobia and the problematization of Mosques: a critical exploration of hate crimes and the symbolic function of "old" and "new" Mosques in the United Kingdom', *Journal of Muslim Minority Affairs*, 37(3): 294–308.

Bachmann, C.L. and Gooch, B. (2017) *LGBT in Great Britain: Hate Crime and Discrimination*, London: Stonewall and YouGov.

Back, L. and Sinha, S. (2016) 'Multicultural conviviality in the midst of racism's ruins', *Journal of Intercultural Studies*, 37(5): 517–32.

Baker, J. (2019) 'Is it a mosque? "The Islamization of space explored through residents" everyday discursive assemblages', *Identities*, 26(1): 12–32.

Bonner-Thompson, C. (2017) '"The meat market": production and regulation of masculinities on the Grindr grid in Newcastle-upon-Tyne, UK', *Gender, Place and Culture*, 24(11): 1611–25.

Bregazzi, H. and Jackson, M. (2018) 'Agonism, critical political geography, and the new geographies of peace', *Progress in Human Geography*, 42(1): 72–91.

Cancellieri, A. and Ostanel, E. (2015) 'The struggle for public space: the hypervisibility of migrants in the Italian urban landscape', *City*, 19(4): 499–509.

Casper, M. and Moore, L. J. (2009) *Missing Bodies*, New York: New York University Press.

Chari, S. (2008) 'Critical geographies of racial and spatial control', *Geography Compass*, 2(6): 1907–21.

Colliver, B. and Silvestri, M. (2020) 'The role of (in) visibility in hate crime targeting transgender people', *Criminology and Criminal Justice*, DOI: 1748895820930747

Corteen, K. (2002) 'Lesbian safety talk: problematizing definitions and experiences of violence, sexuality and space', *Sexualities*, 5(3): 259–80.

Costa, L. (2013) 'Mad patients and legal intervenors in court', in B.A. Le Francois, R. Menzies and G. Reaume (eds) *Mad Matters: A Critical Reader in Canadian Mad Studies*, Toronto: Canadian Scholar's Press, pp 195–209.

Cross, M. (2013) 'Demonised, impoverished and now forced into isolation: the fate of disabled people under austerity', *Disability and Society*, 28(5): 719–23.

Dale, K. (2005) 'Building a social materiality: spatial and embodied politics in organizational control', *Organization*, 12(5): 649–78.

Deacon, L., Macdonald, S.J. and Nixon, J. (2019) 'The loss: understanding experiences of social isolation and loneliness, and the necessity of weekend and evening multi-agency community support', *Social Work and Social Sciences Review*, 20(3): 68–87.

Dickinson, H., Carey, G. and Kavanagh, A.M. (2020) 'Personalisation and pandemic: an unforeseen collision course?', *Disability and Society*, 35(6): 1012–17.

Donovan, C. and Hester, M. (2011) 'Seeking help from the enemy: help-seeking strategies of those in same sex relationships who have experienced domestic abuse', *Child and Family Law Quarterly*, 23(1): 26–40.

Donovan, C., Clayton, J. and Macdonald, S.J. (2019) 'New directions in hate reporting research: agency, heterogeneity and relationality' *Sociological Research Online*, 24(2): 185–202.

Doughty, S. (2020) (04/06/20) 'Newcastle Muslims "living in fear" after Islamic school is trashed and covered in paraffin', *Chronicle Live*, 4 June, Available from: https://www.chroniclelive.co.uk/news/north-east-news/bahr-academy-newcastle-vandalism-police-16027795 [Accessed 7 July 2020].

Forman, P. (2020) 'Materiality, new materialisms', in A. Kobayashi (ed) *International Encyclopaedia of Human Geography* (2nd edn), London: Elsevier, pp 449–55.

Formby, E. (2017) *Exploring LGBT Spaces and Communities: Contrasting Identities, Belongings and Wellbeing*, London: Routledge.

Forster, S. and Pearson, A. (2020) '"Bullies tend to be obvious": autistic adult's perceptions of friendship and the concept of "mate crime"', *Disability and Society*, 35(7): 1103–23.

Fox, N.J. and Alldred, P. (2018) 'Mixed methods, materialism and the micropolitics of the research-assemblage', *International Journal of Social Research Methodology*, 21(2): 191–204.

Gale, R. (2004) 'The multicultural city and the politics of religious architecture: urban planning, mosques and meaning-making in Birmingham, UK', *Built Environment*, 30(1): 30–44.

Gale, R. and Naylor, S. (2002) 'Religion, planning and the city: the spatial politics of ethnic minority expression in British cities and towns', *Ethnicities*, 2(3): 387–409.

Godzisz, P. and Viggiani, G. (2019) *Awareness of Anti-LGBT Hate Crime in Europe*, Warsaw: Lambda Warsaw.

Goffman E. (1963) *Stigma Notes on the Management of Spoiled Identity*, London: Penguin.

Göle, N. (2013) 'Islam's disruptive visibility in the European public space: political stakes and theoretical issues', *Sens public*, 15–16, English version, Available at: http://www.eurozine.com/islams-disruptive-visibility-in-the-european-public-space/ [Accessed 7 July 2020].

Goodley, D. Lawthom, R. and Runswick Cole, K. (2014) 'Posthuman disability studies', *Subjectivity*, 7: 342–61.

Gravell, C. (2011) *Loneliness and Cruelty*, London: Lemos & Crane.

Griffiths, M. and Repo, J. (2018) 'Biopolitics and checkpoint 300 in occupied Palestine: Bodies, affect, discipline', *Political Geography*, 65: 17–25.

Guasp, A., Gammon, A. and Ellison, G. (2013) *Homophobic Hate Crime: The Gay British Crime Survey 2013*, London: Stonewall and YouGov.

Hall, E. (2005) 'The entangled geographies of social exclusion/inclusion for people with learning disabilities', *Health and Place*, 11(2): 107–15.

Hall, E. (2018) 'A critical geography of disability hate crime', *Area*, 51(2): 249–56.

Hall, E. and Bates, E. (2019) 'Hatescape? A relational geography of disability hate crime, exclusion and belonging in the city', *Geoforum*, 101: 100–10.

Hawthorne, C. (2019) 'Black matters are spatial matters: Black geographies for the twenty-first century', *Geography Compass*, 13(11), DOI: 10.1111/gec3.12468

Healy, J.C. (2020) '"It spreads like a creeping disease": experiences of victims of disability hate crimes in austerity Britain', *Disability and Society*, 35(2): 176–200.

Hopkins, P., Clayton, J. and Tell MAMA (2020) *Islamophobia and Anti-Muslim Hatred in North East England*, Newcastle-upon Tyne: Newcastle University.

Hughes, J., Simpson, R., Slutskaya, N., Simpson, S. and Hughes, K. (2017) 'Beyond the symbolic: a relational approach to dirty work through a study of refuse collectors and street cleaners', *Work, Employment and Society*, 31(1): 106–22.

Jackson, P. (2008) 'Afterword: new geographies of race and racism', in *New Geographies of Race and Racism*, London: Ashgate, pp 297–304.

Johansen, B.S. (2015) 'Locating hatred: on the materiality of emotions', *Emotion, Space and Society*, 16: 48–55.

Kitchin, R. (1999) 'Creating an awareness of others: highlighting the role of space and place', *Geography*: 45–54.

Kitchin, R. and Lysaght, K. (2003) 'Heterosexism and the geographies of everyday life in Belfast, Northern Ireland', *Environment and Planning A*, 35(3): 489–510.

Labanyi, J. (2010) 'Doing things: emotion, affect, and materiality', *Journal of Spanish Cultural Studies*, 11(3–4): 223–33.

Latham, A. and McCormack, D.P. (2004) 'Moving cities: rethinking the materialities of urban geographies', *Progress in Human Geography*, 28(6): 701–24.

Leicester Hate Crime Project, The (2014) *Briefing Paper No. 3 Homophobic Hate Crime*, Leicester: Leicester University, Available from: https://www2.le.ac.uk/departments/criminology/hate/documents/bp3-homophobic-hate-crime [Accessed 3 April 2020].

Macdonald, S.J. (2015) 'Community fear and harassment: learning difficulties and hate crime incidents in the North East of England', *Disability and Society*, 30(3): 353–67.

Macdonald, S.J. (2021) 'Therapeutic institutions of violence: conceptualising the biographical narratives of mental health service user/survivors accessing long term "treatment" in England', *Journal of Criminological Research Policy and Practice*, 7(2): 179–94.

Macdonald, S.J., Deacon, L. and Nixon, J. (2018) '"The invisible enemy": disability, loneliness and isolation', *Disability and Society*, 33(7): 1138–1159.

Macdonald, S.J., Donovan, C. and Clayton, J. (2021) '"I may yet be left with no choice but to seek an ending to my torment": disability, hate crime and the intersectionality of hate relationships', *Disability and Society*, DOI: 10.1080/09687599.2021.1928480

Moran, L., Skeggs, B., Tyrer, P. and Corteen, K. (2001) 'Property, boundary, exclusion: making sense of hetero-violence in safer spaces', *Social and Cultural Geography*, 2(4): 407–20.

Moser, I. (2006) 'Disability and the promises of technology: technology, subjectivity and embodiment within an order of the normal', *Information, Communication and Society*, 9(3): 373–95.

Najib, K. and Teeple Hopkins, C. (2020) 'Geographies of Islamophobia', *Social and Cultural Geography*, 21(4): 449–57.

Nayak, A. (2010) 'Race, affect, and emotion: young people, racism, and graffiti in the postcolonial English suburbs', *Environment and Planning A*, 42(10): 2370–92.

Nayak, A. (2017) 'Purging the nation: race, conviviality and embodied encounters in the lives of British Bangladeshi Muslim young women', *Transactions of the Institute of British Geographers*, 42(2): 289–302.

ONS (2021) *Hate Crime, England and Wales, 2020 to 2021*, London: Home Office.

Perry, B. (2001) *In the Name of Hate: Understanding Hate Crimes*, New York: Routledge.

Perry, B. and Alvi, S. (2012) '"We are all vulnerable" The in terrorem effects of hate crimes', *International Review of Victimology*, 18(1): 57–71.

Philo, C. (2000) 'More words, more worlds: reflections on the cultural turn and human geography', in I. Cook, D. Crouch, S. Naylor and J. Ryan (eds) *Cultural Turns/Geographical Turns: Perspectives on Cultural Geography*, Harlow: Prentice Hall, pp 26–53.

Pile, S. (2011) 'Skin, race and space: the clash of bodily schemas in Frantz Fanon's Black skins, white masks and Nella Larsen's passing', *Cultural Geographies*, 18(1): 25–41.

Power, A. and Bartlett, R. (2018) '"I shouldn't be living there because I am a sponger": negotiating everyday geographies by people with learning disabilities', *Disability and Society*, 33(4): 562–78.

Power, A., Coverdale, A., Croydon, A. et al (2022) 'Personalisation policy in the lives of people with learning disabilities: a call to focus on how people build their lives relationally', *Critical Social Policy*, 2(2): 220–40.

Roulstone, A., Thomas, P. and Balderston, S. (2011) 'Between hate and vulnerability: unpacking the British criminal justice system's construction of disablist hate crime', *Disability and Society*, 26(3): 351–64.

Saldanha, A. (2006) 'Reontologising race: the machinic geography of phenotype', *Environment and Planning D: Society and Space*, 24(1): 9–24.

Sanchez, M.C. and Schlossberg, L. (eds) (2001) *Passing: Identity and Interpretation in Sexuality, Race, and Religion*, New York: NYU Press.

Sharp, J. (2021) 'Materials, forensics and feminist geopolitics', *Progress in Human Geography*, 45(5): 990–1002.

Simonsen, K., de Neergaard, M. and Koefoed, L. (2019) 'A mosque event: the opening of a purpose-built mosque in Copenhagen', *Social and Cultural Geography*, 20(5): 649–70.

Simpson, P. (2013) 'Alienation, ambivalence, agency: middle-aged gay men and ageism in Manchester's gay village', *Sexualities*, 16(3/4): 283–99.

Smith A., Byrne, B., Garratt, L and Harries, B. (2021) 'Everyday aesthetics, locality and racialisation', *Cultural Sociology*, 15(1): 91–112.

Swanton, D. (2010) 'Flesh, metal, road: tracing the machinic geographies of race', *Environment and Planning D: Society and Space*, 28(3): 447–66.

Tell MAMA, (2017) *Beyond the Incident: Outcomes for Victims of Anti-Muslim Prejudice. Tell MAMA Annual Report*, London: Faith Matters.

Tell MAMA, (2019) *National Mosques Security Panel*, Available from: https://tellmamauk.org/national-mosques-security-panel/ [Accessed 12 Feb 2020].

Thiara, R.K., Hague, G. and Mullender, A. (2011) 'Losing out on both counts: disabled women and domestic violence', *Disability and Society*, 26(6): 757–71.

Thorneycroft, A. (2017) 'Problematising and reconceptualising "vulnerability" in the context of disablist violence', in N.L. Asquith, I. Bartkowiak-Théronn and K.A. Roberts (eds) *Policing Encounters with Vulnerability*, Cham: Palgrave Macmillan, pp 27–46.

Tyler, D.I. (2013) *Revolting Subjects: Social Abjection and Resistance in Neoliberal Britain*, London: Zed Books.

Tyler, D.I. (2020) *Stigma: The Machinery of Inequality*, London: Zed Books.

Wallengren, S. and Mellgren, C. (2015) 'The role of visibility for a minority's exposure to (hate) crime and worry about crime: a study of the Traveller community', *International Review of Victimology*, 21(3): 303–19.

Wood, C. and Orpinas, P. (2021) 'Victimization of children with disabilities: coping strategies and protective factors', *Disability and Society*, 36(9): 1469–88.

Zouggari, N. (2019) 'Hybridised materialisms: the "twists and turns" of materialities in feminist theory', *Feminist Theory*, 20(3): 269–81.

7

The Role of Space and Place in Learning Disabled People's Experiences of Disablist Violence

Ellen Daly and Olivia Smith

Introduction

It is well established that disabled people in the UK experience high levels of hostility, harassment and violence (Hughes et al, 2012; Clayton et al, 2016). Those with learning disabilities and/or mental health conditions have a heightened chance of victimization than those with physical disabilities only (Sin et al, 2009; Clement et al, 2011). The types of hostility and prejudice faced are wide-ranging, from 'low-level' verbal incidents to physical violence resulting in death, but all can seriously impact on wellbeing (Quarmby, 2008; Chakraborti et al, 2014; Williams and Tregidga, 2014; Carr et al, 2017). Indeed, Kattari (2020) found that disablist microaggressions had long-term detrimental effects on mental health, and previous research shows that the most harmful incidents recalled by disabled people were often 'low-level' intimidatory behaviour and abusive language (Clement et al, 2011; Chakraborti et al, 2014; Richardson et al, 2016; Carr et al, 2017; Macdonald et al, 2017).

Disablist acts have become normalized for many and are made 'mundane' by their frequency, which when coupled with stories of extreme violence experienced by others, creates an underlying sense of fear across disabled communities (Pain, 1997; Beadle-Brown et al, 2014; McClimens and Brewster, 2017). Quarmby (2008) argued that casual disablism remains entrenched in British society and 'disability hate crime' is simply an extreme manifestation of this disablism. This has led to a move away from 'hate crime' terminology, with many academics preferring the alternative 'disablist violence' (see, for example, Chakraborti and Garland, 2012; Thorneycroft and Asquith, 2015). While conceptualizing incidents as 'disability hate crime' enables people to report prejudicial violence and hostility to authorities, it does not reflect the broader understanding of such acts as being shaped by a disablist society and reproduced through social interactions (Goodley and Runswick-Cole, 2011). Additionally, criminal justice responses to hate crime are inconsistent (Sin 2016), and police often fail to see the prejudice, bias and/or hostility in crimes against disabled people (Brereton, 2013; Smith, 2015). The concept of 'disablist violence' is therefore used throughout this chapter in place of 'disability hate crime' to emphasize the social processes that underlie exclusion and have a disabling effect (rather than the impairment itself).

Using data from seven focus groups with learning disabled people and support practitioners, this chapter argues for 'continuum thinking' (Boyle, 2019; see also Kelly, 1988; Hollomotz, 2012) to conceptualize the lived reality of disablist violence. Drawing on parallel literature about gendered violence, the chapter argues that the continuum reveals a pervasive low-level fear that requires disabled people to undertake 'safety work' (Kelly, 2012) and has implications for their free movement around the social world (see Vera-Gray, 2018). Existing research highlights the risk of harm across different social spaces, for example on public transport (Wilkin, 2019), in the home (McCarthy, 2017) or when navigating inaccessible buildings (Guffey, 2017). Criminological research such as the Leicester Hate Crime Project (Chakraborti et al, 2014) identified the varied settings in which hate crime occurs, while Hall (2018) advocated using a geographical imagination to explore how the nature and experience of hate crime shifts in different settings. The chapter argues that conceptualizing disablist violence as a continuum enables better connections between these varied settings, while leaving space to acknowledge different landscapes of hate throughout the social world.

The study

The data were collected in 2017 for a study on the under-reporting of disability hate crime, commissioned by a police force in Southeast England (ethical approval granted by Anglia Ruskin University's Departmental Research Ethics Panel [DREP] for Social Sciences). In total, seven focus groups were run across the force area, as well as one follow-up telephone interview with a support practitioner. One focus group comprised only support practitioners or volunteers for support organizations, while the other six involved a mix of service providers and service users. This mixing made the research more accessible for learning disabled participants by providing familiar faces who could put them at ease and offer follow-up support for any issues that arose. The support workers were also able to help manage group dynamics and spot misunderstandings to facilitate smoother communication. Data collection took place during regular activity sessions provided by the support organizations, meaning that the size and timing of focus groups were determined by the service provision in each area. The groups ranged in size from five to 15, with one large session of 20 when the authors were invited to a support organization's regional team meeting (Focus Group [FG] 2).

The sample included 55 disabled people and 31 support practitioners or volunteers, some of whom also identified as disabled. The disabled participants who were not also support staff all had learning disabilities and some also spoke of mental health conditions; a significant minority were also physically disabled. The support workers in FG2 supported adults with mental health conditions and learning disabilities, as well as older people with long-term health problems. The participants in FG2 therefore spoke from a broader perspective than the other focus groups, which were based in specialist learning disability services. Participants were not asked for specific details of their disabilities, rather they were able to disclose (or not) whatever information they felt was relevant because a list of medical diagnoses may not accurately reflect a disabled person's self-identity (Murugami, 2009). The authors are therefore unable to establish how many participants had particular types of disability.

Participants were self-selecting, with support organizations responding to an open invitation and speaking with their service users about whether they would like to get involved (only doing so if there was clear consensus from the whole group). At least one, but more often two, support workers known to the learning-disabled participants co-facilitated the focus groups and the setting was familiar to those involved. The groups themselves were informal and participants came and went, for example to make cups of tea, to allow for different attention spans and to help someone 'check out' of anything they did not wish to discuss. The points of discussion in the focus groups related to disabled people's experiences of hostility, who they told about it and the reasons for their decisions, their understanding of and feelings about the term 'disability hate crime', and their thoughts about the police both in general and specifically in relation to 'disability hate crime'.

The focus groups were met with enthusiasm from the participants and produced extensive data on a broad range of topics, which were analysed thematically. This chapter outlines emergent themes relating to continuum understandings; limited affinity with the 'hate crime' label; geographically diverse settings of hate crime and the blurring of 'safe' and 'unsafe' space; and the 'safety work' undertaken by learning disabled people and the limits this places on their mobility.

The continuum of disablist violence

All participants had stories of disablist violence, either against themselves or people they knew. Most of the conversations centred around being hurt by frequent 'low-level' comments from others, although these also included threats of violence. For example:

> 'The table next to us [at the pub recently] had actually got up and moved away and said, "Oh I'm not sitting here with them people."' (Practitioner,[1] FG4)

> 'I do find it happens a lot with me because they know I can't walk very well, so they say, "Oh come on then, walk without your walker". ... I said, "If you take my walker away from me I will fall" ... and then they snatch it from me, and that ain't good cos I fell and I hurt myself. ... And they say, "I'll break it!"' (Service user, FG5)

> 'They threaten me, they say things like, "When you get off [the bus] I'm gonna beat you up."' (Service user, FG1)

In line with existing research (Sin et al, 2009), the term 'hate crime' was poorly understood and had limited use for learning disabled people voicing their experiences. For example, in FG6, participants were only able to define 'disability hate crime' in terms of specific past experiences they had been told by police and support workers counted as such. There was also confusion about the role of 'hate' in hate crime, because people may be targeted for a variety of reasons (see Clayton et al, 2016 for more on this):

> 'I think people are still really confused [about what a hate crime is]. ... And I think you can be the victim of anything. Anyone, even me, at any moment in your life when you're feeling vulnerable, can be a victim of anything.' (Practitioner, FG3)

> 'I think [service users] get muddled and think it's only actual physical abuse. ... I think the term "hate crime" does kind of get it across from an informative perspective, but I think the actual word "hate", and then goes "hatred", and then actually it almost is like "oh, this is happening because people hate me". So that has a very negative context for people with a learning disability.' (Practitioner, Follow-up interview)

The term 'disability hate crime' was also critiqued from a conceptual perspective because it further differentiated learning disabled people from others, compounding their feeling of exclusion: 'They should all be classed as hate crimes whether you've got a disability or not ... cos we're not different' (Service User, FG4).

This could be a result of using the word 'disability' rather than 'disablist', which names the individual identity (disability) rather than the system of oppression (disabl*ism*). Such terminology diverges from other types of hate crime where, for example, it is 'racist' hate crime not 'Black' hate crime (Thorneycroft, 2017). When asked about being made to feel different or scared without labelling the incidents, participants instead discussed experiences in terms of "banter" (FG1), "bullying" (FG1), "being picked on" (FG5), and "taking the mickey" (FG4). For example, one learning disabled participant in FG3 argued the term 'bullying' was preferable because it was more widely understood: "So why don't we change the word from 'hate crime' to 'bullying', where people understand more?" (Service User, FG3)

While most learning disabled participants knew the term 'disability hate crime' and did find it helpful in labelling some forms of hostility, it was perceived as unable to fully capture their experiences. This may be a symptom of conceptual inadequacies in the term 'hate crime' or a result of earlier hate incidents being trivialized in one particular space: school.

All focus groups involved stories of disablist harassment in school (see also Mencap, 2011), which for most participants was decades earlier. Specific incidents remained notable even after the intervening years and were often named before more recent or 'serious' offences: "I thought I was doing alright with the students but I didn't ... they all didn't really connect with me when I was at school ... they called me names" (Service User, FG6). "They called me that word, you know, spastic. I'm not. That upsets me that does. I'm not. I'm a normal girl and woman" (Service User, FG6).

A participant in FG5 also talked about teenage boys putting a worm in her food and refusing to remove it, while others in FG6 recalled having their hair pulled or their glasses deliberately broken. This harassment was labelled 'bullying' by school staff, leading to confusion about terminology in adult life when the same incidents became 'hate crime'.

The language chosen by participants similarly minimized their experiences of disablist hostility and obscured the prejudicial and harmful nature of the incidents, for example one participant quickly said that the frequency of incidents made them less impactful: "I got bullied [by] loads of boys at my old school, don't bother me anymore, you get used to it" (FG6). Browne et al (2011) noted that hate crime against LGBTQ+ communities is subject to similar trivialization, often as a form of self-preservation by those experiencing it. However, the cumulative impact of disablist interactions was elsewhere recognized as high:

'This under the radar bullying can build up and that's why you get people committing suicide, because they can't handle the strain of it anymore. And it's just the little words, just the tiny little words when you're on the bus or down the street saying "look at this so and so" or "look at that so and so", they're pulling faces or intimidating.' (Practitioner, FG1)

Indeed, varying forms of hostility were discussed as interlinked and the impact as cumulative. Participants discussed microaggressions such as 'funny looks' alongside mention of threats to kill, sexual and physical violence, and even murder (more on these later). For example, in FG1 the conversation moved quickly from a friend's experience of being stared at, to receiving threats to kill: "It's a visible disability [that my friend has] ... and he was stared at a lot. On the bus, in the street, out shopping ... [and an old man] threatened to kill him on the bus" (Service User, FG1).

Here, it is helpful to learn from 'continuum thinking' and the gender-based violence literature. Kelly (1988) identified many different forms of sexualized violence and abuse that men committed against women, highlighting their interconnectedness as symptoms of patriarchy. In identifying these connections, causal explanations could move beyond individual male perpetrators to recognize that victim–survivors were targeted *because they were women*, and that this had a symbolic meaning beyond the immediate physical and emotional impacts of violence (Boyle, 2019).

Hollomotz (2012) applied the same principles to connect the wide-ranging experiences of disabled individuals in a continuum of disablist violence. The acts of prejudice, hostility and violence discussed in the focus groups spanned the whole continuum of disablist violence; including stares or being ignored, to acts of physical and sexual violence. Continuum thinking is useful because it recognizes the underlying structural inequalities and embedded disablist attitudes that re/create a context that is conducive with disablist practices (see also Goodley and Runswick-Cole, 2011; Clayton et al, 2016). Following Kelly (1988), Hollomotz (2012) stressed that the acts on the hate crime continuum are not linear or hierarchical because the act does not dictate the level of harm experienced (except violence that results in death). A person at one time and space may experience not being listened to as more harmful than name-calling, whereas somebody else, or the same person at another space or time, may find the opposite.

An important part of Kelly's (1988) continuum is the recognition that making connections between different incidents is essential for understanding the lived experience. While it is possible to explore specific types of violence, for example the verbal abuse of disabled people on buses, this cannot adequately be explained without also acknowledging disablism in its structurally and culturally violent forms (see Galtung, 1969). Indeed, learning once more from the violence against women literature, Walling-Wefelmeyer (2019) argued that the continuum of men's harassment towards women imposes gendered self-awareness, with intrusions being simultaneously unexpected and continuous. This means that in relation to 'low level' harassment, there is always risk of escalation, and in relation to physical violence, there is a subtext of societal acceptance that women's bodies are legitimate targets for action (Walling-Wefelmeyer, 2019).

Finally, the impact of continuum violence is that those being targeted receive a message of needing to be 'less', as they are shown to be unwelcome across all social spaces. Vera-Gray and Kelly (2020) discussed the role of street harassment in teaching women that their mere presence is a risk, and highlighted the women's movement as having specifically fought for visible presence (see, for example, Reclaim the Night marches, campaigns for women on banknotes or statues and the response to Sarah Everard's murder; see Strick, 2021). Learning disabled people have a comparable history of being excluded from public visibility, both through explicit policies of segregation and the disabling design of social space (Wilkin, 2019). Several of the participants felt this keenly, for example saying that: "[Disability *and* disability hate crime] seems to be a problem that the government would rather see disappear" (Service User, FG1).

There was resistance to these narratives, however, with several focus groups also involving affirmative discussion about the worth of disabled people: "We are no different to anybody else in this world" (Service User, FG3).

The continuum of disablist violence therefore taught the participants that their presence was problematic or risky, but it did not prevent them from having good self-esteem and understanding their worth. It is now important to understand the embodied impacts of continuum experiences.

Safety work

Vera-Gray (2018) developed Kelly's (1988) arguments by examining the impact of continuum thinking for women's freedoms. While individual women might not make connections between specific incidences of violence in their own lives, Vera-Gray (2018) argued that a pervasive awareness of risk leads to women undertaking 'safety work'. Safety work refers to the habitual strategies that women use to mitigate the risk of men's intrusions, both in terms of reducing occurrences and minimizing harm when they do occur. The focus groups revealed that learning disabled people also undertook safety work to limit the risk of experiencing disablist hostility. For example, in FG4, Service Users variously said: "Don't go out in the dark cos you could get attacked or raped ... it could happen"; "and physically I don't go out, not after 7 o'clock"; "No, I don't. ... I don't go out [at night] for the same reason."

Browne et al (2011) found similar avoidance tactics in a study on LGBTQ+ hate crime, where people reported self-policing their behaviours to avoid conflict; for example, leaving employment where abuse happened in the workplace. The data also reflect Roberts et al's (2020) work on street harassment of female students, where public space was deemed particularly risky under darkness. The conversation in FG4 moved on to areas that were avoided even in daytime, and these discussions were echoed across multiple focus groups: "Don't go to [specific park] ... it's dangerous" (Service User, FG4). "But in my new home I will [only] go out with my carers. ... It is strange, that people think they can do things to us" (Service User, FG3).

This moderated behaviour suggests an underlying sense of fear, and even those who said they had never experienced 'hate crime' still adapted their behaviour. In her work on the geography of women's fear, Valentine (1989, 1990) noted that second-hand information, as well as first-hand experiences, informed women's assessment of threat and thus their decisions about which spaces were 'safe' to occupy. Previous research has shown that disabled people have a heightened fear of crime compared to non-disabled people (Lorenc et al, 2012; Coleman and Sykes, 2016), and Hall (2018) argued that the saturation, that is, the everydayness and ubiquity of disablist incidents, creates a continuous sense of fear. As Vera-Gray (2018) argued in relation to women's fear of crime, this heightened concern should not be dismissed as unwarranted because safety work might indeed offer some protection against victimization. It is therefore not simply a matter of inconsequential habit but rather about the trade-off between safety and freedom (Vera-Gray and Kelly, 2020).

Similarly, Vera-Gray and Kelly (2020) argued that conducting safety work often means invisibilizing oneself, taking up less space and seeking to pass through public places unnoticed. This is more difficult for anyone with visible disabilities, as the appearance of difference can make people hyper-visible and is often a reason they are targeted for hostility (Chakraborti and Garland, 2012). It is also the opposite of what is needed for policy change, as Hardy and Chakraborti (2020) highlighted the contradiction between disabled people being targeted for hyper-visible difference and yet being invisible to many policymakers. Much is written elsewhere about how austerity amounted to a form of structural violence (see Galtung, 1969 for more on this concept), and how culturally violent 'scrounger' narratives have justified both welfare cuts and hate crime (Burch, 2018; see also Garthwaite, 2011). The invisibilization of individual safety work is therefore opposite to the collective action of revisibilization needed to address wider disablist structures.

Furthermore, safety work had additional financial implications that compounded the structural violence of austerity and other socio-economic inequalities. For example, one man who had experienced repeated hostility and harassment on buses decided to use taxis despite the impact on his finances:

Practitioner: [Name] was picked on a lot on the buses by school
                   kids. ... As a result of that you started to use taxis,
                   didn't you [Name]?
Service User: Yeah. (FG4)

Further, two female participants gave up paid work to avoid hostility: "They wasn't very nice to me ... the staff was alright in there, but it was the customers, they was throwing food in there at me. It was awful. That's why I left" (Service User, FG4).

The intersectional experiences of learning disabled women are important here. For them, the threat of disablist violence intersected with the threat of male violence and two female participants talked about their fear of being raped if going out in the dark (see the first and third participant quotes of this section). Another young woman, whose disability was visible, talked about street harassment perpetrated by a man: "I was going to walk to my work ... there was a man sitting down, an old man, he was old man, he was sitting on a bench and I was just walking up, he said, 'Hi lovely, how old are you? You're so sexy'" (Service User, FG6).

Hill Collins (2000) argued that for women located at the intersection of oppressed identities, the matrix of dominations acted as a 'conducive context' for violence (see Kelly, 2016, for more). Others have recognized the impossibility of separating disablism from other systems of oppression, such as sexism (Goodley, 2014; Healy, 2019). Balderston (2013a) found that disabled women were significantly more likely to experience sexual violence than men and abled women, and that they faced additional barriers when seeking justice and support (Balderston, 2013b). For instance, institutional responses often frame disabled women's sexual victimization as resulting from a perceived inherent vulnerability, thus obscuring prejudicial motivations and compounding feelings of exclusion (Balderston, 2013b). Moreover, Pain's (1997) research with disabled women highlighted their heightened fear of victimization that constrained their interactions with the social world. Indeed, for the young woman in the example mentioned earlier, the experience left her feeling distressed: "It can be very hurtful when people say those things to other people, like me. ... I was crying and I was shaken up a bit" (Service User, FG6).

In considering what to do in such situations, a support worker talked about finding places of safety: "I think, erm, quite a lot of you know what you would do now in that situation ... cos we've had quite a few different people come in and talk and explain about finding places of safety, and what to do" (Practitioner, FG6).

These 'safe' locations included shops that participated in a hate crime 'safe space' scheme, statutory services or even just getting home; which ignored the spread of disablist incidents into these environments (more on this later). The need for safety work was reinforced by support workers in all focus groups, who encouraged learning disabled people to ignore hostility: "Best way is to walk on the opposite side of the road and just ignore them ... you won't get in trouble" (Practitioner, FG4). "You just ignore them? Probably wise ... it can escalate" (Practitioner, FG7).

This reflected Brooks Gardner's (1995) description of women's strategies in response to street harassment; whereby the most common tactics were to ignore it or redefine events as harmless. Other tactics by women included the invocation of an absent protector or making a complaint to an external authority (Brooks Gardner, 1995). These were evident in some of the focus groups, as participants talked about knowing they could visit the 'safe space' shops, report incidents to their support workers, or call police, for example: "You can go to shops and they report back to police" (Service User, FG6).

However, one participant highlighted the risk of complaining to authority figures, as it could result in losing freedoms around housing: "Then social services will go, 'oh, are you okay living in the community then, is there a risk? Do you need to be in supported living?'" (Practitioner, FG2).

Another of Brooks Gardner's (1995) coping strategies was for women to 'answer back' when experiencing harassment, but this posed specific risks for learning disabled people. Four of the focus groups discussed how people sometimes resisted hate crime with anger, but found it challenging to do so in a way that was deemed acceptable and led to them being viewed as a perpetrator with the risk of being criminalized: "I feel like when this happens, seems to me [the perpetrators] get away with it. We blow up, we're the ones who get nicked! It's ridiculous. ... We blow up because we got good reason to and the coppers don't do anything" (Service User, FG1).

Resisting disablist harassment therefore had the same risk of escalation described by Walling-Wefelmeyer (2019) but could also lead to further restrictions on movement (for example, being banned from buses). To borrow another concept from Kelly (2003), their 'space for action' was limited. That is, the ability to exercise their autonomy was limited by the omnipresence of harassment and hostility, as was their freedom to resist it (Kelly et al, 2014). For learning disabled people with communication difficulties, 'safety work' consequently involved a more pronounced trade-off between freedom and safety. Vera-Gray and Kelly (2020) posit that women do safety work not only to minimize the risk of something happening but also to minimize the risk that they would be blamed if it did. There is a long history of women being blamed for their victimization, with more sympathy given to those who respond by being passive and upset, rather than active or angry (Bosma et al, 2018).

The examples mentioned earlier demonstrate a similar phenomenon with regards to disabled people, particularly as they are often framed as being inherently vulnerable (Quarmby, 2008). This means that anything other than a passive response to disablist violence is perceived as contrary to expectation and in need of management (Sin et al, 2009; Carr et al, 2017). Not only does the need for passivity tie in with criminological understandings of the 'ideal victim' (Christie, 1986) but also with the long history of disabled people being considered a public nuisance. For learning disabled people, this is particularly significant, as they have been perceived as potentially dangerous and in need of control since at least the Middle Ages, when St Augustine of Hippo suggested people with learning difficulties were possessed by devils (Richardson, 2005).

Our data therefore shows that the concept of 'safety work' can also be applied to learning disabled people's attempts to avoid and/or mitigate disablist hostility. As Vera-Gray and Kelly (2020) argued, safety work requires significant energy, and it is important to consider whether there are any spaces where disabled people can be relieved of this obligation. Hall and Bates (2019, 101) called for recognition of disabled people as social agents traversing and negotiating both discriminatory, exclusionary spaces *and* welcoming, inclusive spaces. The final section of this chapter therefore examines the spatial experience of hate crime, arguing that blurred boundaries between spaces and cultural depictions of disablism lead to an inability to escape the intrusions of disablist hostility even in otherwise safe and inclusive spaces.

(Blurred) spaces of disablist hostility

Our focus groups supported the existing literature in that participants described disablist hostility across a wide range of spaces. Specific incidences were mentioned in pubs, the workplace, streets, public transport, schools, shopping centres, at home, in youth clubs and online. For example, a support worker in FG4 described resistance to feeding disabled adults using a PEG feeding tube: "In like the food court, people actually come over and say, 'ah you can't do that here, that is disgusting'" (Practitioner, FG4).

In this example, ableist notions of decency around food were used to exclude those who cannot conform, reflecting a long-established history of disabled people being segregated for not doing things 'normally' (Hansen and Philo, 2007).

In line with national evidence, public transport was particularly mentioned as a site of frequent victimization (Wilkin, 2019), with six of the seven focus groups describing incidents occurring on local buses, including a participant having chewing gum put in her hair (FG4), a person having eggs thrown at them (FG6), and another having rude and insulting gestures directed towards them (FG6). The range of hostility experienced on public transport once more represent continuum violence and communicate a message to learning disabled people that they are not welcome in those spaces.

When participants described incidents that happened at home, it usually involved people close to the victim as part of wider interpersonal tensions, but some harassment by people in the local community also occurred: "[My friend] was getting mail sent to him like they were gonna kill him and blow him up and smash his windows right in. They was writing things all over his windows" (Service User, FG1).

The varied sites of incidents in the focus groups show that the experience of 'hate crime' is lived out in social relations both publicly and privately. This makes what happens in 'private' space intrinsically linked to public social relations, and Vera-Gray (2018: 33) noted that any attempts to categorize incidents as public or private ignores the main issue: "The division between public and private violence doesn't really matter when you're just trying to stop it from happening again."

Indeed, the public/private divide is arguably blurred for learning disabled people in supported living, where there are not the same boundaries as a 'private' household. Fyson and Kitson (2010) argued that for people with learning disabilities and autism, abuse was prevalent in institutional settings and at home (see also Sin et al, 2009). In the focus groups, many participants discussed incidents of 'mate crime' (see Landman, 2014) perpetrated by 'friends', family members or regular support staff. For example, economic abuse was described by three people in FG2 and the follow-up interview:

'At one point he'd taken somebody in and they were living there. ... I've done quite a few safeguarding cases where that's the case, where it is financial abuse, and they don't see it as financial abuse. Especially the elderly and the more vulnerable, they really don't see that. And it's not just the elderly, but a lot of young people also.' (Practitioner, FG2)

Viewing strangers as the sole perpetrators of hate crime therefore obscures the reality of the continuum of disablist violence (Williams and Tregidga, 2014). Indeed, family members and friends were specifically implicated:

'Quite often it's family that's abusing. I had a client that his daughter had transferred all his benefits to her account, he ended up in about £10,000 arrears with the council for his care home. She'd already done it to him once, "but it's my daughter, I don't want to get her into trouble".' (Practitioner, FG2)

Participants in two focus groups discussed a 'mate crime' that had resulted in the killing of a member of the local disabled community: "He thought he'd made some nice friends, could trust them, they lulled him into a bit of false security really" (Practitioner, FG4).

Social responses to what Doherty (2019) termed 'exploitative familiarity' have been somewhat lacking, although criminal justice agencies increasingly recognize learning disabled people's risk of 'cuckooing' as part of county lines drug dealing[2] (McLean et al, 2019). The disablist violence in private spaces was less identified as being motivated by prejudice or perceived difference so continuum thinking became useful to acknowledge the role of disablism in abuse that otherwise lacked overt hostility. However, it is important not to overly emphasize the difference in experiences between public and private spaces. For example, Balderston (2013a) found that incidents involving sexual violence happened in both public and private spaces.

In FG3, two female participants disclosed sexual assault in public (at work) and private (in sheltered housing) spaces before the recording equipment had even been set up. Another participant talked about a friend being raped by someone she knew: "She had it on her mind all the time, and she didn't know what to do. … It wasn't her fault, it was his fault, the bloke who done it. … It's rape. She got raped, by this man" (Service User, FG5).

Chakraborti et al (2014) found that 22 per cent of their disabled participants had been a victim of sexual violence, and that figure rose to 33 per cent for people who had been targeted because of mental health problems. Five out of 30 (17 per cent) disabled interviewees in Sin et al (2009) also disclosed sexual violence. This underlines the call from Virueda and Payne (2010) and McCarthy et al (2017) to recognize the similarities between 'mate crime' and wider 'public' abuse, as well as intimate partner violence. Vera-Gray and Kelly (2020) argued that public space constitutes a 'conducive context' for the private harassment of women, as the actions available to social actors are shaped by prevailing power structures, which in turn are reinforced by microaggressions or threats in public space.

Online spaces further blur the boundaries of public and private space, as Alhaboby et al (2016) found similarities between online and offline victimization of disabled people. Burch (2018) also demonstrated these commonalities in her analysis of online disablist hate speech, although the extra anonymity of the internet was seen to encourage people to engage in hate speech more often (see also Banks, 2010). Furthermore, perpetrators of online hate can feel galvanized from their online interactions, which could spill into the offline world (Winter, 2019). Online spaces were highlighted in the focus groups as a concern because "there's a lot of cyberbullying" (Practitioner, FG7).

A further example from FG6 demonstrated how disabled people's freedoms and 'space for action' can therefore become limited in online spaces as well as offline spaces: "Stay off social media [to keep safe]" (Service User, FG6).

Research elsewhere has found that young people with learning disabilities are at a heightened risk of online victimization and that the impacts are often more severe than for abled youth (Martínez-Cao et al, 2021). This is of particular concern given the marked shift to the online world during the pandemic, which may have the effect of further limiting the freedoms and 'space for action' for disabled people whose safety work involves avoiding online spaces. Their engagement with the social world is further limited in this way when considering how integrated social media has become into everyday life and that use of social media enables its users to assemble social capital that positively impacts their lives (Bouvier, 2015).

The internet provides a unique merging of public and private space (Bakardjieva, 2005), where social media platforms, for example, act as a public space with messaging options that are hidden from others. For example, a disabled woman in FG6 shared her experiences of being targeted via social media by an acquaintance, known to her offline through a family member, who sexually exploited her online. "I got bullied online ... [he] was picking on me, [asking] 'what do you wear in bed?'" (Service User, FG6).

In her work on men's intrusions, Walling-Wefelmeyer (2019) noted that harassment was connected across social space to the extent that there were no clear boundaries and sometimes no easily identifiable agents when women were recalling incidents. This relates to Galtung's (1969) distinction between direct, structural and cultural violence. While some examples of hate crime are direct interactions between social actors in a particular time and space, for Galtung, violence can also exist 'where there is no such actor [because] the violence is built into the [social] structure' (171). Walling-Wefelmeyer (2019) similarly highlighted the lack of spatial boundaries in male violence against women, as harassment occurred in specific places, but women could also be disrupted by experiences or stories of violence through online communication, in private conversations with friends or even through cultural depictions of abuse when watching television alone. By applying these concepts to the present research data, the authors argue that categorizing locations of disability hate crime can obscure the pervasiveness of disablist violence.

Conclusion

A shift towards continuum thinking is imperative because it better reflects the lived experiences of disabled people. Crucially, it moves away from a view of disablist hostility as an individual problem and thus away from the responsibilization of disabled communities. Moreover, continuum-thinking recognizes and makes visible the safety work of learning disabled people, showing how their freedom of movement around the social world is constrained. The spaces in which hate crime occurs are diverse and cannot easily be categorized into public and private. Continuum thinking reveals a blurring of public and private, safe and unsafe spaces, and exposes the underlying cultural and structural violence that acts as a 'conducive context' for everyday disablist hostility.

This chapter has therefore demonstrated that 'hate crime' is a rights issue. It is about freedoms and the ability to take up space. Learning from feminist campaigns on street harassment, it could now be useful for hate crime scholarship to examine how feminist self-defence classes empowered women to take up space and to explore whether similar actions could be helpful for learning disabled people. There must, however, be consideration of the additional policing of learning disabled people's responses to harassment and hostility. That is, being mindful that, for some, their responses can be misunderstood or seen in isolation and lead to them being seen as the aggressor. In all, taking disabled people's safety work into consideration demonstrates the need for wider societal change, including addressing structural inequalities and power imbalances, in order to foster meaningful change.

Notes

[1] For ease, both full-time employees and volunteers are referred to as 'practitioner', to reflect their role in the focus group. While some practitioners mentioned having disabilities before the sessions started, it was not possible to distinguish between disabled and non-disabled practitioners in the transcripts.

[2] 'County lines' refers to organized criminal networks transporting drugs from one locality to another, usually from urban centres to smaller towns. 'Cuckooing' refers to the practice whereby criminals take over a person's home for exploitative reasons, often to aid in drug-related crimes.

References

Alhaboby, Z.A., al-Khateeb, H.M., Barnes, J. and Short, E. (2016) '"The language is disgusting and they refer to my disability": the cyberharassment of disabled people', *Disability and Society*, 31(8): 1138–43.

Balderston, S. (2013a) 'Victimized again? Intersectionality and injustice in disabled women's lives after hate crime and rape', in M. Texler Segal and V. Demos (eds) *Gendered Perspectives on Conflict and Violence: Part A*, Bingley: Emerald Group Publishing Limited, pp 17–51.

Balderston, S. (2013b) 'After disablist hate crime: which interventions really work to resist victimhood and build resilience with survivors', in H. Mason-Bish and A. Roulstone (eds) *Disability, Hate Crime and Violence*, Abingdon: Routledge, pp 182–97.

Bakardjieva, M. (2005) *Internet Society: The Internet in Everyday Life*, London: Sage.

Banks, J. (2010) 'Regulating hate speech online', *International Review of Law, Computers and Technology*, 24(3): 233–9.

Beadle-Brown, J., Mansell, J., Ashman, B., Ockenden, J., Iles, R. and Whelton, B. (2014) 'Practice leadership and active support in residential services for people with intellectual disabilities: an exploratory study', *Journal of Intellectual Disability Research*, 58(9): 838–50.

Bosma, A.K., Mulder, E., Pemberton, A. and Vingerhoets, A.J.J.M. (2018) 'Observer reactions to emotional victims of serious crimes: stereotypes and expectancy violations', *Psychology, Crime and Law*, 24(9): 957–77.

Bouvier, G. (2015) 'What is a discourse approach to Twitter, Facebook, YouTube and other social media: connecting with other academic fields?', *Journal of Multicultural Discourses*, 10(2): 149–62.

Boyle, K. (2019) 'What's in a name? Theorising the inter-relationships of gender and violence', *Feminist Theory*, 20(1): 19–36.

Brereton, S. (2013) 'Living in a different world: joint review of disability hate crime', *Probation Journal*, 60(3): 345–50.

Brooks Gardner, C. (1995) *Passing By: Gender and Public Harassment*, London: University of California Press.

Browne, K., Bakshi, L. and Lim, J. (2011) "It's something you just have to ignore': understanding and addressing contemporary lesbian, gay, bisexual and trans safety beyond hate crime paradigms', *Journal of Social Policy*, 40(4): 739–56.

Burch, L. (2018) '"You are a parasite on the productive classes": online disablist hate speech in austere times', *Disability and Society*, 33(3), 392–415.

Carr, S., Holley, J., Hafford-Letchfield, T. et al (2017) 'Mental health service user experiences of targeted violence and hostility and help-seeking in the UK: a scoping review', *Global Mental Health*, 4: e25.

Chakraborti, N., Garland, J. and Hardy, S. (2014) *Briefing Paper 1: Disablist Hate Crime, The Leicester Hate Crime Project*, Leicester: University of Leicester.

Chakraborti, N. and Garland, J. (2012) 'Reconceptualizing hate crime victimization through the lens of vulnerability and "difference"', *Theoretical Criminology*, 16(4): 499–514.

Christie, N. (1986) 'The ideal victim', in E.A. Fattah (ed) *From Crime Policy to Victim Policy*, London: Palgrave Macmillan, pp 17–30.

Clayton, J., Donovan, C. and Macdonald, S.J. (2016) 'A critical portrait of hate crime/incident reporting in North East England: the value of statistical data and the politics of recording in an age of austerity', *Geoforum*, 75: 64–74.

Clement, S., Brohan, E., Sayce, L., Pool, J. and Thornicroft, G. (2011) 'Disability hate crime and targeted violence and hostility: a mental health and discrimination perspective', *Journal of Mental Health*, 20(3): 219–25.

Coleman, N. and Sykes, W. (2016) *Crime and Disabled People: Measures of Disability-Related Harassment 2016 Update*, Manchester: Equality and Human Rights Commission.

Doherty, G. (2019) 'Prejudice, friendship and the abuse of disabled people: an exploration into the concept of exploitative familiarity ("mate crime")', *Disability and Society*, 35(9): 1457–82.

Fyson, R. and Kitson, D. (2010) 'Human rights and social wrongs: issues in safeguarding adults with learning disabilities', *Practice: Social Work in Action*, 22(5): 309–20.

Garthwaite, K. (2011) '"The language of shirkers and scroungers?" Talking about illness, disability and coalition welfare reform', *Disability and Society*, 26(3): 369–72.

Galtung, J. (1969) 'Violence, peace and peace research', *Journal of Peace Research*, 6(3): 167–91.

Goodley, D. (2014) *Dis/ability Studies: Theorising Disablism and Ableism*. Abingdon: Routledge.

Goodley, D. and Runswick-Cole, K. (2011) 'The violence of disablism', *Sociology of Health and Illness*, 33(4): 602–17.

Guffey, E. (2017) *Designing Disability: Symbols, Space, and Society*, London: Bloomsbury Publishing.

Hall, E. (2018) 'A critical geography of disability hate crime', *Area*, 51(2): 249–56.

Hall, E. and Bates, E. (2019) 'Hatescape? A relational geography of disability hate crime, exclusion and belonging in the city', *Geoforum*, 101: 100–10.

Hansen, N. and Philo, C. (2007) 'The normality of doing things differently: bodies, spaces and disability geography', *Tijdschrift Voor Economische en Sociale Geografie*, 98(4): 493–506.

Hardy, S. and Chakraborti, N. (2020) 'Visible yet invisible: challenges facing hate crime victims', in S. Hardy and N. Chakraborti (eds) *Blood, Threats and Fears*, Cham: Springer International Publishing, pp 11–23.

Healy, J.C. (2019) '"It spreads like a creeping disease": experiences of victims of disability hate crimes in austerity Britain', *Disability and Society*, 35(2): 176–200.

Hill Collins, P. (2000) *Black Feminist Thought* (2nd edn), New York: Routledge.

Hollomotz, A. (2012) 'Disability, oppression and violence: towards a sociological explanation', *Sociology*, 47(3): 477–93.

Hughes, K., Bellis, M.A., Jones, L. et al (2012) 'Prevalence and risk of violence against adults with disabilities: a systematic review and meta-analysis of observational studies', *The Lancet*, 379(9826): 1621–29.

Kattari, S.K. (2020) 'Ableist microaggressions and the mental health of disabled adults', *Community Mental Health Journal*, 56(6): 1170–79.

Kelly, L. (1988) *Surviving Sexual Violence*, Cambridge: Polity Press.

Kelly, L. (2003) 'The wrong debate: reflections on why force is not the key issue with respect to trafficking in women for sexual exploitation', *Feminist Review*, 73(1): 139–44.

Kelly, L. (2012) 'Standing the test of time? Reflections on the concept of the continuum of sexual violence', in J. Brown and S. Walklate (eds) *Handbook on Sexual Violence*, London: Routledge, pp xvii–xxv.

Kelly, L. (2016) *The Conducive Context of Violence Against Women and Girls*, Available from: https://discoversociety.org/2016/03/01/theorising–violence–against–women–and–girls/ [Accessed 12 August 2020].

Kelly, L., Sharp-Jeffs, N. and Klein, R. (2014) *Finding the Costs of Freedom: How Women and Children Rebuild their Lives After Domestic Violence*, London: Solace Women's Aid.

Landman, R.A. (2014) '"A counterfeit friendship": mate crime and people with learning disabilities', *The Journal of Adult Protection*, 16(6): 355–66.

Lorenc, T., Clayton, S., Neary, D. et al (2012) 'Crime, fear of crime, environment, and mental health and wellbeing: mapping review of theories and causal pathways', *Health and Place*, 18(4): 757–65.

Martínez-Cao, C., Gómez, L.E., Alcedo, M.Á. and Monsalve, A. (2021) 'Systematic review of bullying and cyberbullying in young people with intellectual disability', *Education and Training in Autism and Developmental Disabilities*, 56(1): 3–17.

McCarthy, M. (2017) '"What kind of abuse is him spitting in my food?": reflections on the similarities between disability hate crime, so-called "mate" crime and domestic violence against women with intellectual disabilities', *Disability and Society*, 32(4): 595–600.

McCarthy, M., Hunt, S. and Milne–Skillman, K. (2017) '"I know it was every week, but I can't be sure if it was every day": domestic violence and women with learning disabilities', *Journal of Applied Research in Intellectual Disabilities*, 30(2): 269–82.

Macdonald, S.J., Donovan, C. and Clayton, J. (2017) 'The disability bias: understanding the context of hate in comparison with other minority populations, *Disability and Society*, 32(4): 483–99.

McLean, R., Robinson, G. and Densley, J.A. (2019) *County Lines: Criminal Networks and Evolving Drug Markets in Britain*, Cham: Springer Nature.

McClimens, A. and Brewster, J. (2017) 'Intellectual disability, hate crime and other social constructions: a view from South Yorkshire', *Journal of Intellectual Disabilities*, 23(4): 486–97.

Mencap (2011) *Don't Stick It. Stop It! Bullying Wrecks Lives: The Experiences of Children and Young People with a Learning Disability*, London: Mencap.

Murugami, W.M. (2009) 'Disability and identity', *Disability Studies Quarterly*, 29(4).

Pain, R.H. (1997) 'Social geographies of women's fear of crime', *Transactions of the Institute of British Geographers*, 22(2): 231–44.

Quarmby, K. (2008) *Getting Away with Murder: Disabled People's Experiences of Hate Crime in the UK*, London: SCOPE.

Richardson, L., Beadle-Brown, J., Bradshaw, J., Guest, C., Malovic, A. and Himmerich, J. (2016) '"I felt that I deserved it": experiences and implications of disability hate crime', *Tizard Learning Disability Review*, 21(2): 80–88.

Richardson, M. (2005) 'Critiques of segregation and eugenics', in G. Grant, P. Goward, M. Richardson and P. Ramcharan (eds) *Learning Disabilities: A Life Cycle to Valuing People*, Maidenhead: Open University Press, pp 66–90.

Roberts, N., Donovan, C. and Durey, M. (2020) 'Gendered landscapes of safety: how women construct and navigate the urban landscape to avoid sexual violence', *Criminology and Criminal Justice*, 22(2): 1–17.

Sin, C.H. (2016) 'Commentary on "I felt I deserved it": experiences and implications of disability hate crime', *Tizard Learning Disability Review*, 21(2): 89–94.

Sin, C.H., Hedges, A., Cook, C., Mguni, N. and Comber, N. (2009) *Disabled People's Experiences of Targeted Violence and Hostility*, Manchester: Equality and Human Rights Commission.

Smith, M. (2015) 'Disability hate crime: a call for action', in R. Shah and P. Giannasi (eds) *Tackling Disability Discrimination and Disability Hate Crime*, London: Jessica Kingsley Publishers, pp 36–53.

Strick, K. (2021) 'Reclaim the streets: how Sarah Everard's story sparked a movement around women's public safety', *Evening Standard*, Available from: https://www.standard.co.uk/insider/reclaim-the-streets-sarah-ever ard-womens-public-safety-b923519.html [Accessed 2 August 2021].

Thorneycroft, R. (2017) 'Problematising and reconceptualising "vulnerability" in the context of disablist violence', in N.L. Asquith, I. Bartkowiak-Theron and K.A. Roberts (eds) *Policing Encounters with Vulnerability*, London: Jessica Kingsley Publishers, pp 27–45

Thorneycroft, R. and Asquith, N.L. (2015) 'The dark figure of disablist violence', *The Howard Journal of Criminal Justice*, 54(5): 489–507.

Valentine, G. (1989) 'The geography of women's fear', Area, 21(5): 385–90.

Valentine, G. (1990) 'Women's fear and the design of public space', *Built Environment*, 16(4): 288–303.

Vera-Gray, F. (2018) *The Right Amount of Panic*, Bristol: Bristol University Press.

Vera-Gray, F. and Kelly, L. (2020) 'Contested gendered space: public sexual harassment and women's safety work', *International Journal of Comparative and Applied Criminal Justice*, 44(4): 265–75.

Virueda, M. and Payne, J. (2010) *Homicide in Australia: 2007–08 National Homicide Monitoring Program Annual Report (Monitoring Report 13)*, Canberra: Australian Institute of Criminology.

Walling-Wefelmeyer, R. (2019) 'Scrapbooking men's intrusions: "it's nice to have a place where you can rant about things that people normally tell you you're over-reacting about"', *Women's Studies International Forum*, 75: 102242.

Wilkin, D. (2019) *Disability Hate Crime: Experiences of Everyday Hostility on Public Transport*, Cham: Springer International Publishing.

Williams, M.L., and Tregidga, J. (2014) 'Hate crime victimization in Wales: psychological and physical impacts across seven hate crime victim types', *The British Journal of Criminology*, 54(5): 946–67.

Winter, A. (2019) 'Online hate: from the far-right to the "alt-right" and from the margins to the mainstream', in K. Lumsden and E. Harmer (eds) *Online Othering: Exploring Digital Violence and Discrimination on the Web*, London: Palgrave MacMillan, pp 39–63.

8

Hostility, Hate and Humiliation: Disability Hate Crime on UK Public Transport

David Wilkin

Introduction

Of all the public spaces, public transport is arguably one of the most contested, unfamiliar and ever-changing ones. Public transport is a necessity for many people, yet is also a space of the unknown, of confusion, of strangers in close proximity and it can be a space of foreboding. This chapter enhances our understanding of the lived experience for disabled people within the particular shared space that is public transport and explores both active and passive hate in this space. As Wilson (2011: 646) argues, relationships inside the bus are symbolic of wider society, 'experiences [that] might also further implicate the ways in which we relate to others'. The bus, Wilson argues, is a place of opportunity; a catalyst for wider relationships to flourish. For an able-bodied, normally confident person, public transport has the potential to be a diverse and stimulating meeting place. Public transport is a space where negotiations take place: 'is this seat taken?'; 'sorry, was that your foot?'; 'do you know if?' ... convivial encounters that can be constructive and pleasant, the start of things to come (Bredewold et al, 2019).

Many disabled people have to plan for expending substantial energy in preparation for a bus journey, which they often have no alternative but to make (given limited transport options). Bodily contact, manoeuvrability and the etiquette of sharing this service with strangers all need to be considered. Consider that a disabled person's identity is beyond their control – and they begin their social arbitration not from a position of equality but from having already been labelled by fellow passengers a burden; a nuisance; a potential for delay. The very key to freedom – the bus – can also be the facilitator of experiences of hate, abuse and aggression. Bulky equipment that gets in the way of other passengers, a need for a priority seat, as well as having to ask other passengers to vacate it so that you can use it, all provide potential for hateful encounters, embarrassment and for others to witness your discomfort and impairment. These experiences are daily occurrences for some people who are clearly physically disabled. People with learning difficulties or communication problems may be afflicted by different indignities with distinctive obstacles to surmount. If you have just soiled yourself, or inadvertently revealed a hidden anxiety, you can be transformed from someone with a private and controllable difficulty to someone who becomes a spectacle for others. The contested social landscape of a bus is tough enough, but for disabled people their role as a target may feel too challenging to navigate: "Fuck this; why should I put up with this, I'd rather stay at home" (A former male paratrooper, now an amputee).

As discussed, experiences are drawn from recent research undertaken by the author. This chapter will reveal more about that study, focussing on buses as a space that produces hate for disabled people. This chapter looks at the impacts of such abuse, examines examples of sometimes orchestrated aggression, and considers why bystanders seem to do little to help the victims. The chapter will close by offering some potential solutions generated by disabled people to counter the phenomena, which in UK legal terms, is known as disability hate crime.

Disability hate crime

Since the de-regulation of bus services in the UK in the 1970s it is recognized that services have reduced in rural areas and the cost of using buses and trains has increased – often beyond existing inflation rates. These services have become often unaffordable for many disabled people with limited incomes and while regulatory change has required that adjustments are made for disabled people, attitudes of staff and passengers have resulted in disabled people feeling unwelcome on them (Garcia, 2018). In the UK, between 2014/15 and 2016/17 reports of disability hate crimes to the police increased by 249 per cent (BBC, 2018). During 2015/16, the attrition rate, whereby reported crimes result in convictions, was substantial for disability hate crimes. Only 4 per cent of reported hate crimes against disabled people concluded with a conviction and uplift to the offenders' sentence (Walters et al, 2018). Moreover, reports of hate crimes on UK public transport increased by 82 per cent in the period 2017/18; yet fewer than 25 per cent resulted in the British Transport Police (BTP), who police the UK rail network, charging an offender with such an offence (*The Guardian*, 2018). Despite these facts, the UK government seems reluctant to tackle disability hate crime, reflected in the scarcity of campaigning to reduce it (Mason-Bish, 2010).

Academically, disability hate crime attracts comparatively less attention than the other protected strands (Roulstone and Mason-Bish, 2013; Hamilton and Trickett, 2014; Chakraborti, 2018; Chaplin and Mukhopadhyay, 2018). This is despite the everyday occurrences of abuse, hostility and violence often faced by disabled people in society. Furthermore, academia has predominantly overlooked the particularity of hate crime on public transport – although it is noticeable that geographical specificities of hate do occasionally break through this academic impasse (for an example, see Hall, 2019). However, potential participants who might have communication difficulties, or require more stringent ethical approval pathways or where resilient gatekeepers make working with these groups difficult, are avoided (Sin, 2013; 2015).

Crime on public transport

Public transport has long suffered the indignity of being an area of general criminogenesis (see Clarke and Smith, 2000; Delbosc and Currie, 2012) and a site specific to the criminogenesis of disability hate crime (for example, Equality and Human Rights Commission [EHRC], 2011). However, there is a surprising lack of research specifically concerning disability hate crime on public transport considering it is known to result in upset and fear in the short term and in the longer term, a loss of confidence and avoidance of public transport can ensue (EHRC, 2011). Victimization can result in individual consequences: social isolation, economic deprivation and educational deficit (Beadle-Brown et al, 2014). However, the resulting lower use of public transport inevitably leads to social consequences: negative environmental impact, increased risk of damage to highways, as well as a rise in pollution levels as a result of increased car use (Vilalta, 2011).

There is also a paucity of research considering the motivations of disability hate crime offenders (Chakraborti, 2015). Iganski (2008) argues that these are mainly not planned offences but rather acts conducted by ordinary people, venting frustration, resentment or spitefulness. More generally, Newton and Ceccato (2015) suggest that public transport offers rich pickings for the opportunist criminal. Following Felson's (2002) routine activity theory, Newton and Ceccato (2015) argue that motivated offenders can easily remain anonymous in such congested, contested and unfamiliar spaces, that are often lightly staffed, with poor information and public surveillance. Criminal activities may therefore be undertaken with decreased risk of identification. Delbosc and Currie (2012) assert that up to 10 per cent of the population would use public transport more if personal safety concerns were addressed (Crime Concern, 2004, cited in Delbosc and Currie, 2012: 302), and users felt they could trust it. Delbosc and Currie (2011; 2012) also offered an understanding of how the general public form bonds of trust and how they assess the risk of public travel. For disabled travellers, indicators of trust included: easy access to public transport vehicles; feeling safe from attack when travelling alone; and finding someone to provide assistance if this was needed. Of the study sample, 34 per cent of disabled participants voiced one of these facets as being necessary to instil trust and 18 per cent cited two of the three (Delbosc and Currie, 2011: 557–8). Participants who did not have access to a car or because they were living in poverty were deemed to be at a *transport disadvantage*. These participants were additionally likely to be: unemployed; a lone parent or relying on disability benefit; thus many who had a transport disadvantage were also socially disadvantaged (Currie and Allen, 2007). The Delbosc and Currie (2011; 2012) research concludes by affirming that the health and wellbeing of an individual is closely linked to them not remaining socially isolated. For disabled people, opportunities to avoid social isolation are dependent on them feeling able to trust and use public transport. As Stanley and Stanley (2007) argue, their reliance on public transport thus categorizes them as *captive users*, people with limited or no choice.

Methods of researching hate crime on public transport

This chapter now explores the author's recent research into the experiences of victims of disability hate crime on public transport (Wilkin, 2020). Witness data was also acquired; however, restrictions of space limit this chapter to discussing victim data only. Participant recruitment was initially attempted by asking disability organizations to circulate the researchers' details – this was abandoned when help was not forthcoming. Instead, social media was used, which attracted 277 potential participants within a few days of the canvass. Recruitment was limited to the UK and ultimately 56 participants were included, all self-declaring a disability that ranged from the physical to psychological, both visible and hidden. Of those participants, 26 were interviewed and 30 participated in focus groups.

The data-gathering techniques for researching participants were semi-structured telephone interviews, group interviews and interactive focus groups. Because people with a range of disabilities participated, informed consent for telephone interviews was normally achieved via email. However, techniques needed to remain responsive and flexible. For participants who struggled with written communication, consent was accepted audibly. For those unable to use the telephone for long periods, an alternative email interview was offered. This alternative provided a reasonable replacement for those who might prefer an asynchronous conversation because of cognitive disabilities. One participant who contributed via a YouTube video was later asked supplementary questions via email. It was this type of flexibility that made the study as inclusive as possible. To triangulate data gathered from the 26 interviews, five focus groups, each lasting approximately one hour, were conducted. Focus groups are potentially less intimidating than a one-to-one conversation. Although focus group data were comparable to that from the telephone interviews, the interactive atmosphere group provided differing aspects of data from that generated in the interviews (Morgan, 2012). Because of communications difficulties, improvised role play activity was often used in the focus groups. Ethical approval was sought and secured from the University of Leicester Ethics Committee. This included multiple protection arrangements for both the participants and the researcher.

Experiences of hate crime on public transport

The following evidence reveals experiences of hate crimes and incidents, the victims' responses to these attacks, staff behaviours and also the impacts of hostility and abuse. For more detailed accounts of victimization and witness accounts see Wilkin (2020).

All 56 participants in the study indicated, following an explanation of accepted terms, that they had experienced hate offences (cited in the guidance issued by the College of Policing (CoP, 2014) on public transport. The CoP guidance differentiates a hate crime incident as one not including a criminal offence while remaining abusive in nature. Of the participants, 45 (80 per cent) stated that they had been a victim of a hate crime and 11 (20 per cent) of a hate incident. The majority of incidents experienced by participants took place on buses (74 per cent), followed by those on trains (21 per cent) and incidents in a taxi (3 per cent). Victim participants thought that the bus offered everything potential abusers might wish for: a readily formed audience in a small space; an opportunity to abuse and vanish; a single member of staff; and no alarm cord to pull. Victims explained that being on a bus is like being in a small room – you are more likely to be abused as you have no escape. Furthermore, the acoustic qualities of the space make the abuse more impactful, and some victims cited that abusers seemed to perform – to an audience or potential fellow abusers – more easily in a smaller space. There is certainly potential here for future research to consider further the implications of the specific spatial context of a closed, moving, acoustic space with a captive audience, for practices of hate.

Analysis reveals that the techniques of abuse used against victims are generally either active or passive. Passive abuse occurs where the abuser makes non-verbal gestures, addresses the victim using jibes or *banter*, or does not assist the victim when help is clearly needed or requested. These opportunistic slights could be obvious eye-rolling, headshaking or similarly supposedly *forgettable* gestures. But these were not forgettable to participants in this study. Many victims consider these microaggressions to be a form of abuse, even though they are not classified as hate crimes. These microaggressions were reported by 28 per cent of the participants as being very damaging, cumulative micro-abuse, which, over time, began to negatively affect the victim. For example: "I was going to work one day when there was a very large suitcase in the wheelchair bay. I searched around the bus for the owner. Two women huffed and looked out of the window; obviously disinterested in my dilemma" (A female wheelchair user).

Although defined as passive, these situations have a potential to escalate into active and potentially violent ones. After the participant herself moved the suitcase to allow wheelchair access to the designated wheelchair bay the exchange escalated into a verbally violent incident (6 per cent of participants reported similar escalations):

'[the] two women just leaped like vultures, swooped on top of me screaming at me just "how dare I touch somebody else's bag" they just screamed abuse at me! … For about 10 minutes. They were saying [to another passenger with a baby] "that horrible disabled woman would have picked up the baby and thrown it on the floor". They were truly nuts!' (A female wheelchair user)

Other reported passive techniques included challenging a victim's disabled status and voicing resentment based on the perception that disabled people receive enhanced benefits, privileges or hold an expectation to occupy reserved spaces. Victims were also abused because they took up more room or had mannerisms resulting in others needing to adjust their seating position or behaviour. Abuse seemed to be opportunistic, when the circumstances contrived to be *right* for abuse to take place. In this category 40 per cent of participants reported incidents; here is one example: "[in justification] I told the lady that I had just recovered from a brain tumour and she said 'oh well, you're not disabled anymore'" (A middle-aged female using power chair).

Seemingly 'innocent' comments made by fellow passengers can also cause considerable offence, and 17 per cent of participants reported such occurrences. These were the hardest to describe as hate-related incidents or crimes because the intent was difficult to determine. For example: "how did you have a baby?" (A middle-aged female using power chair).

Conversely, active abuse included: name-calling; swearing; devaluation; threats of, and ultimately the use of, violence. Participants thought that these were opportunistic and unplanned; for example, some participants were targeted when they had boarded already delayed services, then becoming a magnet for the frustrations of others. Some participants reported that they feared the bus or train being delayed because of this. This facet affected 30 per cent of participants: "One gentleman called out 'I didn't know we had to accommodate cripples on the bus'. And the other one said 'well I'm late for a meeting – why should we have to wait for him to get on the bus'?

'They disrupt people's days and they seem to enjoy it'" (An autistic walking stick user).

A non-disabled person remaining in designated priority seats and areas was often problematic, triggering 62 per cent of incidents on buses. Many of these involved buggies and prams parked in wheelchair bays causing consternation and conflict. Non-disabled travellers seemingly did not understand, or want to understand, the needs of the disabled person. The conflicts between buggy/pram users and disabled people requiring the use of a designated space might explain why 50 per cent of perpetrations in the authors' research were conducted by females. This is an unusual statistic as most hate crime perpetrators are white males (Iganski, 2008).

Regarding priority seating, a male autistic participant with fibromyalgia, which resulted in uncontrollable weight gain, tried to occupy a seat on a train and was told: "'You're fat and you'll take up two seats. ... There's a section for the incapable in the next carriage'" (An autistic walking stick user).

The transition and escalation from passive to active hate can be difficult to predict and/or navigate. The experience of the participant discussed previously exemplifies this. Jibes, or *banter*, from a group of young males which may have been expressed as humour soon became abusive and violent:

'He said "there's fuck all wrong with you, you must have [walking sticks] to sign on [claim benefits] with, you're just a fat cunt." Then they all laughed at me. ... When these lads walked away, they said to a man reading his paper "your tax money goes on that cunt".' (An autistic walking stick user)

One female participant with Tourette's syndrome (who uses a wheelchair) bangs her chest with her fist and begins chanting when she has a tic. She was often targeted through active hate aboard buses. She hoped that the confines of a bus would help her attract support from fellow passengers – but that rarely came. Instead, the bus – a small, unfamiliar, insecure space – seemed to her to be the perfect stage to ridicule someone on: '"The bus smells of shit since you got in; you've got shit on your bum because you are disabled. ... Bang harder on your chest so that you have a heart attack and end up in a coffin you stinkin' bitch"' (A female with Tourette's using a wheelchair).

The confines of the moving bus results in both entrapment of the participant, who cannot escape her tormentor, and a captive audience who, by their silence, give the perpetrator the message that they can continue with their hate.

This section has illustrated how abuse towards disabled people is manifested on public transport in the UK. Hostility ranged from the seemingly everyday, continuous name-calling, staring and jostling, to threats and actions of extreme violence. The following section illustrates how collaboration has been used during acts of hostility.

Group abuse: collaboration and justification techniques

As discussed previously, the enclosed space of public transport can create a captive audience to whom perpetrators 'play to' and are sometimes 'egged on' by. In some episodes of abuse recounted in this study, perpetrators were able to enrol members of the 'audience' to actively join in with hate. The initial, or principal, offender is able to recruit formerly inoffensive fellow passengers to become involved in the incident. Recruitment efforts were not always successful; however, participants reported attempted recruitment in 71 per cent of incidents on buses and trams and in 23 per cent of incidents on trains, totalling 52 per cent of the participant data. Collaboration involved the principal offender using a range of recruitment techniques including 'humour', *banter* and supposed *justification*. The reaction of the formerly non-offending passengers followed one of three paths: successful recruitment, where the once formerly unoffending passengers ally themselves with the principal offender; oppositional, where action sympathetic to the victim occurs; or non-intercessional. In the last category, fellow passengers took the option not to get involved in the emerging situation. The following example illustrates the principal offender loudly abusing a participant while justifying the offending and getting a result when another passenger joins in with the hate:

> 'She started screaming at me in front of everybody calling me a parasite living on hand-outs. … She was looking at the other passengers, like seeking back-up. I was broken into tears, I was in the middle of the aisle and everybody was looking at me, I was crying and I was being berated by this mad and selfish woman. … They were all looking at me and the mother was still seething and moaning about 'cripples being a fucking nuisance'. Most others seemed to have some sympathy with me … one man said that I should be 'ashamed of myself'. But why? All I want to do is catch the bus! She wanted everyone to know that I was a 'sponger".' (An older female with a wheelchair using daughter)

One female wheelchair-using participant had a panic attack on a train journey and some of the other passengers tried to encourage her to alight from the train to avoid a delay to the service. Similar justification techniques that were agreed with among fellow passengers were noted in 33 per cent of other occasions. In the following excerpt it seems that as soon as one person speaks and gives a justification for why the participant should be treated with hate, this gives confidence to others that they can join in. These are mostly and initially men, but a woman escalates the situation by suggesting – in banter? – physical violence:

'I announced that I couldn't go anywhere until I got help to get off. At this point a man came along and looked out of the train for me and said that nobody was coming to assist. … Another man said 'we can't wait here forever' … another guy came up and said that I was making everybody late – he said this loudly so that everyone could see that I was the cause. … When I managed to remonstrate, he said 'but you are delaying us'. That, incredibly, was followed by jeers from the other passengers. A woman said "we should tip her on the platform". I was so very scared. They were contemplating assaulting me so as not to delay the fucking train.' (A female wheelchair user with anxiety)

Portraying the disabled passenger as a *freak*, or similarly devaluing them, was another justification technique cited in 12 per cent of incidents. Examples included making derogatory remarks about the disabled passenger and highlighting their otherness. Mannerisms, for example facial differences and walking disabilities, were often used to illustrate these differences. In the following example, however, a wheelchair was the catalyst for abuse:

'Then he [the driver] said "you lot are a joke". That got a few on the bus laughing … he got a couple of appreciative nods too. … I've had the first abuser say that I was blocking the aisle and that "if there was a fire then we would all be dead". Then I would be "done for murder" … then somebody else chimed-in and called me a "selfish bitch".' (A female wheelchair user)

This was an example where the single point of authority aboard the bus *performed* to the audience, which solicited laughing from the other passengers. In the following excerpt, the disabled passenger felt like a *freak* when being discussed by a female bus driver. This technique was seemingly used to appease fellow passengers and to justify the abuse:

'She turned to the rest of the passengers and she said "I'm very, very sorry about this but it's the law I have to let her on the bus." I did get on and I did not say another thing to her I was just so shocked. I was just rattling. … I don't even blame the other passengers, they either laugh with the driver or what – the bus doesn't move? We're there for ever?' (A female wheelchair user)

In 3 per cent of incidents techniques of expulsion were utilized by the principal offender, including by drivers, drawing on justifications as to why the disabled person should leave the vehicle (delays to the service, blocking other transport users from getting to/using seats) and making this known to fellow passengers.

It was difficult to establish when conditions were favoured by allies to commence collaborative abuse. Circumstances seem to come together: the smallness of the space on the bus or train carriage; the availability of an audience; or perhaps the already heightened tension caused by delay or disruption: "Everyone was already pissed off the bus was nearly an hour late; it just needed one to start. I knew it was coming my way, and it did. He laid into me for a good ten minutes" (A former male paratrooper, now an amputee).

Recruited allies seemed to wait until it appeared safe to do so before joining the abuse:

> 'It looks to me as if they can see that the environment is safe for them to abuse us first. Once a few start then the way becomes clear for others to join in with alacrity. The way is clear for them to enjoy themselves with a warmed-up audience already in position.' (A female in a wheelchair, as is her husband)

The same participant thought that these allies were motivated by potentially trying to protect themselves from becoming additional targets for the primary perpetrator: "They can't help it I don't think. If perhaps they didn't laugh they themselves think that they might be laughed at – how would they like that. They are just siding with the popular crowd" (A female in a wheelchair, as is her husband).

Impacts on the victim

The key impacts described by participants that result from experience of hate include fear, embarrassment, humiliation and isolation, combined with often overwhelming physical weakness – a sudden tiredness brought about by numerous experiences of abuse and the relentless nature of unpredictable mistreatment. The longer-term implications of these harms are life changing. Due to ongoing abuse, some participants voiced a reluctance to continue using public transport. Immediately following an abusive attack, 67 per cent stated that they lost confidence and any hope that the day would go well. Concerns that anxiety in public would cause an embarrassing loss of control were also noted by 40 per cent of the sample. However, many stated that they did not want to be in a place where abuse might occur in the first place; 85 per cent stated that they would rather not use public transport again and were seeking an alternative. This is deeply impactful for many as public transport is their key to freedom: to be social; to broaden their skills and knowledge; and to see friends and family. For participants, including those severely disabled, it was telling that many preferred to find other means, often incurring additional hardships, for example the additional expense of using taxis and other means of transport, rather than continue their journey by public transport. Decisions about using public transport can involve a great deal of anxiety. For many, their choice would be to not use it and to spend money on taxis. However, this comes with economic costs that many cannot afford:

'I don't want to use public transport any more. I get a taxi if I can afford to but the reason I'm on the bus in the first place is that I can't always afford a taxi and I have to get to certain appointments. I really feel like staying-in.' (An older female with a wheelchair-using daughter)

Having to take an unknown bus route presented particular anxieties about safety that were preferably avoided. Again, often participants did not have a choice if they could not afford a taxi and relied on buses to get to hospital appointments. If appointments were made for clinics in unfamiliar hospitals participants explain they have to manage their anxiety and take the bus: 'I didn't like using it in a place I didn't know or using routes I have never used before. I turn into a ball of anxiety. The choice is not to go anywhere strange, but these days hospital appointments can be anywhere, miles away' (A female wheelchair user and support coordinator).

Some participants made decisions about their safety and the avoidance of risk that had impacts for their social life: particular bus routes and/or particular parts of their local areas at particular times of the day became no-go spaces – even if this meant that they had to give something up they had enjoyed:

'That's simple to answer. I avoid buses at that time of day and in that part of town. I use a taxi if I need to go somewhere official and I cannot really afford that. I won't go on that bus again. It was the most frightening 30 minutes of my life. I won't go near that part of XXX again if I can help it. That means that I miss my art class but so be it.' (An autistic user of walking sticks)

Why target disabled people?

With little primary evidence from perpetrators of disability hate available (Chakraborti, 2015), we are forced to theorize about perpetration (see Chapter 2). Disability has long been linked to concepts of deviancy and abnormality (Quarmby, 2013). One reason for the vilification of disabled people and therefore their propensity to be victims of hate crime might lie in how disabled people are depicted within the media (Mason-Bish and Trickett, 2019), mainly in newspapers. Ralph et al (2016) revealed a tendency for the press to denigrate disabled people for their questionable credibility for state support. In this study, it was clear how government targeting of disability benefits for systematic review and reduction, and the accompanying discourses of undeserving benefits claimants, played out in some of the participants experiences of hate (see also Chapter 7).

Becker argues that for people to be perceived as deviants they do not necessarily need to break conventions, laws or rules. All they need to be is to be seen as an 'outsider' or somewhat different (Becker, 2013: 260). What is important for the maintenance of difference is that boundaries are established between what is the *ingroup* and the *outgroup*, the *normal* and the *deviant*, to demarcate and legitimize victimization. These boundaries need to be defended to support power relationships while denigration of the victim takes place (Perry, 2003; Craig, 2012). Furthermore, Vaes et al (2012) argue that a process of dehumanization is important for the demarcation of ingroup/outgroup boundaries. Any devaluation of the *deviant* will assist the ingroup coagulation process. For example: "He said that I was 'a parasite'! A 'drain on humanity'! Yes. That's what I thought, bloody cheek! He was doing this to make the crowd on the platform laugh – but I considered this really insulting" (A female wheelchair user with anxiety).

The opportunistic nature of routine activity theory contributes to this discussion by emphasizing that if the conditions are apposite, then such incidents or crimes are more likely to occur (Felson, 2002; Iganski, 2008). This occurs provided that any capable guardianship of the victim is in a lowered state – in other words, that the victim is perceived to be susceptible to an attack. As Iganski (2008) argues, predetermined hate offending might, or might not, be a primary motivation, the offender may just be seizing an opportunity to vent their feelings on the victim. In a collaborative attack, if the principal offender uses a *routine opportunity* to do this, then why should this attitude not be shared by fellow passengers to assist in that offending. The crowded nature of the public transport vehicle might additionally enhance any opportunity to offend (Newton and Ceccato, 2015; Purifoye, 2015). In other words, the opportunity, the reduced guardianship of the victim and the space within the vehicle being conducive to conduct abuse, might offer a formula not to be missed. Moreover, research by Reynald (2010) states that the factor of reduced capable guardianship is a critical element to the perpetrator deciding whether to commit an offence. Reynald (2010) asserts that capability for guardianship is enhanced if the potential victim feels comfortable and familiar within their environment – the more familiar with their surroundings they are, the more likely the victim is to feel able to protect themselves. Public transport, typically with very low staffing, is, by its nature, an ever-changing place operating through differing geographies, where strangers come and go. The moods of fellow passengers are susceptible to personal experiences, the quality of the journey, delay, information availability, and other influences. Therefore, there is seemingly little chance that the victim will be able to feel comfortable in a place which is constantly in a state of flux, thus they are susceptible to reduced guardianship.

Where recruitment of collaborators is attempted, why do those who were not recruited mainly fail to take an opposing view or do anything to intervene to protect the victim? As a matter of speculation, this may be to protect their personal safety. An example of this non-intervention follows:

> 'For 10 long minutes everyone on the lower deck listened to a public shaming of my body my life and my worth. And then it followed, the ignorance, the judgementalism, the shit from other peoples' minds, the total, total silence that left me more exposed and isolated than any of the vitriol that had been directed at me. I desperately needed someone on that bus to acknowledge what had taken place – that didn't happen. …
>
> On the bus I felt incapacitated, in part, by the inaction of my fellow passengers. …
>
> I didn't need them to know exactly what to do to help. But I did want them to be present and to acknowledge what was happening to me.' (A female with Tourette's using a wheelchair)

Having discussed how sometimes primary perpetrators are able to recruit others from their audience to join in with hate, the chapter now turns to why fellow passengers do not get involved as an ally of the disabled person.

Bystander non-intervention

When researching bystander non-intervention in public or when disabled people are being targeted, the only studies have been restricted to examining behaviour among adolescents (for example, Mulvey et al, 2016) or the bullying of children with Special Educational Needs (for example, Thornberg et al, 2018). Arguably, this type of study is too distant from the targeting of disabled adults on public transport and therefore would offer little toward this discussion. However, non-intervention can perhaps be understood by delineating the dynamics of the *outgroup*. Although not wanting to be an active member of the *ingroup*, formerly unoffending passengers may not want to reveal themselves as being sympathetic to the outgroup; in other words, siding with the disabled victim. This action could potentially result in them also being victims of the principal offender and of any collaborators that may have successfully been recruited. While not wishing harm upon the victim therefore, they will not go as far as allying themselves with the victim and therefore potentially incurring the wrath of the abusers.

An ambivalence to ameliorate these situations, therefore, may be due to a fear of personal harm; a fear of being embarrassed because they have misunderstood the situation; not wanting to look foolish; or perhaps a feeling that the situation is not of their making. Indeed, the situation may be perceived as being none of their business. Research by Sheleff (1978, cited in Cohen, 1993: 656), suggested the following three explanations for bystander non-intervention: diffusion of responsibility (why should I intervene?); inability to identify the victim (we help our family, friends or ingroup, we do not help those not in our 'universe'); and inability to conceive an effective intervention (what should I do?). Any of these might help to understand why fellow passengers are reluctant to offer assistance to a victim on public transport; reminding ourselves that bystanders are also temporary visitors to a place of transience and are among strangers.

Additionally, Reynald (2010) conducted empirical research to understand why bystanders decline to become involved in defending victims. Reynald's (2010) research focused on the propensity of bystanders to intervene within low, medium and high crime geographical areas. Reynald (2010) found that bystanders are generally successful in deterring crime once they decided to become involved. Indeed, Reynald's (2010) research found that most bystanders, in most situations, were willing to take some type of action. That action, however, may simply be monitoring the evolving situation or reporting it to a third party while not becoming directly involved themselves. Reynald (2010) additionally found that in high crime areas, any bystander was statistically only half as likely to want to become involved at all. Other factors involved in the decision to intervene included the size and perceived physical characteristics of the assailant and an assessment of the personal safety of the bystander. Courageous behaviour to intervene on behalf of others does take place; however, much of this altruistic behaviour remains mainly unexplained (Shepela et al, 1999). In public transport spaces there is an argument for saying that the staff should be trained and supported to intervene when disabled passengers are under attack. The staff's structural position in that space as 'authority figure', able to issue sanctions against perpetrators of hate (for example, ejecting them from the bus/train or contacting the police), could also shift the atmosphere (see Chapter 5) towards a more benign and supportive space for all passengers.

Future considerations

This chapter has examined disability hate crime and non-crime incidents on public transport, and made the point that even though many disabled people rely on public transport because of their reduced economic circumstances, they often use it with extreme trepidation, and many would prefer not to use it. Two kinds of hate are discussed: passive and active. The particularity of the public transport space, its mobility, its enclosed nature, its entrapment of those being victimized and its creation of a captive audience, are all discussed for their exacerbating effects on disability hate occurring and escalating. The role of collaborators who join in with the primary perpetrator is an added factor. Consideration was also given to why, if some people will join in with hate, others will not be allies to the disabled person. The implications of the wider socio-economic and political context in which disabled people have been positioned as undeserving benefits claimants and a drain on the public purse was discussed, along with the more micro-level potential for bystander intervention and the particular role public transport staff might have. Negotiating short-term relationships within the specific spatial confines of the bus or train, and how strangers interact within the pressures of that unfamiliar space in possibly disrupted circumstances, could be all important – and certainly signals the need for more research in this area (Transport for London, 2017). The research reported in this chapter found that most public transport hate attacks took place on buses. Future research might reveal whether route geography makes any difference to criminogenesis or incidence of hate. Furthermore, we could question if the availability of onboard security influences the occasioning of crime or the seating layout and design. Compartmentation and higher seat back-profiles could potentially reduce exposure, and thus control by the abuser, compared with the single open space often found within buses.

An overwhelming proportion of the participants had little confidence in public transport staff members being able to recognize or to manage hate incidents. Staff members questioned by the author shared this paucity of knowledge (Wilkin, 2020). Therefore, Disability Equality Training should be delivered to public transport frontline staff and supervisors to give them the tools to recognize and help to manage incidents of hostility (EHRC, 2018). Effective and evaluated training would align with the EHRC (2018) guidance that: 'Public transport providers and regulators across Britain should work together … to ensure that all staff members have the knowledge and skills to meet the needs of disabled passengers' (EHRC, 2018: 209).

Participants voiced their frustration at not being confident to report incidents or being in fear of the consequences of reporting. Awareness of third party reporting (TPR) capabilities should be widely publicized. The provision of such reporting processes would align with core recommendation six of EHRC (2011: 167). Accumulated data gathered through TPR avenues would augment that already in the public arena and will add value to knowledge and understanding of hate crimes. Moreover, and overwhelmingly, participants voiced that education was fundamental to make the public transport space a more welcoming one. Formal school education should reflect a broader understanding of disability and the rights of disabled people. Publicity on public transport should also be aimed at widening awareness of disabilities and addressing disability hate crime.

For disabled people, public transport, most often the bus, is often a landscape of fear, abuse and one to be avoided. It may be difficult for able-bodied public transport users to comprehend the difficulties faced by many people with disabilities. But wider understanding is just what is needed to bridge the gap of comprehension between those who are victimized, those who generate the harm and those who might be able to help.

References

BBC (2018) *Radio Five Live Investigates Disability Hate Crime*, Available from: https://www.bbc.co.uk/programmes/b098mtqm [Accessed 29 May 2020].

Beadle-Brown, J., Richardson, L., Guest, C., Malovic, A., Bradshaw, J. and Himmerich, J. (2014) *Living in Fear: Better Outcomes for People with Learning Disabilities and Autism, Main Research Report*, Tizard Centre, Canterbury: University of Kent.

Becker, H. (2013) 'Outsiders', in E. McLaughlin and J. Muncie (eds) *Criminological Perspectives* (3rd edn), London: Sage, pp 256–67.

Bredewold, F., Haarsma, A., Tonkens, E. and Jager, M. (2019) 'Convivial encounters: conditions for the urban social inclusion of people with intellectual and psychiatric disabilities', *Urban Studies*, 57(10): 2047–63.

Chakraborti, N. (2015) Conversation between Professor Neil Chakraborti and the author, October.

Chakraborti, N. (2018) 'Responding to hate crime: escalating problems, continued failings', *Criminology and Criminal Justice*, 18(4): 387–404.

Chaplin, E. and Mukhopadhyay, S. (2018) 'Autism spectrum disorder and hate crime', *Advances in Autism*, 4(1): 30–6.

Clarke, R. and Smith, M. (2000) 'Crime and public transport', *Crime and Justice*, 27: 169–233.

Cohen, S. (1993) 'Human rights and crimes of the state', in E. McLaughlin and J. Muncie (eds) (2013) *Criminological Perspectives* (3rd edn), London: Sage, pp 646–65.

College of Policing (2014) *Hate Crime Operational Guidance*, Coventry: College of Policing.

Craig, K. (2012) 'Examining hate-related aggression: a review of the social psychological literature on hate crime as a distinct form of aggression', in B. Perry (ed) *Hate and Bias Crime: A Reader*, London: Taylor and Francis Group, pp 135–48.

Crime Concern (2004) *People Perceptions of Personal Security and Their Concerns about Crime on Public Transport: Research Findings*, London: Department for Transport.

Currie, G. and Allen, J. (2007) 'Australians with disabilities: transport disadvantage and disability', in G. Currie (ed) *No Way To Go: Transport and Social Disadvantage in Australian Communities*, Clayton, Victoria: Monash University Publishing, pp 7.1–7.13.

Delbosc, A. and Currie, G. (2011) 'Exploring the relative influences of transport disadvantage and social exclusion on well-being, *Transport Policy*, 18(4): 555–62.

Delbosc, A. and Currie, G. (2012) 'Modelling the causes and impacts of personal safety perceptions on public transport ridership', *Transport Policy*, 24(24): 302–9.

Equality and Human Rights Commission (EHRC) (2011) *Hidden in Plain Sight: Inquiry into Disability-related Harassment*, Manchester: Equality and Human Rights Commission.

Equality and Human Rights Commission (EHRC) (2018) *Is Britain Fairer? The State of Equality and Human Rights 2018*, Manchester: Equality and Human Rights Commission.

Felson, M., (2002) *Crime and Everyday Life* (3rd edn), Thousand Oaks, CA: Sage.

Garcia, V. (2018) An interview between the researcher and Victoria Garcia, Accessibility and Communities Manager for Brighton and Hove Buses and Metrobus, 9 March.

Guardian, The (2018) 'Less than 25% of hate crime reports on UK railways lead to charges', *The Guardian*, 25 January, Available from: https://www.theguardian.com/uk-news/2018/dec/25/hate-crime-reports-uk-railways-charges-british-transport-police-figures [Accessed 10 May 2020].

Hall, E. (2019) 'A critical geography of disability hate crime', *Area*, 51(2): 249–56.

Hamilton, P. and Trickett, L. (2014) 'Disability hostility, harassment and violence in the UK: a "motiveless" and "senseless" crime?', in N. Hall, A. Corb and P. Giannasi (eds) *Routledge International Handbook on Hate Crime*, New York: Routledge, pp 207–25.

Iganski, P. (2008) *Hate Crime and the City*, Bristol: The Policy Press.

Mason-Bish, H. (2010) 'Future challenges for hate crime policy: lessons from the past', in N. Chakraborti (ed) *Hate Crime: Concepts, Policy, Future Directions*, Cullompton: Willan, pp 58–77.

Mason-Bish, H. and Trickett, L. (2019) 'Introduction to the special issue on the politics of hate: community, societal and global responses', *Crime, Law and Social Change*, 71(3): 241–43.

Morgan, D.L. (2012) 'Focus groups and social interaction', in J.B. Gubrium, J.A. Holstein, A.B. Marvasti and K.D. McKinney (eds) *The Sage Handbook of Interview Research: The Complexity of the Craft* (2nd edn), Thousand Oaks, CA: Sage, pp 161–76.

Mulvey, K.L., Palmer, S.B. and Abrams, D. (2016) 'Race-based humor and peer group dynamics in adolescence: bystander intervention and social exclusion', *Child Development*, 87(5): 1379–91.

Newton, A. and Ceccato, V. (2015) 'Theoretical perspectives of security and safety in transit environments', in V. Ceccato and A. Newton (eds) *Safety and Security in Transit Environments*, Basingstoke: Palgrave Macmillan, pp 23–36.

Perry, B. (2003) 'Accounting for hate crime: doing difference', in B. Perry (ed) *Hate and Bias Crime: A Reader*, London: Routledge, pp 97–108.

Purifoye, G. (2015) 'Nice-nastiness and other raced social interactions on public transport systems', *City & Community*, 14(3): 286–310.

Quarmby, K. (2013) *Scapegoat: Why We Are Failing Disabled People*, London: Portobello.

Ralph, S., Capewell, C. and Bonnett, E. (2016) 'Disability hate crime: persecuted for difference', *British Journal of Special Education*, 43(3): 215–32.

Reynald, D. (2010) 'Guardians on guardianship: factors affecting the willingness to supervise, the ability to detect potential offenders, and the willingness to intervene', *Journal of Research in Crime and Delinquency*, 47(3): 358–90.

Roulstone, A., and Mason-Bish, H. (eds) (2013) *Disability, Hate Crime and Violence*, Abingdon, Oxon: Routledge.

Sheleff, L. (1978) *The Bystander*, Lexington, MA: Lexington Books.

Shepela, S.T., Cook, J., Horlitz, E. et al (1999) 'Courageous resistance: a special case of altruism', *Theory and Psychology*, 9(6): 787–805.

Sin, C.H. (2013) 'Making disablist hate crime visible', in A. Roulstone and H. Mason-Bish (eds) *Disability, Hate Crime and Violence*, Abingdon, Oxon: Routledge, pp 147–65.

Sin, C.H. (2015) 'Hate crime against people with disabilities', in N. Hall, A. Corb, and P. Giannasi (eds) *Routledge International Handbook on Hate Crime*, New York: Routledge, pp 193–206.

Stanley, J. and Stanley, J. (2007) 'Public transport and social exclusion: an operator's perspective UK', in G. Currie (ed) *No Way To Go: Transport and Social Disadvantage in Australian Communities*, Clayton, Victoria: Monash University Publishing, pp 14.1–14.11.

Thornberg, R., Landgren, L. and Wiman, E. (2018) '"It depends": a qualitative study on how adolescent students explain bystander intervention and non-intervention in bullying situations', *School Psychology International*, 39(4): 400–15.

Transport for London (TfL) (2017) Interview between the TfL Operational Standards team representative and the researcher, 14 August.

Vaes, J., Leyens, J., Paola Paladino, M. and Pires Miranda, M. (2012) 'We are human, they are not: driving forces behind outgroup dehumanisation and the humanisation of the ingroup', *European Review of Social Psychology*, 23(1): 64–106.

Vilalta, C. (2011) 'Fear of crime in public transport: research in Mexico City', *Crime Prevention and Community Safety*, 13(3): 171–86.

Walters, M.A., Owusu-Bempah, A. and Wiedlitzka, S. (2018) 'Hate crime and the "justice gap": the case for law reform (United Kingdom)', *Criminal Law Review*, 12: 961–86.

Wilkin, D. (2020) *Disability Hate Crime: Experiences of Everyday Hostility on Public Transport*, London: Palgrave Macmillan.

Wilson, H. (2011) 'Passing propinquities in the multicultural city: the everyday encounters of bus passengering', *Environment and Planning A*, 43(3): 634–49.

9

Safe Spaces or Spaces of Control? Racial Tensions at Predominantly White Institutions

Denise Goerisch

Introduction

Rabbit, a first-generation Hmong student, and I sat in my small windowless office in the library of Robin State University (RSU).[1] We talked for an hour about her first semester at RSU. She recounted stories about the flooding in her residence hall, the moment she found out she won a prestigious national scholarship and being accepted into the Honours programme. Rabbit shared that she was a part of the Robin Ready programme, which helped first-generation students of colour navigate their first year of college. Rabbit credited Robin Ready with being an essential resource that made her feel as if she belonged on campus: "I made a lot of my friends through Robin Ready. … It made me very familiar with campus when school started. It just really made me feel that, like, RSU is a place that – you know, RSU is where I should be" (15 January 2015).

For Rabbit and many students of colour at RSU, Robin Ready was a safe space. Rabbit was also a part of other organizations and initiatives that tried to create and support safe spaces for diverse students. However, by the beginning of her second year of college, Rabbit became disillusioned with RSU and was unsure if she truly 'belonged' due to racial hostility from white students, faculty, staff and university leadership. She seriously questioned if there were truly any safe spaces for students of colour at RSU.

Over the past 20 years, US universities have become increasingly racially diverse with nearly half of the student population identifying as students of colour (Dedman, 2019). For many students of colour at predominately white institutions (PWIs), such as RSU, programmes like Robin Ready provide spaces of belonging and inclusion. Many US students from historically underrepresented groups (for example, students of colour, women, LGBTQ, first generation to the attend university) appreciate the overall goals of university spaces and programmes dedicated to promoting diversity and inclusivity at PWIs (Strayhorn, 2018). These spaces create essential emotional and financial support structures as well as a strong sense of community. However, many believe that these spaces and programmes can act as a mechanism to segregate students of colour from the rest of the campus, thus potentially rendering these students and their experiences of racialized discrimination and violence invisible to the larger campus population as well as not holding those who perpetuate racialized violence and microaggressions accountable (Leonardo and Porter, 2010). Many PWIs state they value diversity, but associated actions tend to focus on developing cultural competencies among the white student population and maintaining hegemonic order rather than protecting students of colour from bias incidents or hate crimes (Hughes, 2013). Within the context of US higher education, a 'bias incident' typically refers to language or behaviours that create an unsafe or unwelcoming environment, which can include racial slurs (Prutzman, 1994). Hate crimes are typically crimes motivated by bias towards another group such as causing or threatening physical harm (Prutzman, 1994). Bias incident is more commonly used rather than hate crime within higher education in the US in order to signify that these are isolated occurrences and not indictive of a pattern of systemic, racial violence (Hughes, 2013). By defining bias incidents as isolated occurrences, the continued violence experienced by marginalized students is erased and diminished.

There is a debate about who university safe spaces are actually for: marginalized students or white students who have the privilege not to engage with racial discourse (Leonardo and Porter, 2010). Students in this study debated whether or not such spaces act to keep them safe from racial hostility or if these spaces act to contain particular student groups which may, albeit inadvertently exacerbate existing racial tensions. Through an examination of these spaces and programmes, this chapter contributes to the growing geographic literature on safe space, particularly how safe space is identified, (re)claimed and sought after within the landscape of the University.

The theorization of safe space has been widely discussed within geography (The Roestone Collective, 2014), particularly as it relates to difference (Held, 2015), education (Hall 2004; Freitag, 2013), cyberspace (Maliepaard, 2017; Brownlie, 2018), activism (Goh, 2018), and children and young people (Djohari et al, 2018). Recently, Djohari et al (2018) called upon geographers to reconceptualize definitions of safe space as it pertains to children and young people, particularly surrounding activism, education, and the home. Safe spaces are broadly defined as physical locations that are free from harm, provide the opportunity to openly express new ideas, experiment with identities and ways of being, and to make mistakes (Djohari et al, 2018). These spaces are particularly important for students of colour as they are perceived as being free from the dominant hegemonies that silence or restrict marginalized groups (Djohari et al, 2018). In discussions of safe space within the context of educational spaces, geographic literature is limited to debates surrounding the classroom (Freitag, 2013) or play spaces situated within and out of schools (Holloway and Pimlott-Wilson, 2014).

For college students, their everyday educational experiences extend beyond that of the classroom. College is presented as a holistic experience, where students often live, learn, and work on campus (Strayhorn, 2018). For many students, there are few options for safe space beyond the boundaries of the campus due to financial, mobility, or socio-cultural constraints, so they seek out such spaces on campus (Trowler, 2019). For marginalized students, specifically students of colour, navigating such spaces can be difficult, especially as many safe spaces are designated, controlled, and surveilled by university administration. As such, no space can truly be safe when those in positions of power and privilege are present (Freitag, 2013). This can create uncertainty around inclusivity, freedom of expression, relationship building and community formation for marginalized individuals and groups. It is important to examine how safe spaces are often created in relation to institutions' reactions and responses to physical and emotional distress and harm (Freitag, 2013). However, the development of these spaces may not necessarily protect the marginalized but segregate and close off certain spaces and opportunities, thus potentially further othering those effected (The Roestone Collective, 2014). In doing so, the mere creation of designated safe space does not hold those in power accountable when boundaries are transgressed by privileged individuals or groups, and violence and hostility erupts.

This is not to say that safe spaces do not or cannot exist on campus, but these spaces should be shaped and adapted by those occupying and experiencing them rather than being subject to them by those in power (Djohari et al, 2018). It is important to recognize how safe spaces are co-created, co-imagined and co-experienced, and born out of ongoing, renewing and ever-evolving relationships with others (Djohari et al, 2018). Even when institutions and those in power try to establish permanent safe spaces, those seeking out those spaces may find discursive ways to challenge and extend the physical, social and emotional borders that make up these prescribed safe spaces. In doing so, this enables those utilizing these spaces to re-claim them.

Based on an 18-month ethnographic study conducted at a small, public university in the US Midwest, this chapter explores minority students' experiences in university-sponsored spaces and programmes designated for students of colour to develop a deeper understanding of the complex pathways students of colour must navigate and negotiate to survive at PWIs. This chapter therefore complicates definitions and mappings of safe space within the context of the racialized landscape of the University.

Researching safe spaces

From 2014 through 2016, I conducted an ethnographic study about college affordability with low to middle income (LMI) college students at RSU. Emerging from this study were the ways in which race and ethnicity were deeply embedded in the everydayness of affording college and became the focus of my time at RSU. The study was part of a larger team ethnographic project, where each of the four ethnographers was physically located at a different public university in Wisconsin, US, to investigate the myriad of ways that college is affordable or not to LMI college students.[2] We closely examined the financial limitations that many college students face as well as the relational, social, cultural, emotional and psychological costs of college placed upon LMI students (Kendall et al, 2020). We each worked with between 11 and 14 LMI students and engaged in various ethnographic activities. We conducted multiple in-depth semi-structured interviews on topics that ranged from personal histories to college experiences to academic and financial realities. We also spent several days following or walking with students as they went about their days while on campus, including attending classes, hanging out in social spaces, studying, and eating with them. During the summer between their first and second years of college, we spent a day with students to check in and visit with their families. We analysed pertinent documents such as academic transcripts and financial aid award summaries as well as photographs students took which captured their college experiences. In addition to working with the LMI students, we interviewed faculty, staff, and administrators to develop a better understanding of the social, political, and economic histories and contexts of our field sites. These interviews helped us identify key issues related to college affordability and socio-economic inequalities that are evidenced in racial tensions and violence at RSU. I also conducted participant observation in 'public spaces' on campus such as the student union, library and green spaces.

From 2014 to 2016, I worked closely with 11 LMI students at RSU.[3] Students were recruited either through a previous study conducted by our organization, the Wisconsin HOPE Lab, or word of mouth. The 11 students I worked with were largely first-generation college students and Pell grant recipients, a federal needs-based grant, which signifies that most of these students came from low-income families. Of these 11 students, 7 identified as students of colour, 6 of whom identified as Hmong, a Southeast Asian ethnic group, and one identified as Latina, and it is these students' accounts that this chapter is largely based on. These participants' majors included education, history, psychology and social work. During their first year, they all lived on campus and all, but one, worked on campus at a local daycare centre for young children. During their second year, two participants moved off campus due to financial limitations and both were the only students of colour to work off campus.[4]

The Hmong have often been described as a people without a nation and are members of the Unrepresented Nations and Peoples Organization. Since the ending of the Vietnam War, there has been an influx of Hmong refugees, estimates at over 3 million, who have migrated to the US, with many settling in the upper Midwest region (Vang, 2016). All the Hmong students in the study were the children or grandchildren of refugees and these identities often played a role in their motivations for attending college as they wanted to 'give back' to the sacrifices their parents made (Hang, 2015). While college enrolment rates have been steadily increasing over the past two decades among the Hmong population, the group has the lowest rates of education attainment among other Southeast Asian groups in the US (Xiong, 2019). Hmong students often face incredible barriers to degree completion such as socio-cultural, socio-economic, and language challenges (Hang, 2015). Like other students of colour, Hmong students face everyday microaggressions, racial discrimination and religious persecution on predominately white campuses (Vue, 2021).

As a white woman in my then early 30s, I was always cautious about entering spaces that participants identified as 'safe'. While I was allowed to be in these spaces, I always sat with a sense of discomfort being in spaces that students of colour identified as being safe, which largely meant being physically separated from white students, faculty, staff, and administrators. This discomfort better helped inform me of my privileges within these spaces and on campus. It enabled me to reflect upon my own college experiences as a white, first-generation, working-class student and how dramatically different my experiences were from what some students are currently facing in the US. While many of the students I worked with were forthcoming in their experiences, many of them made it quite clear that while I could empathize with what they experienced, I could never understand their experiences and how they engage with safe space on campus, which I fully acknowledge. Additionally, sitting with this discomfort better informed my understanding of safe spaces. When we conceptualize safe space in higher education, it is often about constructing physical spaces to protect marginalized groups. However, in the case of the safe spaces at RSU, this discomfort reminded me of how safety or the illusion of safety transcends physical boundaries. This is not to say that physical space is not important, but when analysing the collected data, I realized how safety was constructed not by the students occupying those spaces but those in power and how that sense of safety could be used to control and surveil marginalized students.

I always asked for consent to enter these spaces and was always introduced to others in the space who frequently introduced me as a researcher doing research about college affordability and social inequality. This led to many interactions with participants' friends and acquaintances in these spaces. These interactions often led to worthwhile discussions about racial and economic inequality but also led to a lot of questions about what I planned to do with the research. Reciprocity has widely been discussed and debated within geography, particularly around ethics (Goerisch, 2017). While the students greatly appreciated the monetary incentives they received for participation in the study, they hoped that the research would create concrete change for them and future RSU students. Participants and students asked when and where they could read about the research or whether I was going to present it to university administration. In 2016 when the study concluded, I wrote a report that was sent and presented to the provost. He was horrified by the experiences of students of colour on campus, particularly around aggressions in the classroom experienced by women students of colour. The result of this report was that Robin Ready, which was to be defunded due to the 2015 Wisconsin Higher Education budget crisis, was funded as well as reinstating support staff positions for students of colour that had been previously cut (Goerisch, 2019). There was also a promise of a review of how bias incident reports are conducted at RSU; it is unclear if this was carried out.

Race, space and violence at PWIs

Despite growing numbers of marginalized students, specifically students of colour, on college campuses, US universities and colleges often lack the infrastructure to effectively support them. US college campuses have always existed as unsafe, violent spaces for students of colour, especially Black and Indigenous students, due to long-standing histories of slavery, Jim Crow, the illegal acquisition of tribal land, white supremacy and settler colonialism (Johnson and Joseph-Salisbury, 2018). Racism and white supremacy still persist on college campuses in the forms of racialized violence, racist stereotypes, racist mascots, microaggressions and harmful policies that directly impact students of colour (Black, 2002; Harwood et al, 2012; Johnson and Joseph-Salisbury, 2018). University responses to campus racism have varied from cultural training workshops, to implementing policies to better protect students of colour, to the creation of safe spaces (Jones, 2019). However, many of these responses either lack infrastructure or become the responsibility of marginalized faculty, students and staff to sustain them, which absolves university leadership from making any real structural change (Calafell, 2014; Jones, 2019). When structural change does happen, it is sporadically enforced or benefits those who are already in positions of privilege (that is, white affluent students), thus not only perpetuating racialized violence but also exacerbating it (Scarritt, 2019). At RSU and other PWIs, residence halls, student unions, and classrooms are among the spaces where students of colour encounter the most racialized violence and, perhaps, the most diverse forms of racialized violence.

All of the students of colour in the study experienced racial microaggressions at RSU. Many cited the ones in the classroom to be the most hurtful and alarming, especially when they initially perceived their white professor or peers to be allies who suddenly betray them. Racial microaggressions are a form of systemic, everyday racism that are meant to keep those at the racial margins in their place (Johnson and Joseph-Salisbury, 2018). It is a form of racism that is increasingly normalized and supported by white supremacy and the institutions that it supports (Johnson and Joseph-Salisbury, 2018). Many of the students of colour in the study noted that in lectures when professors showed images of poverty and crime, the images exclusively showed people of colour, specifically Black and Latinx bodies. The subtlety, frequency and everydayness of microaggressions often overwhelm students of colour, making it difficult to track and report, resulting in what is known as racial battle fatigue (Corbin et al, 2018). For many of the participants, racial microaggressions in the classroom perpetuated by faculty was a significant source of stress. More often than not, students of colour are discouraged by university leadership from reporting microaggressions because they often result in inactions from university leadership and can actually be framed as having long-term negative effects for the student (Nadal et al, 2014). For example, Veronica, a Latina, reported to the ombudsman that her history professor, a tenured white woman, made derogatory remarks directed towards undocumented immigrants. Since it was only Veronica's word against the instructor, nothing came of the report.[5] Veronica was incredibly frustrated and regretted not withdrawing from the class or being able to move into a different class of the same course, which was required for her major. The lack of support and flat out discouragement to challenge racial bias in the classroom contributed to the growing racial tensions at RSU between white students, faculty, and staff and marginalized students, faculty, and staff.

Beyond the classroom, students of colour faced not only microaggressions in the residence halls but hostile, racialized violence that put them at physical and emotional risk of harm. Students spend a great deal of time at their residence hall and/or associated spaces (for example, cafeterias, shared study spaces, gyms and so on). Studies have shown that there are benefits to living in residence halls such as achieving higher grades, participating in campus life, higher graduation and retention rates, and developing a sense of belonging and community (López Turley and Wodtke, 2010). However, for students of colour, who often experience both subtle and explicit racism in the residence halls, these benefits are significantly lessened (Harwood et al, 2012). For many of the Hmong students, the residence halls were, perhaps, the most violent spaces. Most of the Hmong students in the study experienced some form of racialized violence while living in the residence halls, which ranged from microaggressions to racial slurs to segregation, to biased treatment from residence hall and university leadership.

Many of the Hmong students in the study experienced racial slurs that made them feel unsafe in the residence halls. During her second year of college, Rabbit learned of two incidents that made her seriously question the safety of Hmong students at RSU. Rabbit's roommate, Tina, who was also Hmong, was verbally assaulted with racial slurs by two white women in the elevator of her residence hall. Since she was unable to identify her attackers, no action was taken. Due to feeling unsafe and betrayed by RSU administration, Tina transferred to another university the following semester. Rabbit heard about a similar experience from her friend Sally. Sally and other Hmong students were part of a study group that reserved a space in their residence hall that was shared by other groups. A white Bible study group made derogatory remarks towards Sally's study group, which resulted in an argument. Later, the white Bible study group filed a bias incident report against Sally's study group, which resulted in several of the members being questioned by university administration. While no action was taken against the Hmong study group, this incident only increased the racial tensions present at RSU as the bias incident committee had taken the white Bible study group complaint seriously, while completely dismissing Tina's complaint regarding the racial slurs in the elevator. Allegations of racism are often minimized or dismissed by residence directors and advisors as well as university administration, which not only makes students of colour feel invalidated but also unsafe in a space they call home (Harwood et al, 2012).

In addition to these two incidents, as well as countless microaggressions in the residence halls, there was another major incident involving social media. Many of the Hmong students held small gatherings in their residence hall basements where they brought traditional Hmong food and played popular Hmong music. After one such gathering, an anonymous message was posted to the now defunct social media platform, Yik-Yak. Yik-Yak was a social media app that enabled users within a five-mile radius to post anonymous messages. In the message, the original poster writes: 'Why is it Asian invasion every f***ing day and night in willow brook basement this semester, I swear its they bring their kids and everything. … Wtf.' The message devastated the Hmong community at RSU as many students felt their culture and community were under attack. Following the posting, Hmong students gathered both in and out of the residence halls to grieve the loss of space and community they had in the residence halls, as well as discussing how to organize to take action against attacks on social media. A group of Hmong students took the message to university leadership and asked the university to investigate the attack. University leadership said since the post was anonymous there was no way for them to investigate the incident. At other universities, such as Western Washington University, leadership was able to investigate similar attacks and classified them as hate crimes, which led to arrests or suspensions (*Burlington Free Press*, 2015). RSU leadership classified this as a bias incident rather than a hate crime as they felt there was no physical violence or threat of violence. RSU launched a social media campaign that concerned itself more with bullying than developing policies and procedures to protect students of colour from attacks on social media, such as classifying these attacks as a hate crime (Figure 9.1). Many students of colour were frustrated by the university's response and saw this as a failure to recognize that racism even exists on campus. As Rabbit put it, "it would be nice if they [faculty and administrators] actually acknowledged racism on campus" (12 December 2015). Most discussions of hate crimes and place have focused on the geographic location of the crime, however, more debates surrounding meaning-making, hate, and place have emerged (Sumartojo, 2004). Hate and hate crimes are tied to space and place in terms of threat, identity, and motivation (Medina et al, 2018). By failing to recognize the post as an act of hate and labelling it as a bias incident, RSU leadership contributed to the on-going racial tensions by absolving white

Figure 9.1: RSU poster to encourage students to take a pledge against hate

Note: In addition to an online campaign, RSU hung up a poster to encourage students to take a pledge against hate. Many students of colour felt this was an empty gesture and asked for institutional change.

Source: Author's own image

supremacy, and further marginalizing and disenfranchising Hmong students and other students of colour.

Newly emerging from these discussions is the relationship between hate and virtual space. Following the incident on Yik-Yak and the complete lack of response from university leadership, many of the Hmong students felt they were not only unsafe physically on campus but also in online spaces. Virtual spaces have been constructed as possible safe spaces for BIPOC, LGBTQ+, disabled and other marginalized groups (Maliepaard, 2017).[6] Virtual or online spaces can be seen as transformative or liberating as they can potentially provide anonymity, a sense of freedom of expression and are relatively easy to access in comparison to finding safe spaces in their everyday lives (Maliepaard, 2017). Virtual space can provide a space to celebrate identity and provides symbolic and political power for marginalized groups (Maliepaard, 2017). Virtual spaces can also provide the opportunity to connect with others and create meaningful and powerful relationships and networks (Brownlie, 2018). Practices, interactions and relationships conducted in virtual space then can be translated to offline experiences, which may better prepare participants to create transformative change in their lives and communities (Brownlie, 2018). Even though online space is often constructed as a space to express oneself without repercussion and with anonymity, these same features increase the risk of feeling unsafe. Many virtual spaces, especially on social media platforms, can be harmful spaces for oppressed peoples and a space where they are constantly surveilled and monitored (Brownlie, 2018). Many Hmong students felt unsafe online and felt they had to be strategic as to how, where and when they engaged with social media. Following the attack on social media, RSU highlighted stories and images of students of colour to promote racial diversity on their social media platforms to demonstrate how inclusive and safe they were. While showing diversity is incredibly important, particularly for current and incoming marginalized students, these sort of social media campaigns not only provide a false narrative of the presence of racial diversity at RSU but also give an inaccurate representation of safety for students of colour (Hamer and Lang, 2015).

Following these incidents, very few students of colour, especially Hmong students, ventured into associated spaces of the residence halls during their first and second years of college. Many stayed in their rooms out of fear of experiencing violence. Hmong students took other precautions, such as taking the stairs rather than the elevators. As many lived on the upper floors of their residence hall, this added a lot more time and energy to their day. While Tina did leave RSU, for many Hmong students, this was not an option educationally and/or financially. Many of the Hmong students in the study felt they needed to finish their degrees out of a sense of responsibility and obligation to their parents and families. Moving off campus was also not an option for students as off campus housing, especially in the middle of the academic year, was incredibly difficult to find, with many students signing leases for off-campus housing over a year in advance.

RSU, like many PWIs is a hostile environment for students of colour. With little to no response from university leadership to address racially motivated bias incidents and hate crimes, students of colour are only left with the opportunities offered by safe spaces. These are often offered by colleges in lieu of creating policies to address systemic racism. While there are many benefits to the existence of such programmes and spaces, they also have limitations that can exacerbate racial tensions rather than calm them.

Conceptualizing safe spaces for students of colour

Universities often present themselves as spaces of diversity and inclusion especially as a way to recruit and retain students of colour. While college campuses are constructed as diverse, this does not necessarily mean that universities are safe for students of colour. There is definitely a need for safe spaces for students of colour at PWIs given the racialized violence and microaggressions that persist on college campuses. Safe spaces can provide students of colour with a refuge from harm as well as be spaces to foster community and belonging. While the intent of these spaces is well-meaning (and many students appreciate having these spaces), the development and maintenance of these spaces do generate larger questions about how universities treat and protect marginalized students, faculty and staff. As students continued their time at RSU, they seriously doubted the effectiveness and purpose of such spaces, given how little institutional change they witnessed. For many students of colour, if universities want to be diverse and inclusive, especially for students of colour, the campus, especially residence halls and classrooms, will need to be holistically reconceptualized as a safe space rather than segregating students of colour to specific spaces. Here, I highlight the evolution of two safe spaces identified by RSU students of colour: the Office of Multicultural Affairs/Robin Ready Lounge, known colloquially as the Lounge, and the Hmong Student Center. Both spaces were seen as a refuge and the only two spaces the students felt 'safe' from the harsh racial realities and politics present at RSU. However, due to budget cuts and misguided university leadership, safe spaces for students of colour, especially Hmong students, became compromised and sites of racial tension.

Given their attention to diversity, inclusion and opportunities for marginalized students, faculty, and staff, universities are often perceived as 'micropublics' (Andersson et al, 2012). A micropublic is considered a shared space wherein different cultural groups can come to terms with differences in daily encounters and negotiations (Amin, 2002; Knibbe and Horstman, 2019). Micropublics can offer an opportunity for shared belonging and citizenship but can also engender and exacerbate fears and tensions (Amin, 2002; Knibbe and Horstman, 2019). The need for safe spaces outside of the home can create contestations and further fuel existing and emerging racial tensions (Madanipour, 2004). Thus, micropublics set up boundaries based upon inclusionary and exclusionary practices. It is important to understand how and why these borders are established and who exactly they serve. Within the setting of the university, physical safe spaces may be established to better protect students who are marginalized and oppressed by dominant groups, but they also exclude opportunities and possibilities for those same marginalized and oppressed groups, especially if there are forces setting out to dismantle and challenge their existence and purpose.

As a response to anti-racist protests on college campuses and student demands (Blow, 2015), universities develop programmes and designate spaces that emphasize racial justice and multiculturalism (New, 2016). The creation of these programmes and spaces has been met with both praise and criticism. Several have noted that the establishment and use of programmes and spaces dedicated to one demographic group, such as University of Connecticut's residence hall specifically directed towards Black men, is to help address low graduation and retention rates among that demographic by creating community and vital support networks (DeRuy, 2016). Most of the criticism around these kinds of programmes and spaces has come from white students and policymakers who argue that the development of BIPOC-specific spaces are a form of segregation (DeRuy, 2016). However, it is not so much about universities segregating BIPOC students from white students but the tendency for white students to continue to claim access to safe spaces as their own (DeRuy, 2016). Sometimes universities respond to this criticism by opening up presubscribed safe spaces to white students, faculty and staff, which compromises the safety and community-building within those spaces.

One such space was Robin Ready, briefly mentioned in the Introduction to this chapter. As a programme that primarily serves first-generation students of colour, Robin Ready provides several support services and opportunities for employment and travel. Through this programme, students took classes together as well as participated in different academic and professional development activities that focused on equity and diversity. Robin Ready also had a designated gathering space through the Office of Multicultural Affairs, which the students called, the 'Lounge.' In the Lounge, students hung out, ate meals together, studied, napped and organized events. The Lounge, located in one of the newer buildings on campus, contained several tables, workspaces, couches, armchairs, large monitors, computers and printers. Many of the participants spent large portions of their day in the Lounge, only leaving to get food from the student union and attend class or student organization meetings. The room was usually full and rarely quiet. Due to the large windows leading out into the main hallway of the building, students felt that while the room had beautiful natural light and made the space feel more open, they felt they were in a fishbowl constantly on display to others, leaving them with little privacy. Despite this, students felt the space created a sense of home and belonging, at least during their first year of college. Many of the students identified the Lounge as a safe space as they were able to freely express themselves. Nora, a Hmong student, claims: "That room is kinda a safe space for us, where we talk about all these racial issues that happened to us. ... If you are being suppressed, you need to vent in some way" (10 May 2015).

Safe spaces within educational institutions can provide vulnerable students with support that is not available elsewhere on or off campus. According to Djohari et al (2018), safe spaces are a diverse set of social and therapeutic practices and conditions that can be found throughout social institutions and informal networks, emerging in education, youth work and therapeutic support groups, in addition to activists seeking to raise consciousness or encourage political mobilization.

Feelings of home and community quickly fell apart during their second year of college for the students of colour in the study. In 2015, then Governor Scott Walker cut over $250 million in higher education. The cuts negatively impacted RSU, and especially Robin Ready. Before the start of the fall 2015 semester, rumours swirled that Robin Ready, the Office of Multicultural Affairs, and the Women's and LGBTQ Center would be combined into one resource office in order to save money. Students of colour were concerned that the Lounge and the programmes housed in the Office of Multicultural Affairs, like Robin Ready, would be co-opted by white students. When Veronica learned of the potential merger, she was afraid that she and other students of colour "would walk in here [the Lounge] and it will all be different and they won't know what it means for them" (9 July 2015).

She feared that the Lounge would become a 'one-stop shop for diversity' and that students of colour would get the 'short end of the stick.' Fortunately, these offices and programmes were not combined, but Robin Ready did open up their programme to include more white students.[7] White students felt that the Lounge (which was operated by the Office of Multicultural Affairs) should be inclusive to them. Many of the students of colour in the study and their friends no longer felt safe in the space, especially as many of these white students made ignorant derogatory remarks regarding race and people of colour. Nora, who made friends with a few of the white Robin Ready students, warned them to not make "off-colour" jokes about race in the Lounge as doing so compromises the space for students of colour: "They [white students] have to understand that we [Hmong students] are going to talk about racial issues and that will make them [white students] uncomfortable" (10 May 2015).

Safe spaces assume that threats of racialized violence and exclusion have been addressed but safe spaces may exacerbate these pre-existing tensions. For example, safety from harm does not necessarily mean freedom from it (Bowstead, 2019). Safe spaces can be seen then as potentially restrictive and controlling as they continue to harm rather than provide protection or refuge (Bowstead, 2019). In response to the inclusion of racist white students, many of the Hmong students decided to no longer utilize the Lounge as they no longer saw it as a safe space, forcing them to claim other spaces on campus, which were few and far between. Several Hmong students decided to reclaim a previously unused space in the old administration building to house the 'Hmong Student Center'. Initially, the space was overcrowded with tables and chairs, chalkboards, empty bookcases and cabinets. The room held one computer and printer station. There was a small kitchenette that included a microwave and sink. The temperature was rarely regulated in the room making it sweltering hot during the winter. Despite the location, the room usually had about 10–20 students in at a time, with more students present during mealtimes. During the fall semester, students moved chairs and tables to make the space more inviting and for it to be used as both an informal and formal gathering space for Hmong Club and Hmong student-focused initiatives. As the space was tucked away in an obscure, outdated building that few passed through, students had more privacy. Students typically met here to discuss different institutional initiatives such as creating a Hmong Studies programme. Most importantly, Hmong students felt they could speak Hmong to one another, which was often met with stares and racist slurs when occurring in the presence of white students.

While the university allowed the students to use the space, the space was not controlled in the same ways as the Lounge. The Lounge may have been a space for students of colour, but it was also used to highlight diversity and inclusion at RSU. As a recruitment mechanism, prospective students of colour were often shown the Lounge on campus tours. The Lounge was also physically linked to the Office of Multicultural Affairs, which meant that administrators, staff and faculty frequented the space. While students were friendly with many of them, the students still felt wary of anyone who was not a student in the space. Students felt they could not be free to express themselves openly given the potential intrusion of others, especially white staff and students. By contrast, with the Hmong Student Center, while restricting who could access the space (Hmong students), students felt a sense of relief in how open they could be. This is why the Hmong Student Center was the site of organizing and critical discussions surrounding race and policy at RSU. Highlighting the differences in these two safe spaces, demonstrates how universities and students perceive, construct, and utilize safe space. More importantly, these spaces highlight how external forces such as budget cuts negatively impact the maintenance of these spaces and can actually exacerbate racialized tensions and violence at PWIs, especially in terms of who has claims to space.

Conclusion

As universities are perceived as spaces where diversity and inclusion are more likely to be experienced and encountered by young people, safe space is inherently necessary for marginalized students within the college landscape. Safe spaces for young people can be effective in community and relationship building, developing a broader sense of self and awareness, and they can be used to create social change as demonstrated through the two spaces highlighted in this chapter: the Lounge and the Hmong Student Center. Many universities may have good intentions when constructing safe spaces for students of colour. However, the maintenance of these spaces presents challenges due to internal and external forces: institutional policies, trends in higher education, budget cuts and shifting student demographics. As demonstrated in this chapter, these forces made the establishment and retention of safe spaces contingent and relied on students of colour to be vigilant and active in asserting their need for safe space.

Universities need to openly acknowledge that racism, xenophobia and other forms of hate exist on their campuses and pursue measures to alleviate hate. In order for there to be safe spaces on college campuses, university leadership needs to do more than just provide physical space for students of colour. Students need to be included not just in the creation of these spaces but the evolution of the spaces when different forces potentially pose changes, especially if those changes compromise the safety of those utilizing those spaces. However, the burden of labour should not just fall to students. Universities should extend the same policies for ensuring safety to virtual space, especially as more universities are moving towards online courses and use of digital media in the classroom and beyond. University leadership needs to be accountable for maintaining the safety of these spaces. Rather than focusing energies on quick fixes and empty gestures, university leadership needs to work towards making campus as a whole a safer space for students of colour by carrying out more just and equitable policies and spending, especially related to bias incident reporting and programmes for students of colour.

Notes

1. Pseudonyms have been given to places, people, organizations, and programmes to maintain confidentiality.
2. The study was approved by the University of Wisconsin Madison's Institutional Review Board. We received proper permissions from all four universities prior to the start of the study.

3   I began the study with 12 participants; however, due to other responsibilities and the recommendations of academic advisors, one student dropped out of the study midway through our first semester together.

4   At some point during the study, all the white students worked off-campus in a variety of positions: food delivery, retail, health services and homecare. Only one of the white students held an on-campus position as a residence hall front desk clerk.

5   An ombudsman confidentially listens to complaints, concerns or inquiries about alleged acts, omissions, or improprieties and offers options for resolution.

6   BIPOC refers to Black, Indigenous, Person of Colour.

7   Prior to 2015, there were white students, who identified as first-generation and low-income, in Robin Ready but they were in the minority as the programme catered towards students of colour.

References

Amin, A. (2002) 'Ethnicity and the multicultural city: living with diversity', *Environment and Planning A*, 34: 959–80.

Andersson, J., Sadgrove, J. and Valentine, G. (2012) 'Consuming campus: geographies of encounter at a British university', *Social & Cultural Geography*, 13(5): 501–15.

Black, J.E. (2002) 'The "mascotting" of Native America: construction, commodity, and assimilation', *American Indian Quarterly*, 26(4): 605–22.

Blow, C.M. (2015) 'Race, college and safe space', *New York Times*, 16 November, Available from: http://search.proquest.com/docview/207 4600858/abstract/E0881C4FCC734823PQ/1 [Accessed 17 June 2020].

Bowstead, J. (2019) 'Safe spaces of refuge, shelter and contact: introduction', *Gender, Place and Culture*, 26(1): 52–8.

Brownlie, J. (2018) 'Looking out for each other online: digital outreach, emotional surveillance and safe(r) spaces', *Emotion, Space and Society*, 27: 60–67.

Burlington Free Press (2015) 'Western Washington University student charged with hate crime', 10 December, Available from: https://www.burlingt onfreepress.com/story/news/local/bellingham/2015/12/10/western-was hington-university-student-charged-hate-crime/77120194/ [Accessed 22 June 2020].

Calafell, B.M. (2014) '"Did it happen because of your race or sex?": university sexual harassment policies and the move against intersectionality', *Frontiers*, 35(3): 75–95.

Corbin, N.A., Smith, W.A. and Garcia, J.R. (2018) 'Trapped between justified anger and being the strong Black woman: Black college women coping with racial battle fatigue at historically and predominantly white institutions', *International Journal of Qualitative Studies in Education*, 31(7): 626–43.

Dedman, B. (2019) 'College students are more diverse than ever. Faculty and administrators are not', Association of American Colleges and Universities, Available from: https://www.aacu.org/aacu-news/newsletter/2019/march/facts-figures [Accessed 12 July 2020].

DeRuy, E. (2016) 'There's a fine line between "safe spaces" and segregation', *The Atlantic*, 17 August, Available from: https://www.theatlantic.com/education/archive/2016/08/finding-the-line-between-safe-space-and-segregation/496289/ [Accessed 28 July 2020].

Djohari, N., Pyndiah, G. and Arnone, A. (2018) 'Rethinking 'safe spaces' in children's geographies', *Children's Geographies*, 16(4): 351–5.

Freitag, M. (2013) 'A queer geography of a school: landscapes of safe(r) spaces', *Confero: Essays on Education, Philosophy and Politics*, 1(2): 123–61.

Goerisch, D. (2017) '"Doing good work": feminist dilemmas of volunteering in the field', *The Professional Geographer*, 69(2): 307–13.

Goerisch, D. (2019) 'Doing less with less: faculty care work in times of precarity', in C.W. Byrd, R.J. Brunn-Bevel and S. Ovink (eds) *Intersectionality and Higher Education: Identity and Inequality on College Campuses*, New Brunswick: Rutgers University Press, pp 122–35.

Goh, K. (2018) 'Safe cities and queer spaces: the urban politics of radical LGBT activism', *Annals of the American Association of Geographers*, 108(2): 463–77.

Hall, E. (2004) 'Social geographies of learning disability: narratives of exclusion and inclusion', *Area*, 36(3): 298–306.

Hamer, J.F. and Lang, C. (2015) 'Race, structural violence, and the neoliberal university: The challenges of inhabitation', *Critical Sociology*, 41(6): 897–912.

Hang, D. (2015) '"I am a Hmong American": an exploration of the experiences of Hmong students in college' (diss.), Kingston, RI: University of Rhode Island.

Harwood, S.A., Huntt, M.B., Mendenhall, R. and Lewis, J.A. (2012) 'Racial microaggressions in the residence halls: experiences of students of color at a predominantly white university', *Journal of Diversity in Higher Education*, 5(3): 159–73.

Held, N. (2015) 'Comfortable and safe spaces? Gender, sexuality and "race" in night-time leisure spaces', *Emotion, Space and Society*, 14: 33–42.

Holloway, S.L. and Pimlott-Wilson, H. (2014) 'Enriching children, institutionalizing childhood? Geographies of play, extracurricular activities, and parenting in England', *Annals of the Association of American Geographers*, 104(3): 613–27.

Hughes, G. (2013) 'Racial justice, hegemony, and bias incidents in US higher education', *Multicultural Perspectives*, 15(3): 126–32.

Johnson, A. and Joseph-Salisbury, R. (2018) '"Are you supposed to be in here?" Racial microaggressions and knowledge production in higher education', in J. Arday and H.S. Mirza (eds) *Dismantling Race in Higher Education: Racism, Whiteness and Decolonising the Academy*, Cham: Springer International Publishing, pp 143–60.

Jones, V. (2019) 'Discourse within university presidents' responses to racism: revealing patterns of power and privilege', *Teachers College Record*, 121(4): 1–32.

Kendall, N., Goerisch, D., Kim, E.C., Vernon, F. and Wolfgram, M. (2020) *The True Costs of College*, New York: Palgrave Macmillan.

Knibbe, M. and Horstman, K. (2019) 'The making of new care spaces: How micropublic places mediate inclusion and exclusion in a Dutch city', *Health & Place*, 57: 27–34.

Leonardo, Z. and Porter, R.K. (2010) 'Pedagogy of fear: toward a Fanonian theory of "safety"', *Race, Ethnicity and Education*, 13(2): 139–57.

López Turley, R.N. and Wodtke, G. (2010) 'College residence and academic performance: who benefits from living on campus?', *Urban Education*, 45(4): 506–32.

Madanipour, A. (2004) 'Marginal public spaces in European cities', *Journal of Urban Design*, 9(3): 267–86.

Maliepaard, E. (2017) 'Bisexual safe space(s) on the internet: analysis of an online forum for bisexuals', *Tijdschrift Voor Economische en Sociale Geografie*, 108(3): 318–30.

Medina, R.M., Nicolosi, E., Brewer, S. and Linke, A.M. (2018) 'Geographies of organized hate in America: a regional analysis', *Annals of the American Association of Geographers*, 108(4): 1006–21.

Nadal, K.L., Wong, Y., Griffin, K.E., Davidoff, K. and Sriken, J. (2014) 'The adverse impact of racial microaggressions on college students' self-esteem', *Journal of College Student Development*, 55(5): 461–74.

New, J. (2016) 'U of Connecticut creates new living-learning center for black male students', *Inside Higher Ed*, 2 February, Available from: https://www.insidehighered.com/news/2016/02/02/u-connecticut-creates-new-living-learning-center-black-male-students [Accessed 18 June 2020].

Prutzman, P. (1994) 'Bias-related incidents, hate crimes and conflict resolution', *Education and Urban Society*, 27(1): 71–81.

Roestone Collective, The (2014) 'Safe space: towards a reconceptualization', *Antipode*, 46(5): 1346–65.

Scarritt, A. (2019) 'Selling diversity, promoting racism: how universities pushing a consumerist form of diversity empowers oppression', *Journal for Critical Education Policy Studies*, 17(1): 188–228.

Strayhorn, T.L. (2018) *College Students' Sense of Belonging: A Key to Educational Success for All Students*, New York: Routledge.

Sumartojo, R. (2004) 'Contesting place antigay and lesbian hate crime in Columbus Ohio', in C. Flint (ed) *Spaces of Hate: Geographies of Discrimination and Intolerance in the USA*, New York: Routledge, pp 87–108.

Trowler, V. (2019) 'Transit and transition: student identity and the contested landscape of Higher Education', in S. Habib and M.R.M. Ward, (eds) *Identities, Youth and Belonging: International Perspectives, Studies in Childhood and Youth*, Cham: Springer International Publishing, pp 87–104.

Vang, C.T. (2016) *Hmong Refugees in the New World: Culture, Community and Opportunity*, Jefferson: McFarland.

Vue, R. (2021) 'Trauma and resilience in the lives and education of Hmong American students: forging pedagogies of remembrance with critical refugee discourse', *Race, Ethnicity and Education*, 24(2): 282–301.

Xiong, S. (2019) 'Access, use, and efficacy of campus services among Hmong American community college students', *Journal of Applied Research in the Community College*, 26(1): 73–88.

10

'It's Not Hate to … [Say] That Gay Sex Leads to Hell': Contesting Hate, Reiterating Heteronormativities

Kath Browne and Catherine Jean Nash

Introduction

The liberalization of sexual and gendered rights in the 21st century dramatically altered the socio-sexual landscapes of the Global North in what has been described as a 'world we have won' (Weeks, 2007). Hate speech definitions include sexual orientation and gender identities in hate crime legislation in the UK and Canada. Recording of hate crimes against predominantly LGBT populations has been instigated in the UK and individuals are encouraged to report hate incidents (UK Citizens Advice, nd), all of which has revealed patterns of violence and abuse (UK Home Office, 18 October 2019). At the time of writing, Ireland did not have hate crime legislation, but in 2020 undertook a consultation on the possibility of some form of legislation (Irish Department of Justice, 2020). Yet the threat of being labelled a 'hater' still holds sway due to cultural perceptions about the acceptance of sexual and gendered rights. This was particularly evident after the 2015 referendum approving the legalization of same sex marriage and in the 2018 referendum enabling access to abortion. Mapping the incidents and nature of hate crimes allows us to document what we might call landscapes of hate and thereby demonstrate the impacts of these experiences of hate on particular groups or individuals and, in some cases, offer a means of redress. Many may argue that non-discrimination and hate crimes legislation fosters more inclusive landscapes. However, in this chapter, we focus on those groups who remain opposed to or resistive of sexual and gendered equalities and seek to reinstate heteronormative structures. In contesting such inclusive landscapes in the UK and Ireland, these groups seek to avoid being labelled 'haters' or being potentially captured under hate legislation.

Contemporary sexualities and gender scholarship has long recognized the failings of legislative equalities including hate crimes legislation, to fully deliver sexual and gender liberations for all. There are extensive studies of the effects of these changes on sexual and gendered others such as lesbian, gay, and increasingly bi, trans and intersex (LGBTI) people, as well as scholarship considering queer contestations of these changes (for example, Browne and Bakshi, 2013; Richardson, 2017; Nash et al, 2018). As discussions of homonormativities have demonstrated, sexual and gendered equalities offer, for some queers, recuperations within normative neoliberal, racialized, monogamous domesticated family ideals while excluding other queers (Bell and Binnie 2000; Stychin, 2001; Duggan, 2002). Scholars offering homonational critiques have further demonstrated effectively how LGBT rights and equalities can be used to reiterate geopolitical hegemonies, and justify invasions as well as violence and torture (Puar, 2007). In terms of hate crime and safety, it has long been noted that the criminalization of (or disapproval of) what might be understood as 'hate' does not necessarily create safety for sexual and gender minorities (Browne et al, 2011).

In discussions of hate crime, the focus is often on those who are subject to it, rather than those who might be accused of it. In this chapter, we argue that in exploring the landscapes of sexual and gender equalities through a lens of 'hate', we can investigate the approaches and practices of those who can be read as perpetuating/perpetrating 'hate' against sexual and gendered minorities. We show that they seek to avoid both criminalization and social perceptions of being 'haters'. Rather than identify 'hate', locate it and categorize it, which is a useful focus for other work, hate here is seen as a naming rhetoric that seeks particular ends (often criminal or societal sanction/redress). The focus here is on how those who are accused of hate through their opposition to sexual and gender rights and equalities, seek to reposition themselves in relation to this narrative. We will show that they do this by reasserting or attempting to recuperate heteronormativities, but in ways that are distinct from late 20th-century state-supported 'homophobias'. We use the term heteroactivism to name and conceptualize these forms of resistances to sexual and gender equalities, including LGBT rights (Browne and Nash, 2017; Nash and Browne, 2020). These activisms seek to reaffirm the 'rightful' place of heteronormative marriage with familial and kinship relations as the best institution for raising children and for the betterment of society as a whole while avoiding any label suggesting they are 'haters' (Browne and Nash, 2015; 2018). Heteroactivists challenge and resist what they see as the growth in state/legislative oppression of their understandings and presentations of sexual and gender norms (Browne and Nash, 2020).

We begin our examination of heteroactivist engagements with 'hate' by setting out the key tenets of heteroactivist ideologies and practices that we have explored in our research since 2012. We then review our data sources, namely participant observation and field notes collected through our attendance at a three-day heteroactivist conference in August 2018. We also considered emails from a key UK heteroactivist organization, to their membership. Drawing on this data, we explore how heteroactivists frame objections (in words and deeds) to sexual and gender equalities while pushing against or working to avoid accusations of 'hate speech'. We show how they frame their arguments as motivated by love and related representations of themselves and those who agree with them as innocent citizens subject to the dangers of both formal criminal sanctions and the social and political consequences of being associated with and perpetuating hate speech. In doing so, this chapter contends that landscapes of hate are contested and recuperated by those who might be named as perpetuators of hate, in ways that are geographically specific. We conclude by asserting that engagement with heteroactivists needs critical attention, including addressing the social divisions surrounding sexualities and genders. We also briefly discuss our current research entitled 'Beyond Opposition',[1] which attempts to think through how we might engage differently with those who have concerns about LGBT socio-legal changes.

Heteroactivism in contemporary sexual landscapes

Only recently have academics begun to focus on political and social resistances to sexual and gendered equalities and rights in places where these rights seem to be in ascendancy (Browne and Nash, 2017; 2020; Kuhar and Paternotte, 2017). Those who continue to assert the superiority of heteronormativity can no longer rely on (and indeed cannot in contexts with hate speech legislation) the vilification of homosexuality as the purview of the paedophile, the mentally ill or the criminal (Browne and Nash, 2015). In this chapter, we demonstrate how heteroactivists work to distance themselves from accusations of hate, homophobia and other terms that might render their arguments out of place in the contemporary public sphere (Nash and Browne, 2020).

In our research to date, we have explored heteroactivism in locations such as Canada, the UK and Ireland, where there is state-supported, as well as broad public support for, sexual and gender equalities (Browne and Nash, 2017; 2019; Nash and Browne 2019; 2020). In these places, heteroactivists are struggling with how their moral values, that is, those asserting the sanctity of heteronormatively gendered, opposite sex marriage, are no longer central in the national consciousness and in legislative (and policy) programmes. They argue that they are often violently excluded from public debates within a newly constituted 'civic' society and the necessity not to appear as a 'hater'. Heteroactivism therefore is a spatially nuanced concept that offers significant analytical capacity to explore heteronormative activisms in ways that are sensitive to cultural specificities.

Religion is often positioned as key to landscapes of hate associated with sexualities and genders, demonstrated by, for example, US Christian Right anti-gay activism (Stein, 2001; Burack, 2015) and the trope of the 'homophobic Muslim' (Boulila, 2019; Haritaworn, 2015). Yet, the conflation of Christianity/Islam with anti-gay/anti-LGBT stances has long been contested (Browne et al, 2010; Yip and Nynäs, 2016). While heteroactivisms can be created through religion, specifically Christianity and is often racialized as white, heteroactivism often moves beyond biblical formulations to what can be seen as broader secular calls for free speech or parental rights (Nash and Browne, 2020) and, as we assert in this chapter, discussions of hate. While the groups we highlight in this chapter draw on Christian belief systems, the acceptance of sexual and gender equalities within Christianity is varied and contested (see, for example, Browne et al, 2010; Yip and Nynäs, 2016). Here, we examine the arguments of Christian heteroactivists in the UK whose contestations seek to avoid accusations of hate by utilizing, in part, *secular* calls for free speech or parental rights rather than relying on biblical claims (Nash and Browne, 2020).

Where heteroactivists come from religious orientations, there is also an awareness of the limitations of biblically based arguments within mainstream societies with both legislative and social support for sexual and gender equalities. The argument that some Christians are suffering unjustly has been a key trope for some heteroactivists (Nash and Browne, 2020). This is more often a backdrop rather than a central feature in their arguments, particularly for those publicly promoting some version of Christian morals but to audiences that are no longer persuaded by biblical admonishments or prohibitions. This focus on the secular marks a key consideration for heteroactivists, some of whom continue to base their adherence to heteronormativity on religious underpinnings but know that this is no longer sufficient in working against accusations of hate or prejudice (Nash and Browne, 2020).

Heteroactivism, as a political and social practice, cannot necessarily or automatically be tied to a particular religion nor is it necessarily associated to political (right-wing/populist) affiliations (Browne and Nash, 2017). While transnational connections are apparent, heteroactivism, as a concept, resists the idea that activities spread through the 'diffusion' or a 'globalization' of, say, the US Christian Right (see Butler, 2006; Murray, 2009; Weiss and Bosia, 2013). In exploring particular key heteroactivist tropes that circulate around notions of hate and its binary opposite, love, this chapter investigates the creation of sexual and gendered landscapes in geographically nuanced ways without a reliance on religious or political affiliation as key analytical lenses. Instead, we show how resistances created through complex interconnected networks are seeking to reiterate specific forms of heteronormativities, centralizing their arguments regarding sexualities and genders.

Methods

This chapter draws on extensive data collection, analysis and writing from a larger research project.[2] Here, we focus specifically on two case studies to develop our arguments. In particular, we use participant observations from an international heteroactivist conference held by the Lumen Fidei Institute in Dublin in 2018. We attended this two-day event, took detailed notes and recorded our discussions at the end of each day, which we draw on in our analysis here. Second, we analyse emails from a key heteroactivist organization in the UK, Christian Concern, to highlight key tropes that are illustrative of our core arguments. This in-depth investigation details how these organizations work with and disseminate their ideas through often contradictory discourses of hate and love.

The Lumen Fidei Institute

The Lumen Fidei Institute, according to their website, 'is an association of Catholic lay people engaged in cultural and educational matters'. As a 'not-for-profit' organization, they assert that 'all monies raised will be use for the purpose of promoting the work of the Institute'.[3] As an activist organization, Lumen Fidei produces a number of articles and books, holds members meetings and organizes numerous events to promote their message.

In August 2018, and as a challenge to the Pope's visit to Ireland in conjunction with the World Meeting of Families (WMoF), Lumen Fidei Institute ran a 'Conference of Catholic Families' (Lumen Fidei, 2018). This conference opposed what they regarded as the liberalizing agenda of WMoF and one that abandoned those who upheld a traditional Catholic view of the family. We covertly attended the two-day event, which consisted of a range of speakers, both laity and clergy. (By 'covertly', we mean we attended the event using our own names and affiliations but did not overtly identify ourselves as researchers. In accordance with Research Ethics clearances from both Maynooth University and Brock University, we merely observed and did not engage in any discussion with participants nor did we pose any questions or participate in the conference in any way other than observers; see Maguire et al, 2019 for a fuller discussion). The conference hall was full for most of the sessions at around 400–450 people. Eleven white, male speakers from the UK, Ireland, Canada, Germany and Hungry and one woman (a US nun seeking to found a convent in Ireland and who attended in the place of a male speaker) presented papers. The audience was predominantly Irish and overwhelmingly white. In this chapter, we focus on five lay speakers who centralized gender and sexuality in their presentations, and being from Canada, the UK and Ireland, they cannot simply vilify homosexuality/LGBT people and/or 'wayward' women.

The lay speakers were compelling, powerful speakers who were organized, passionate and well-trained, and who often included the personal in their talks. Audience members were lively participants, often clapping, cheering and providing enthusiastic standing ovations for all speakers. Throughout the conference, the speakers worked hard, supported by the audience, to denormalize LGBT rights and sexual and gender equalities including queer identities, same sex marriage, trans issues and abortion. They lamented that their views are no longer the accepted as the 'norm' or in sync with hegemonic national values, despite the fact that, in their opinion, their views reflected common sense. Speakers were emboldened by the support of the audience, and the presumption that they were speaking to an 'us' and a 'we' that agreed with their opinions and viewpoints. This 'us' and 'we' were created through framing others as outside the accepted group, and as 'a danger to us', 'our' families, 'our' lives, 'our' faith and 'our' nation. These approaches created space and distance for both the speakers and the audience to participate in nuanced discussions of hate/love. This was undertaken by creating specific discourses that contested the new sexual and gender orders seemingly accepted by the Catholic church particularly in Ireland.

Christian Concern

Christian Concern[4] is a UK organization that seeks to 'speak and influence' in ways that promote 'the love, justice, truth, freedom and hope of Jesus Christ to the heart of (British) society' (Christian Concern, 2021a; 2021b). They are involved in media, court cases and training to assert their understandings of Christianity and support those who feel wronged by sexual and gender equalities, for example, where individuals have lost their employment or positions in key organizations, had their bank accounts closed or have confronted school policies around same-sex marriage or trans inclusions to their detriment. Christian Concern also holds conferences, similar to those of the Lumen Fidei conference, seeking to educate and build resistance to LGBT inclusions and abortion rights.

Christian Concern sends out regular emails, including newsletters, weekly updates and bulletins, as well as immediate requests for prayer or funding.[5] We explored these emails over ten months, from February to November 2020, with a focus on Christian Concern responses to Hate Crime Bills in England and Wales and in Scotland, and new NHS guidelines on violence and abuse including homophobia. We also examine Christian Concern's defence of a pastor who described the cancellations of Pride as 'wonderful news'. We offer a close reading of key texts to detail how they construct their oppositional arguments that contribute to the constitution of landscapes of hate.

Our analysis involved coding data from Christian Concern emails and our notes on the Lumen Fidei conference, creating the key themes that will be discussed later in the paper which focus on the wording used and the creation of specific arguments to develop understandings of how the concept of 'hate' is used within a particular strand of heteroactivism. The quotes we use here are drawn from these various sources and are all clearly marked. Some are related to fieldnotes that use both quotes from speakers in the first person and observations from us in the third person. Some are direct quotes where talks were recorded and transcribed by us. We highlight how there is an effort to resist accusations about their role in creating landscapes of hate by contesting accusations of hate and using claims about 'love' to make room to openly discuss 'hate'. This is important in contexts such as Ireland, where what is regarded as 'hate speech' has become unacceptable in broader popular cultures, and in the UK, illegal.

It's not hate

Heteroactivists can protest against accusations of hate in various ways in order to position their words and actions in legal ways, as well as contesting legislative initiatives that, they argue might make their beliefs and (speech) practices illegal.

This can be seen clearly in the discussion of Scotland's introduction of a Hate Crime Bill in 2020. In response, Christian Concern published an article by Kiska on its website, on 29 May 2020, entitled 'Scottish Hate Crime Bill Over-Regulates Free Speech'. Robert Kiska was particularly exercised by part 2 of the Bill that creates, in his opinion:

> a new offence for stirring up hatred in relation to the enumerated protected characteristics (age, disability, religion, sexual orientation, transgender identity, and variations in sex characteristics). While Sections 11 and 12 of the Bill create exceptions for speech which criticises or discusses religion or sexual orientation, those exceptions do not apply where the speech involved is deemed to be abusive or threatening. Section 14(7) of the proposed bill creates a protected characteristic for gender identity, thus going well beyond the protections afforded both by the Equality Act 2010 and Gender Recognition Act 2004. (Kiska, 2020)

Kiska is concerned about the extension of the category of protected characteristics, to include gender identity. Gender identity (specifically its inclusion of non-normative gender expression, including trans people) has become an important rallying point for resisting LGBT equalities. The creation of a clause that allows for critiques of religion and sexual orientation but not for gender identity, for Kiska, 'goes beyond' legislation and does not fall within what is critiquable. Heteroactivist resistances in places like the UK/Ireland and Canada often seek to make space for critiques of new legislative proposals and for cultural transformation, in ways that pre-empt the possibility that their critiques can be read as hate or perceived as abusive and threatening.

In a related case, in an 11 November 2020 email, Christian Concern noted they had been 'successful' in campaigning to keep the 'following clarification of free speech' in the UK Coroners and Justice Act in 2009 (UK Bill but it applies to England and Wales).[6] The purpose of the Act was named as creating 'effective, transparent and responsive justice and coroner services for victims, witnesses, bereaved families and the wider public' (Corner and Justice Act, 2009; Liberty Central, 2010). There was a debate on the inclusion of a 'Free Speech clause'. This clause was included and read: 'For the avoidance of doubt, the discussion or criticism of sexual conduct or practices or the urging of persons to refrain from or modify such conduct or practices shall not be taken of itself to be threatening or intended to stir up hatred' (Public Order Act, 1986, amendment made in 2008).

This, Christian Concern argues, enables them to legally criticize 'someone's sexuality' without this being 'branded as hate speech' (Christian Concern, Email: 11 September 2020). The discussion of practices and conduct rather than identities is the focus of this clause, and Christian Concern understood it as a victory for them because it opens up room to criticize, ask to refrain from or modify 'sexual conduct and practices' without these contestations being deemed 'threatening' and thus illegal.

The equation of 'threatening' with hate speech illustrates Christian Concern's perception that framing 'hate speech' as threatening impinges on their activities. In the Scottish Bill, even critiques of sexual orientation and religion are not to be permitted where that speech is 'abusive or threatening.' In this case, the definition of abuse and threat and who determines speech as abusive/threatening (and thus 'hate') becomes key. What constitutes a legislative hate crime is based on the perception of those who experience it, not the intent of the speaker. In Kiska's words 'hate is subjective' and this leads to the argument that people are being overly sensitive. This is a push against definitions of hate crime that they believe are grounded on 'feelings'. These 'feelings' are afforded little merit and importantly should not be subject to legal recourse:

the intention of the speaker is initially judged by how the listener perceives the message being spoken. In other words, there is a rebuttable presumption of guilt based on the feelings of the 'victim', no matter how sensitive they are ... overly sensitive local authorities and law enforcement will nonetheless continue to arrest otherwise innocent civilians for exercising their lawful right to speech. ... For the sake of our fundamental freedoms, Scotland deserves better. (Kiska, 2020)

It is not only individuals who are seen as 'overly sensitive' but also, and importantly, 'local authorities and law enforcement'. Whereas in the late 20th century, Section 28 of the UK Local Government Act 1988 allowed local authorities to regulate activities based on understandings of lesbians and gay men as dangerous to children through the 'promotion of homosexuality' (Bell and Binnie, 1999; Stychin, 2001). Kiska now reads these same authorities as a threat to 'otherwise innocent civilians'. To claim innocence, these civilians are assumed to be heterosexual (and white), and acting within their lawful right to contest LGBT equalities. Framing themselves and their supporters as civilians, and as individuals 'outside' the culture war, is to contrast them with LGBT activists who have their own 'agendas' to undermine heteroactivists' rights and freedoms. This creates the idea that there are combatants and that they, in their critiques and contestations, are not combatants. Instead, they are 'citizens' speaking their minds innocently and without their own agenda.

An imagined landscape of sexual and gender militants (organized and funded) attacking citizens is evoked and these citizens, operating in this landscape, are 'innocent'. Hate speech provisions thus become an imminent threat. As Kiska also argues:

The result of 'hate' speech provisions is a reduction in the fundamental right to freedom of speech and freedom of expression. Instead of being free to disagree with one another, have robust debate, and freely exchange ideas, 'hate' speech laws have shut down debate and created a heckler's veto. In the end, a chilling effect is created that leads to self-censorship and an overly sensitive society. (Kiska, 2020)

The claim to free speech is an important trope as it is regarded as foundational and fundamental to sustaining freedom and democracy. The claims about the creation of an 'overly sensitive society' moves from individual and organizations to society itself. Hate speech legislation is thus seen as undermining 'robust debate' and the free 'exchange of ideas'. For Kiska and other heteroactivists, this has a 'chilling effect', invoking the idea of authoritarian states vetoing or rendering invisible those who disagree. They argue for the ability to say anything, anywhere, and as a right regardless of upset speech might cause. Thus, they contend that as innocent citizens, they are being unfairly targeted because by exercising their free speech rights they are being accused of creating landscapes of hate.

Yet free speech and its legislative underpinnings are geographically differentiated and delineated. As the Scottish Bill shows, free speech can be curtailed for being what is defined as 'abusive' and 'threatening', in contrast to Christian Concern's reading of the UK Coroners and Justice Bill, which suggests even abusive and threatening critique can be excluded from definitions of hate. Nonetheless, free speech is seen as underpinning the foundations of 'democracy' and 'civilization'. This means that heteroactivists speak of the 'cost' of prohibiting 'hate crime' becoming 'too high'. The protections that are needed are for 'innocent citizens', not those who are 'sensitive' scare-quoted 'victims'. This sets up a querying of claims of harm related to speech, particularly speech acts related to critiquing sexual orientation and gender identities.

Christian Concern claims that hate speech laws are often premised, as they are with the proposed Scottish Bill, on the unsubstantiated assertion that there is a cause and effect relationship between speech and social harm. Such laws, they argue, are further premised on a second faulty argument that prejudice is so prevalent and insidious in any given jurisdiction that criminal sanction becomes a necessary encumbrance on free speech. Given this, they claim that the move to criminalize speech as a deterrent against prejudice is unnecessary and contrived, and a social regulation of their speech.

> The reality is that in Scotland, there is currently no issue with 'hate' speech. Speech is sufficiently regulated by public opinion. If someone makes a statement which evidences prejudice of almost any kind, the result for the individual will almost always be loss of reputation, public shaming, and even loss of business income or employment. (Kiska, 2020)

In presuming that prejudice will be dealt with through 'public opinion', 'shaming' and 'loss', heteroactivists argue that hate speech legislation is unnecessary and indeed an 'encumbrance' to free speech. And yet, when businesses and individuals are shamed or lose their reputation, Christian Concern expends significant effort in defending such business and individuals including through legal action as well as reworking narratives that might create forms of public shaming. Christian Concern's robust defence of individuals violating 'public opinion' underscores their view that such speech should not be criminalized because it is not harmful and, despite their claims to the contrary, there should not be any social regulation making such speech unacceptable.

Dangers of criminalization and the label of 'hater'

Criminalizing hate speech is also seen as leading to other dangers. Because critiquing sexual orientation and gender identities might constitute a hate crime if certain legislation was passed, heteroactivists fear that 'innocent victims' could then potentially be spied upon by police. Under the title 'freedom', Christian Concern warn: 'The government has so far pushed a new bill – the Covert Human Intelligence Bill – through all stages of the House of Commons. ... Christians are already being accused of 'hatred' or being 'hate groups'; this bill could now give the government licence to spy on Christians' (Email: 23 October 2020).

The dangers that Christian Concern see with 'hate speech', specifically the potential for any critique of sexual and gender identities to be criminalized, are outlined in the linked webpage (Moseley, 2020). This argues that 'public bodies such as the police, the Department of Health and the Food Standards Agency' would be able 'to authorize criminal conduct by spies'. Moseley (2020) contends that because 'the line between hate crime' and 'hate incidents' already gets blurred by the police', the rights of 'innocent citizens' are infringed. This could further enable covert engagement by police who have the power to engage in criminal behaviour with 'campaign groups that have in the past been accused of "hate incidents"'. Once they have joined the group, Moseley (2020) argues, they can commit illegal acts and push groups 'beyond what it would normally envisage'. In this way, Christian Concern are suggesting that the police would join groups that oppose sexual and gender rights and encourage behaviour that is subject to criminal sanction. The police would gain this right through naming what they see as 'critiques' of sexual and gender lives and rights as hate crime. This, Christian Concern argue, becomes even more likely with the potential criminalization of conversion therapy. Thus, criminalization of some speech as hate is seen as creating a legislative and policing landscape where 'innocent' people are criminalized and further encouraged to engage in criminal behaviours because of their public opposition to sexual and gender equalities.

Criminalizing hate speech, it is also suggested, will lead to a loss of treatment from the British public health service, the NHS. Where rules regarding violent or aggressive behaviour are believed to be extended to 'homophobic remarks' made at the time of treatment, Christian Concern asks the question: 'Could criticisms of rainbow lanyards worn by some NHS staff be considered homophobic too?' (Christian Concern, Email: 21 February 2020). The implication here is that rainbow lanyards should be critiqued and that this critique should fall under freedom of speech regardless of the impact of those remarks. Any hurt or harm felt from those remarks are seen to arise when individuals are 'too sensitive' and as Christian Concern contends, should not impact on treatment. Moreover, it presumes that homophobic remarks are related to criticism rather than abuse and verbal violence such as when 'objecting to a Pride flag is homophobic'.

Perhaps the most serious claim that we have come across challenging the criticism of LGBT lives as hate is the argument that this enables sexual abuse. The claims made at the Lumen Fidei conference take a different approach from previously, widespread cultural understandings of all gay men as paedophiles, dangerous and evil. Instead, John Lacken (Lumen Fidei, 2018) argued that it is the 'promotion and acceptance' of the 'homosexual lifestyle', and specifically priests who are 'active homosexuals', who are dangerous and 'a major part of the current crisis around sexual abuse in the Catholic Church'. In seeking to understand contemporary problems in the church, including 'problems with women being abused as well', Lacken argues the primary problem is not power abuse, but same sex attraction. The scandal of power abuse in the church, including sexual abuse is linked directly to homosexuality and same-sex attraction is equated to two forms of abuse: of children, largely boys; and the homosexual activities of seminarians and others within the church hierarchy. Lacken calls out those in the church hierarchy, who are afraid of being called 'haters and homophobic', which he argues, paralyses the church from taking any effective action.

Heteroactivists position themselves as marginalized and oppressed by new sexual and gender equalities because they proclaim the truth as Catholics/ Christians both within the church itself and in society. This reaffirms their place as truth holders who are persecuted by powerful others, including the state. The 'powers that be' within the Catholic church opposing 'the truth' are identified as the organizers of WMoF. In contrast, John Lacken positions the Lumen Fidel Institute Conference as outsiders, arguing that 'true teaching on the family and married life is here, not in the RDS [the conference centre where the WMoF was being held]'. The invitation to the WMoF of James Martin (an outspoken supporter of LGBT people within the church), was presented as a particularly egregious example of the failings of the Catholic church to uphold Catholic teachings. Members of Lumen Fidel who attended Martin's talk reported to the Lumen Fidel Conference expressing horror and revulsion at his suggestion that LGBT people be included in the church's bereavement counselling and other church duties. Anthony Murphy, the lead organizer said, 'I would be bereaved', and expressed particular ire at the suggestion of the Eucharist being handled by LGBT people. Thus, those who support 'traditional marriage' (in their terms between a man and a woman) not only know the truth, but they are also the holders of it. Proclaiming the truth against those who seek to 'destroy' the church resists dominant (and oppressive) 'powers that be' within as well as without.

Reclaiming hate as love

Reclaiming hate, in a context of love, is not as oxymoronic as it might first seem and it is undertaken by heteroactivists to counter key trends in contemporary sexual and gender politics, where love is seen as loving 'who you want' and 'haters' are presented as preventing and objecting to love itself. The Lumen Fidei conference directly responded to and opposed the ideal of love for LGBT people put forward by WMoF and specifically by James Martin. John Henry-Westen, a Canadian who was, at the time, a key figure in Lifesite News (a transnational Catholic heteroactivist organization/website/activist site),[7] entitled his speech 'It's hate not to tell LGBT Catholics gay sex leads to Hell'. This is part of a broader strategy that seeks to counter equality, diversity and other forms of inclusion. As we noted in our fieldnotes:

> John Lacken [a speaker at the conference] called the volunteer flyers for WMoF released on Valentine's day, that focused on love and couples, 'homospeak' and in a mocking tone said that they 'value and embrace diversity'. [The audience laughs] He went on to say that killers are diverse. (Fieldwork notes, quotes are approximations)

In reclaiming hate as something that the Catholic church should do to prevent sexual violence, they seek to create space to attack inclusion from a position they defined as 'love'. John Henry-Westen contended:

> 'The usual tactic is to be called a hater and a bigot because of my stance on same sex attraction.' On a radio show he had argued 'I love my brothers, because it is hate not to tell them [that same sex sex/ attraction is wrong]. ... He said that he was praying for hate – love what God loves, hate the things that God hates. ... He suggests that the church needs more hatred. ... It is hate *not* to tell Same Sex Attracted Catholics that gay sex leads to hell. (John Henry-Westen, quotes are approximations from fieldwork notes)

Henry-Westen argues that calling people 'a hater' and 'a bigot' is how 'supposedly' tolerant open and inclusive societies such as Canada, the UK and Ireland are currently dealing with resistances to sexual and gender rights. He derides this as mere 'name calling' while reiterating the importance of their truth. He argues that the church's (and Lumen Fidel's) hatred of gay sex is done for love, because 'gay sex leads to hell'. Not only this, LGBT lives are understood as being dangerous for LGBT people and this is, he argues, supported by research done by and for LGBT people:

> 'There are many studies that show the ill effects of same sex attraction. It reduces lifespan by 20 years, it leads to sexual health issues. *Xtra*, a homosexual magazine, shows the health issues of LGBT people, including suicide and substance abuse. Health issues are endemic to

the community. Believe the LGBT community. It harms your body, mind, heart and soul this lifestyle.' (John Henry Westen, fieldnotes, quotes are approximations)

The use (or misuse) of LGBT community-based research reframes the effects of prejudice and marginalization as the natural implications of LGBT lifestyles. Western argues it is therefore hate *not* to tell people about the inherent health risks of a LGBT lifestyle. Loving children is crucial to his contentions and training them in what he sees as these truths protects them from what he claims is the damage created by LGBT lives, which Westen argues, *from* LGBT research and media, are the dangers of these 'lifestyles'.

Here the dangers to children go beyond predatory homosexual infiltrators in the church to broader contestations of how ideas about sexual and gender liberation is infiltrating school (and other) settings. The threat posed by emerging landscapes of sexual and gender rights and equalities, it was argued at the Lumen Fidei conference, need to be opposed in order to 'protect' *their* children. Protecting their children, and not all children, is linked to the loss of control of national morals, as well as the perceived loss of authority of Catholic schools (Nash and Browne 2019). In this conference, the updated curriculum of primary schools (with positive representations of LGBT people), in particular, was held up as posing the biggest threat (see also Nash and Browne, 2019; 2020). Young children are seen not only as vulnerable but as impressionable to the detriment of their moral upbringing. Thus, the loss of control within primary schools is an imminent threat to 'our children':

The worst snares are laid for children. Books in primary school – 'Tale of two dads' [said in a mocking tone with a faux US accent]. *Heather Has Two Mums, Mama, Mummy and Me*. The Heather book defies biological facts – she does have a daddy. [Audience titters]. He mocks Todd Parr. It is 'delivered in a playful way' and derisively reads the blurbs of his books. 'This is used in primary schools to poison the image of marriage in children. It upsets children and confuses them. A 5-year-old asked their parents if it is OK to have two mummies.' It turns out that the '5-year-old was afraid because Daddy would have to leave it was OK to have two mummies'. (John Lacken, quotes are approximations from fieldnotes)

Lacken seeks to denormalize that which is made normal through books that are aimed at children and that encourage inclusion and acceptance not only of LGBT people but also of difference more broadly. The 'love' constituting the central themes of these books, is described as improper and as 'poison'.

This is a threat not only to the safety of (presumably heterosexual) children and families, but to their moral fibre by creating confusion and upset in children who no longer have the stability of 'the truth'. The threat here is not predatory gay men, but the inclusive landscapes of schools. They see that a lack of hatred for LGBT 'lifestyles' (rather than people, which is a key distinction) results in an equivalence of same sex marriage with 'traditional' marriage. The presumed innocent citizen – a child at school on this context – is once again read as being threatened through legislative and inclusive social landscapes. This seeks to move heteroactivists from a position of hater, to a position of those who love and seek to protect children from the dangerous moral landscapes of 21st century that support sexual and gendered inclusions.

In their desire to detach the 'hater' from those proclaiming 'the truth', Christian Concern asked the following question: 'Which is more hateful?

- telling people that the Bible calls homosexual behaviours sin;
- calling for businesses to discriminate against church members;
- calling for a church to be burnt'. (Christian Concern, Email: 11 September 2020)

These questions and the call to identify the 'real haters', focuses attention on those who would burn down churches and discriminate against church members for reading biblical passages. In the questions posed, the supposed innocence of the language of 'telling people' is juxtaposed with the language of 'calling for' to illustrate a contrast between the innocent articulation of 'the truth' by heteroactivists compared to LGBT people spreading dangerous hatred against them. The impetus for this argument was a comment made by a pastor that suggested the cancellation of pride was 'Wonderful news' (Christian Concern, Email: 8 September 2020). When postings in response to this statement suggested 'let's burn a church (clown face)', they were reported to the police and 'Josh [the pastor] was warned that he could be breaking a law, and told he ought to keep his views in a *"safe environment"'* (Christian Concern, Email: 11 September 2020). The 'safe environment' does not assume that these views will not be shared but instead asks for a compartmentalization of them outside of the public sphere of social media. In the retelling of this story, the naming of 'Josh' humanizes him, and demonizes both those as a 'mob', who would burn down the church and those who criminalized him for 'telling' what he sees as 'the truth'. The posing of 'which is more hateful?' as a rhetorical question then allows for resistance to and dissent from LGBT inclusions, and welcomes the cancellation of Pride. It does so by reversing the rhetoric of discrimination. In this reading, those who are protected by hate speech legislation protecting denigration of gender identity and sexual orientation are the ones who will discriminate. The landscape of hate is not, in this telling, created by the pastor celebrating the cancellation of Pride but instead by the 'mob' and those who would 'discriminate against all 'church members'.

Conclusion

There are few explorations of the experiences of those accused of hate crimes. In examining a particular group of heteroactivists, this chapter has explored how they seek to push against accusations of hate and the criminalization of their speech/actions as 'hate crime'. While the focus has been organizations that understand themselves as Christian, many of the arguments they make are secular and based in/on the societies in which they exist. Heteroactivists rework linguistic understandings of both legal and cultural terms in order to evade accusations of criminal 'hate speech' as well as social opprobrium. They argue that their speech is not homophobic by attempting to narrow the definition of hate speech. They do so in multiple ways, and in the UK, this includes challenging legal definitions, often through seeking 'freedom' to critique sexualities and gender identities. They seek to show that labelling such critiques as hate has negative consequences for them and for broader society, which becomes less 'free'. Creating themselves, and those who agree with them, as the innocent citizens who would be subject to unjust prosecution, they also seek to rework 'hate and love'. This operates to make space not only to develop arguments that counter sexual and gender equalities but also to link themselves with love rather than hate, and indeed as loving through hating that which is 'evil'. The use of the term 'mob' to rework a narrative of hate illustrates key responses to heteroactivism, and how these responses are re-read and used to further heteroactivist causes.

Another key means of addressing heteroactivists' discussions is to show that they are hateful and harmful, however much they might protest. This is important and empowering work, yet it can also feed into the heteroactivist tropes and discourses discussed here. Creating inclusive landscapes by naming and contesting hatred, prejudice and discrimination and legislating for inclusion is pitted against free speech by heteroactivists. Further, the right to challenge and debate the dangers of these laws by those who seek to reiterate heteronormativity is framed as the pinnacle of social life and civilized societies. They seek to create controversy around these inclusions by reworking the discourses of hate and homophobia and proclaiming love and care for the foundations of civilized and free societies. Heteroactivists contest positions that set them up as the creators of landscapes of hate and they have been effective in setting up oppositions which mobilize, enemies/allies, right/wrong.

It is crucial that society continues to address hate through hate crime legislation and to challenge other forms of heteroactivism that seek to deflect or overturn positive social change for LGBTQ people. Perhaps alongside these efforts, we also need to consider how 'hating the hatred' reiterates modes of being, knowing and doing that reinforce particular frames of power for engaging with each other. We know that oppositional politics are important, empowering and necessary, especially for those who are made vulnerable through the reiteration of hegemonic power relations.

While our work to date documents and analyses heteroactivist arguments, we have become increasingly interested in how we might approach 'the other' differently. Our current research project entitled 'Beyond Opposition' works to consider other forms of engagement with those who fundamentally disagree around changes to sexual and gender cultures and laws (see www.beyondopposition.org).[8] Oppositions are often so engrained, reiterated and reinforced, that it is difficult to think in non-binary, post-oppositional ways (Keating, 2013; Bhattacharyya, 2015). It requires deep engagement with self and it cannot be for everyone, as those engaging in mediation, conflict resolution and transitional justice will testify. As Anzaldúa and Keating (2002, 3) argue, such border crossings are not a safe space as it 'moves us into unfamiliar territory and does not grant safe passage'. This danger is not one-sided, it will be dangerous for all, because it involves reworking power relations and reconsidering hegemonies. It is necessarily destabilizing; however, perhaps we can also explore the potentials. 'Beyond Opposition' asks questions such as: 'What would it mean to engage the "hateful other" in new ways that refuse oppositionalities and instead seek to rehumanise the other?' and 'How might this operate to defuse social polarizations and divisions?'. Such questions ask for a different approach to 'hate' and 'haters', recognizing the political import of the moves to name and stop 'hate', and also the limitations of these namings.

Notes

1. Beyond Opposition Research Project, available from: https://beyondopposition.org/
2. Social Sciences and Humanities Research Council Grant (2015–2019) entitled Resisting recognition: Transnational activism in Canada and Great Britain (435-2014 – 0071) and Social Sciences and Humanities Research Council Insight Development Grant (2012 – 2014), entitled Shifting resistances: emerging international challenges to lesbian, gay, bisexual and trans rights in Canada and Great Britain (430-2012-0032).
3. https://www.lumenfidei.ie/the-lumen-fidei-institute/
4. (https://christianconcern.com/about/). This aspect of the research was undertaken through signing up to lists as part of the SHRCC study and also covered under ethical approvals for the Beyond Opposition research (www.beyondopposition.org). Christian Concern aligns itself with the Anglican church in the UK but is also critical of it for its inclusions around sexualities and genders.
5. We receive Christian Concern and other organizations' emails where they are open for all to sign up to.

⁶ Coroners and Justice Act 2009, c. 25, UK. Available from: https://www.legislation.gov.uk/ukpga/2009/25/contents

⁷ https://www.lifesitenews.com/

⁸ This project has received funding from the European Research Council under the European Union's Horizon 2020 research and innovation programme (Grant agreement No.817897).

References

Anzaldúa, G. and Keating, A.L. (2002) *This Bridge We Call Home: Radical Visions for Transformation*, London, New York: Routledge.

Bhattacharyya, G. (2015) 'Racialized consciousness and class mobilizations', *Ethnic and Racial Studies*, 38(13): 244–50.

Bell, D. and Binnie, J. (2000) *The Sexual Citizen: Queer Politics and Beyond*, Cambridge: Polity Press.

Boulila, S.C. (2019) 'Race and racial denial in Switzerland', *Ethnic and Racial Studies*, 42(9): 1401–18.

Browne, K. and Bakshi, L. (2013) *Ordinary in Brighton?: LGBT, Activisms and the City*, London and New York: Routledge.

Browne, K. and Nash, C.J. (2015) 'Opposing same-sex marriage, by supporting civil partnerships: resistances to LGBT equalities', in N. Barker and D. Monk (eds) *From Civil Partnership to Same-Sex Marriage 2004–2014: Interdisciplinary Reflections*, London, New York: Routledge, pp 71–88.

Browne, K. and Nash, C.J. (2017) 'Heteroactivism: beyond anti-gay', *ACME: An International Journal for Critical Geographies*, 16(4): 643–52.

Browne, K. and Nash, C.J. (2018) 'Resisting marriage equalities: the complexities of religion', in N. Bartolini, S. MacKian and S. Pile (eds) *Geographies of Spirituality*, London and New York: Routledge.

Browne, K. and Nash, C.J. (2020) 'In Ireland we "love both"? Heteroactivism in Ireland's anti-repeal ephemera', *Feminist Review*, 124(1): 51–67.

Browne, K., Bakshi, L. and Lim, J. (2011) '"It's something you just have to ignore": understanding and addressing contemporary lesbian, gay, bisexual and trans safety beyond hate crime paradigms', *Journal of Social Policy*, 40(4): 739–56.

Browne, K., Munt, S.R. and Yip, A.K.T. (eds) (2010) *Queer Spiritual Spaces: Sexuality and Sacred Spaces*, Aldershot: Ashgate.

Burack, C. (2015) 'From heterosexuality to holiness: psychoanalysis and ex-gay Ministries', *Psychoanalysis, Culture and Society*, 20: 220–7.

Butler, J. (2006) *Born Again: The Christian Right Globalized*, London: Pluto Press.

Christian Concern (2021a) 'About section', Available from: https://christianconcern.com/about/ [Accessed 25 February 2021].

Christian Concern (2021b) 'Pastor told not to offend gay Pride as mob threaten to burn down his church', Available from: https://christianconc ern.com/news/pastor-told-not-to-offend-gay-pride-as-mob-threaten-to-burn-down-his-church/ [Accessed 25 February 2021].

Duggan, L. (2002) 'The new homonormativity: the sexual politics of neoliberalism', in R. Castronovo and D.D. Nelson (eds) *Materializing Democracy: Towards a Revitalized Cultural Politics*, Durham, NC: Duke University Press, pp 175–94.

Haritaworn, J. (2015) *Queer Lovers and Hateful Others*, London: Pluto Press.

Irish Department of Justice (2020) 'Legislating for hate speech and hate crime in Ireland report', Available from: http://www.justice.ie/en/JELR/ Pages/Legislating_for_Hate_Speech_and_Hate_Crime_in_Ireland_Rep ort [Accessed 25 February 2021].

Keating, A.L. (2013) *Transformation Now! Toward a Post-Oppositional Politics of Change*, Champaign, IL: University of Illinois Press.

Kiska, R. (2020) 'Scottish Hate Crime Bill over-regulates free speech', *Christian Concern*, 8 May, Available from: https://christianconcern.com/ news/scottish-hate-crime-bill-over-regulates-free-speech/) [Accessed 25 February 2021].

Kuhar, R. and Paternotte, D. (2017) *Anti-Gender Campaigns in Europe: Mobilising Against Equality*, London: Rowman and Littlefield.

Liberty Central (2010) 'Coroners and Justice Act 2009', *The Guardian*, 23 March, Available from: https://www.theguardian.com/commen tisfree/libertycentral/2009/jan/19/coroners-justice-bill [Accessed 25 February 2020].

Lumen Fidei (2018) *A Conference of Catholic Families*, Available from: https:// www.lumenfidei.ie/a-conference-of-catholic-families/ [Accessed 25 February 2020].

Maguire, H., McCartan, A., Nash, C.J. and Browne, K. (2019) 'The enduring field: exploring researcher emotions in covert research with antagonistic organizations', *Area*: 51: 299–306.

Moseley, C. (2020) Beware government bill seeking licence for criminality, Available from: https://christianconcern.com/comment/beware-governm ent-bill-seeking-licence-for-criminality/ [Accessed 19 August 2021].

Murray, D. (2009) *Homophobias*, London: Duke University Press.

Nash C.J. and Browne K. (2019) 'Resisting the mainstreaming of LGBT equalities in Canadian and British schools: sex education and trans school friends', *Environment and Planning C: Politics and Space*, 39(1): 74–93.

Nash, C.J. and Browne, K. (2020) *Heteroactivism: Resisting Lesbian, Gay, Bisexual and Trans Rights and Equalities*, London: Zed Books.

Nash, C.J., Maguire, H. and Gorman-Murray, A. (2019) 'LGBTQ communities, public space and urban movement: towards mobility justice in the contemporary city', in N. Cook and D. Butz (eds) *Mobilities, Mobility Justice and Social Justice*, London and New York: Routledge, pp 188–200.

Puar, J. (2007) *Terrorist Assemblages: Homonationalism in Queer Times*, Durham, NC: Duke University Press.

Public Order Act (1986) c. 64 Part 3A Inflammatory material Section 29JA, amended 08/05/2008, Available from: https://www.legislation.gov.uk/ukpga/1986/64/section/29JA/1996-10-17 [Accessed 19 August 2021].

Richardson, D. (2017) 'Rethinking sexual citizenship', *Sociology*, 51(2): 208–24.

Stein, A. (2001) *The Stranger Next Door: The Story of a Small Community's Battle Over Sex, Faith, and Civil Rights*, Boston: Beacon Press.

Stychin, C. and Herman, D. (eds) (2001) *Sexuality in the Legal Arena*, London: Athlone Press.

UK Citizens Advice (nd) 'Sexual orientation and transgender identity hate crime', Available from: https://www.citizensadvice.org.uk/law-and-courts/discrimination/hate-crime/sexual-orientation-and-transgender-identity-hate-crime/ [Accessed 25 February 2021].

UK Home Office (2019) *Hate Crime, England and Wales (2018/19)*, 18 October, Available from: https://assets.publishing.service.gov.uk/government/uploads/system/uploads/attachment_data/file/839172/hate-crime-1819-hosb2419.pdf [Accessed 25 February 2021].

Weeks, J. (2007) *The World We Have Won: The Remaking of Erotic and Intimate Life*, Oxon: Routledge.

Weiss, M.L. and Bosia, M.J. (2013) *Global Homophobia: States, Movements, and the Politics of Oppression*, Champaign, IL: University of Illinois Press.

Yip, A.K.T. and Nynäs, P. (2016) 'Re-framing the intersection between religion, gender and sexuality in everyday life', in A.K.T. Yip and P. Nynäs (eds) *Religion, Gender and Sexuality in Everyday Life*, London and New York: Routledge, pp 1–16.

11

Speaking Back and Seeing Beyond the Landscapes of Hate

Rick Bowler and Amina Razak

Introduction

This chapter sets out some thoughts on the difficult business of resisting the desensitization, colonization and violence in everyday encounters with British racism which continues to occupy and whitewash space in northern landscapes of England. It has been argued that whiteness 'circulates as an axis of power around the world' (Shire, 2008: 8) and this requires vigilance because white people and dominant culture can operate from a 'social desensitization to racism' (Meer, 2020: 10–11). This desensitization creates divergence between the lived experience of racialized minorities and the matter-of-fact assumption in public discourse that race does not matter (Harries, 2018).

The reality of racism is that it is deeply woven into the day to day conduct of everyday life. Its logic masks the lived racialized experience for Black and Global Majority (BGM) people who in everyday settings encounter violent racism and more commonplace racial microaggressions.[1] This real-world view where racisms are understood to be an everyday phenomenon (Essed, 1991), highlights the importance of speaking back and seeing beyond the extreme and mundane encounters in public places of English northern landscapes. This is important because in these everyday moments of encounter where difference and similarity are assessed and identified (Darling and Wilson, 2016: 1), the foundations are established for enabling or limiting the scope of acts of racism to flourish. Darling and Wilson (2016: 2) argue that: 'encounters are centrally about the maintenance, production and reworking of difference [while also offering] points of possible transformation and an opening to change'.

The narratives offered in this chapter pinpoint examples of these encounters and identify commonplace experiences of racism that appear unfamiliar to white people in majoritarian white spaces because whiteness 'is made' (Garner, 2015: 20) and becomes 'the default setting for human' (Garner, 2010: 119). These logics of race woven into whiteness are the absent presence in the stories told to the public through the formal education curriculum from which most white people learn about Britain's racial reality (Tomlinson, 2019). The logic of white supremacy justified by the racial science of eugenics posited ideas about the innateness and permanence of 'race' despite the reality that 'neither race nor racism has foundations in science' (Rutherford, 2020: 186). These racial logics are reproduced in everyday settings (Bowler, 2013, 2018; Meer, 2020).

The chapter draws upon lived experiences, including from the authors, to expose the conditions in which the commonplace racial microaggressions alongside violent forms of racist hate appear. In Britain, a hate crime counts when officially recorded by and convicted within the Criminal Justice System. In everyday settings racially targeted hate is regularly encountered at multiple scales and in multiple forms, which are shaped through the logics of white supremacy. This framing of hate identifies that 'Cultures of racism are ... created and reinforced in localities that become hostile environments' (Chakraborti and Garland, 2009: 125).

Our interest is in identifying moments and building momentum to challenge and change those cultures of racism that are the foundations for landscapes of 'race'-based hate. The storied experiences in the chapter identify racist encounters as normative. We argue that if the only focus for public officials is on acts of violent racism this clouds the deep roots of everyday racial thought (re)produced in the spaces where whiteness as a colonial and neo postcolonial supremacist belief system is left unchallenged (Schwarz, 2011; Garner, 2015). It is the everyday conditions that make the environment hostile and 'hateful extremism' grow (Khan, 2019). This then makes speaking back so difficult. It blocks the understanding that everyday encounters where differences collide, are also moments where transformative possibilities are made, and this is where seeing beyond is of critical importance.

The sections that follow set out ideas on anti-racist youth work education, the current context and the historic amnesia woven into Britain's response to its own racial formation (Shire, 2008). We then offer two sections on speaking back and seeing beyond. The first, 'Author Reflections', are strategic narratives utilized to situate ideas for practical applicability about the importance to speak back and see beyond the everyday racism woven into dominator cultural habits of being. The second, titled 'Gendered and Cultural Forms', draws upon data from young people and youth workers from research undertaken by the authors (Razak, 2009; Bowler and Razak, 2017, 2019, 2020). We conclude with thoughts about the importance of nuancing simplistic binaries, being mindful of transformative possibilities, and recognizing intersectionality in seeing beyond.

The conceptual and contextual landscape

> hate is produced in a context where the blame for an economic crisis is placed on its victims, and in the process generates further victims of hate. (Burnett, 2017: 217)

Anti-racist education acknowledges that in conceptualizing how the system of racism underpinned by white supremacist logics can be eliminated, it is important to engage critically with the reality that 'whiteness ... is not a natural, unchangeable phenomenon' (Alcoff, 2015: 117). It is this understanding that affords BGM people and their allies a means of seeing beyond how 'race infects and distorts' (Eddo-Lodge, 2017: 81).

In anti-racist youth work the concepts of waking up and walking with (Bowler, 2013) are important for the participation of minoritized and socio-economically disadvantaged young people in their communities and wider society (Craig, 2018). The current British government has embarked in a culture war where their concept of 'woke' (Hunt, 2020) is used as a device to diminish anti-racist education and deny the extent of systemic and structural racism (Olusoga, 2021; Treloar and Begum, 2021; UN, 2021).

The authors' conceptual frame utilizes stories from the margins to expose racism's reality (Chakrabarty et al, 2014). Dominant narratives connecting the Empire to Brexit leave British racism imbricated in the structure and culture of our contemporary politics (Tomlinson, 2019). The absence of racism in the British nation story is made known in the author narratives, to offer an alternative lens from which to 'redress the racist epistemological strictures of a discursive orientation toward whiteness' (Jaima, 2019: 211). We do this because we recognize that speaking back to racism in everyday life is also acknowledging that 'the dominant culture is also the dominator culture' (hooks, 2013: 24).

An anti-racist youth work approach (Aluffi-Pentini and Lorenz, 1996; Bowler, 2013, 2018; Bowler and Razak, 2019, 2020) underpins the lens from which the authors understand the daily encounters of racism identified in this chapter. Anti-racist youth work builds an empowered agency in young people to speak back and see beyond the racisms that pervade their everyday relationships and opportunities. The experience of reaction, immobilization and being proactive to racisms everyday reality, are critical considerations in understanding racisms' reach. They necessitate consideration of resilience, resistance and agency (Maynard and Stuart, 2018) in speaking back and seeing beyond under a context of hateful extremism and ongoing government neglect.

It has been argued that since the financial crisis of 2008 UK governments have abandoned anti-racist policy (Craig, 2018; Garner, 2015). This has enabled government to devise and implement a national narration of hostility to racialized minorities that has encouraged hateful extremism.[2] In the chasm where white privilege and heritage are given space to thrive, the 'fantasy of British uniqueness' (Naidoo, 2008: 1) occupies the mindset of white working-class people precariously trying to make sense of the austerity ravaged post-industrial places in northern England (Cooper and Whyte, 2017; Winlow et al, 2017).

The lack of a governmental anti-racist strategy leaves community engagement for BGM people as marginal to policy (Afridi, 2018) and critical pedagogical work with young people absent of funding and support (Bowler, 2013, 2018). The lack of a governmental youth policy has enabled the decimation of the infrastructure of support to young people and communities (Hughes et al, 2014; Bond and Hallsworth, 2017; Weale, 2020). The socio-economic impact of Brexit remains unknown but widening social divisions including a rise in far-right activity, remain unhealed (Bowler, 2017; Burnett, 2017; Booth, 2019).

Neoliberal governance has limited the space for social and communitarian considerations about the material reality of inequality (Hall et al, 2015). We are now living in a country where 56 per cent of people in poverty are in work (Barry, 2020) and where the poverty rate is twice as high for BGM groups than for white groups (Social Metrics Commission, 2020). People living in poverty have few structural opportunities to participate in speaking about their own lived experiences and the identification of their own concerns. In the North of England, racial diversity and racial inequalities are growing (Runnymede Trust, 2019). This growth in diversity and inequality runs alongside a rise in far-right racist activity (Winlow, et al, 2017; Lowles and Ryan 2020), where ongoing colour coded racism has been amplified by cultural and Islamophobic racisms (Hopkins, et al, 2020).

In Britain, many white politicians, and public figures, including identified racists, claim they are not racist at all, yet systemic and structural racism persists (Lammy, 2020; Meer, 2020). The obfuscation of the truth about the racial reality of Britain's heritage has the appearance of a neutral default position. It is, more accurately, a strategic reproduction of whiteness, articulated by many people through a particular set of habits and meanings, where they have come to believe the political deception that being white is being British and BGM people are not (Schwarz, 2011).

There are no innate essential characteristics to nationhood and identity, the racialization of nationhood is entirely a social formation and this contestation about who belongs in everyday public space are the instances of encounter when speaking back to racism and seeing beyond 'white nation fantasies' (Hage, 2000) become critical moments for change.

The creation of a Home Office 'hostile environment working group' in 2012 by the UK Conservative-led coalition government, discursively produced stories demonizing minority groups (Grierson, 2018). This hostile public culture combined with the policy of austerity to mark as abject 'the migrant and the home-grown scrounger' (Burnett, 2017: 218). This combination increased resentment and social division between and within minoritized ethnic and religious communities and white people. The current racial reality in the North East of England is a region being targeted by far-right demonstrations of hateful extremism with the city of Sunderland attracting the majority of these (Hopkins et al, 2020).

In identifying the targeting of Muslims by far-right activists, a North East England based report on Islamophobia and Anti-Muslim Hatred identified that 27.5 per cent of Muslim and 33.3 per cent of non-Muslim respondents experienced racist incidents daily, with 80.9 per cent of Muslim respondents targeted by unknown perpetrators (Hopkins et al, 2020). In a report on young people growing up in Sunderland, Finlay et al (2020) echo the work of Bowler and Razak (2017, 2019) to identify that racism and Islamophobia are everyday experiences for BGM young people in Sunderland, limiting the places these young people feel safe to go. It is also clear that women are the group most targeted by the hateful extremism of the far right (Bowler and Razak, 2017, 2019; Hopkins et al, 2020).

Speaking back and seeing beyond: author reflections

Racism always intersects with gender, age, ethnicity, faith, culture, education, family, disability, sexuality and class. The authors were born, grew up and educated in Britain. They both have experienced and continue to experience regular reminders that the dominator culture hails their bodies as not belonging. Speaking back and seeing beyond are thus essential standpoints to challenge the politics that maintain social division, hateful extremism and the 'white racial strategies' (Preston, 2009: 193) sutured into British/English exceptionalism.

The decision to speak back and see beyond the system of racism takes cognizance of the need to offer 'meaningful resistance to dominator culture' [by] 'asserting agency' (hooks, 2013: 37). The purpose for us to share these personal experiences of racisms and our struggles with speaking back and beyond is to expose the 'hidden racialized power dynamics' (Bilge, 2013: 2) embedded within everyday British life and the trauma of it.

As we set out in the Introduction to this chapter, the importance of maintaining a focus on the 'broader, more banal, flow of "everyday" encounters, exclusion, violence or solidarities' (Alexander and Byrne, 2020: 3) is to recognize that hate seeps into these moments and therefore encounters need to be understood as one of the sites for struggle in anti-racist education work (Bowler, 2013; 2018).

Rick: What do you think about speaking back?

Amina: I think speaking back is contextual. I think it depends on where you are, what context you are in and if enabled to be able to speak back. I think there are two ways of speaking back. Reactive is in response to racism and proactive is in challenging it.

Rick: You had a recent experience with racism.

Amina: Yes, with the [white] man at the petrol station. I wanted to speak back to him, I wanted to react to his abuse to me and my daughter, but I couldn't, given the nature of where I was, who I was with. I was with my 8-year-old daughter [in a predominantly white public space] and I felt vulnerable, so I felt unable to speak back. I chose another avenue to speak back to him, which was reporting the incident to the police. I moved from the reactive to recognize the physical danger myself and my daughter were in, to being proactive. I was seeking a way to speak back, telling him that his racist mind set, and violent masculinity was not going to stop me from occupying the place of belonging in my city.

Rick: Have you felt this before?

Amina: When I think back on my life, growing up into my teenage years, my early adult years, I had many direct personal experiences of it [racism] and I often would speak back in a reactive way. As an adult there have been many instances [of racism] where I've chosen not to speak back and I've just thought well this is a factor of everyday life, put it away, compartmentalize it and forget about it. It is very painful [emotionally, epistemically] it's when other [racist] incidents occur. It brings back all the experiences that you've had in your life, from the ones that you had at school all the way into adulthood.

           The power of lifelong experiences of daily microaggressions, chip away at you slowly, they have the power to do more damage. These microaggressions inflict small wounds and I mean, small wounds all the time, and those [racist experiences] are the ones that are more damaging, especially if they are inflicted by people that you know or work with. I think those are more difficult to manage. In speaking back, we don't think about the trauma of racism. We don't think about the impact of racism on ourselves, and I think that as BGM people, we don't come to think of racism as trauma but racism as being everyday life and we compartmentalize it.

Rick: Whom do we talk to about this?

Amina: We might tell somebody that we had a racist experience [a friend or family member] but we don't give the space for it, for us to have a discussion, to explore. We often silence ourselves. It is difficult to find the time to share. It is a complicated experience to articulate. We might describe the event. We might tell somebody that for example I went to the shops, and I was abused. We don't talk about how that made us feel. We don't talk about how we are going to deal with that emotionally. I think if we (BGM people) were to talk about the trauma of daily racism and be listened to then it would be less painful, and we wouldn't be so traumatized. What do you think?

Rick: Listening to you sparked off for me how emotional and painful racism is. As you were speaking, I was thinking how the impact of racism is gendered and intersectional. These forms of racist abuse impact upon masculinity. I have spent my whole life encountering specific forms of violent masculine posturing. As you were talking of your experiences with racism, I was sad to remember times when I was terrified as a child, a teenager and then into my adult life. I was also thinking about your reactive and proactive explanations of speaking back. It is meaningful and made me think of racist attacks I have put away.

I remember coming back from work after a long day and two [white] men on the bus became overtly racially abusive to me. It started with racist name-calling. I was tired and was thinking about wanting to get home to my family, but their aggression and harassment got louder. I was tired and frightened. As I got off the bus, we had a confrontation. They suddenly seemed less frightening. They went a different way from me. I was relieved but my blood pressure was sky high, and the blood was running through my body. My heart rate was so high, and I think it's like you say it, as you get through one incident it now is attached to all the others. It is the constant nature of the racist encounters. They can be weekly, monthly, big or small, the microaggressions at work, on the bus, in the street, it's constant and it wears you down.

Amina: It does wear you down.

Rick: It happens so many times in your life. It acts like an added burden. It made me think much more about repressed trauma and everyday racism. When I became a parent, I was not expecting my children to experience racism. That amplifies hurt and brings back the pain. It is as you said earlier, what age? That is the question we start asking ourselves. What age are they going to be before they have their first racist incident, that first public marking of them as racially different? The older they are the luckier, because they are fortunate to hold off what is seemingly an inevitable intrusion and attack on their personal being, and a silencing of them because they're not supposed to belong here. That is what Kobayashi and Peake (2000) identify as whiteness occupying space.

I agree with you about how the impact of racism is suppressed, our experiences of racial violence, the everyday microaggressions, denial, dismissal, they are so often left in silence. I hardly talk about the emotional impact of this stuff, I talk about it with close family and friends who can hold me, but I don't really talk to my colleagues about the emotional impact of racist trauma. I teach about racism but always with a protective eye on how 'this thing' [racism] can be engaged with.

Amina: There's no space to begin to articulate how we feel, and this is something you think about and live with every day. Those emotions constantly linger in the back of your mind about how you feel, how people behave and make you feel and like you said, there are only certain people you can have those discussions with. Those honest discussions can be hard even with other BGM people because when you bring up racism it's often dismissed as something we have just to deal with. So, you never really explore the emotional effect of racism and the impact it has on our mental health and emotional/physical wellbeing and none of that is discussed.

Rick: The training as an academic into the institutional practices of teaching and learning or professional conduct, the idea that one could be emotional is somewhat kept out. I know it's there in feminist praxis, in sensitive methodological design and in critical race theory but it remains somewhat marginal knowledge from the so-called business of 'facts' 'efficiency' and 'outputs' that saturate dominator culture.

Amina: When interviewing BGM people about their racial reality we must be aware that very often they have been denied, abused, terrified and othered, we have to humanize our approach and allow for understanding and care. The young people from YAV (a youth project in Sunderland) were so thoughtful about seeing a possibility for a change, they wanted to create safe spaces to talk with other young people about their experiences of the world they are growing up in.

I think YAV through the work they do have helped them to engage in what Yosso (2005) has called 'aspirational culture', so these young people aspire to meet other young people and share their experiences in safe pedagogical spaces.

Rick: It made me realize how easy it is for white standards to prevail in everyday settings. I have encountered so many conversations where the white person who is ostensibly the access point to the system, reads our experience as not about challenging the unjust system. They in effect silence and block transformational possibilities.

Amina: Seeing beyond has come up in several interviews. One of the YAV youth workers in her interview spoke of how she feels unable to see beyond the weight of persistent racism. This was powerful because in her own life she cannot see a future where racism will not impact on her family and her life. She told me she could not see a time in which racism will cease to exist. I found that sad and I feel sad to hear young people say that.

It seems that white people don't see racism. But when you alert them [white people] to racism they become defensive. It's almost as though you've accused them of being a racist, and they don't want to engage in that conversation. I don't know where we go to resolve this, but it is called 'white fragility' (DiAngelo, 2019).

Rick: I think we must find a way beyond and that's what I thought was so powerful about the young people's voices. The people who listen to those voices need to learn to hear experience and aspiration in the contexts they are made. Everything is in context. There are times when we choose not to speak back, because the context and the backlash will be too difficult, dangerous, terrifying, or we feel very vulnerable. Under the current forms of governance that's not recognized.

Amina: Yes, but what practical things need to happen to see beyond? I sometimes cannot see beyond. I feel disempowered and don't know what we can do to change things. Looking at experiences of speaking back, I have often experienced a backlash, I wanted to see beyond but when I spoke back the response from the white system was, defence, defence, defence and no action. I found the positive attempts to help identify and challenge racism became the problem, as I spoke back, I was challenged by the embedded dominant culture, they weren't attuned to hear my voice or to recognize the failings, this process disempowered me.

Speaking back and seeing beyond: gendered and contextual forms

Much of the racist abuse and hateful extremism in the situated geographies of northern England targets women and their assumed religion (Bowler and Razak, 2017; Finlay et al, 2020; Hopkins et al, 2020). The lived experience of many of our research participants spoke of this gendered reality. We identify two typical responses to racism; reactive and proactive with responses very often contextual but also gendered in nature. Reactive is an immediate response to the situation and proactive is a measured response formulated through resistance, resilience, and agency. Using this framework, we bring to the fore the realities of empowerment or disempowered agency, the deep nuances of racism and the realities of the daily silencing of the voice and experiences of BGM young people. Ethical approval for the research drawn upon in the extracts that follow was given by the University of Sunderland and University of Edinburgh. Pseudonyms are used throughout.

Reactive speaking back

'Reactive' responses to racism can take many forms as the author reflections identify. One such response is to adopt the 'it just happens' stance thereby reducing racist experience to a factor of everyday life. This was common for both young women and men:

Ruby: It's so common, you don't think to report it
Zafar: If it happens I'll just deal with it, it's normal. I'm the only coloured person there [in school] it is normal
Sami: You just get used to it.
Boys: [chorus of voices] Yeah.

Gender is important in the reactive responses to racism. Young women expressed reactions to racism that consisted of non-interaction, complete avoidance, or limited exchange:

Rumi: I used to hate going on the buses this was before I wore my scarf, people were being mean chucking McDonald's burgers and things at me and the driver wouldn't do anything and I would say to my parents I can't wait to drive and get my own car then I won't have to face people. ... I was just walking through town coming out of Debenhams into the car park, it was after 5:30 and they said here comes another one, dirty muzzies. I didn't react or anything.

Mehek: I usually try taking the Metro early in the morning before 6:30 because if you go on it after 6:30am [it] gets packed and there are loads of English people [white] around and I feel uncomfortable, and one day I had to go after 6:30, I was the only person in hijab and only non-white person in that cabin, all of them were literally staring at me. ... I had to get down.

While the data suggests that young women prefer to take a non-belligerent approach, young men are likely to become involved in physical altercations with racism directly challenging masculinity (Razak, 2009). Physical responses to racism reinforce and project powerful fearless, aggressive masculinity, they assert and regain control, but this can be contextual and dependent on possible outcomes:

Mansoor: My big sister shall I say used to have trouble every now n again so I used to try and help her, I used to come home n 'see this happened that happened', 'oh I'm gonna go n chin him' y'know, 'how dare you call my sister a paki'.

Shazad: I could tolerate people being prejudiced towards me because of my colour because of my religion maybe because of the way I walked or dressed etc. I was *not* tolerant towards something like that about my family, the only time I would react in a way perhaps I shouldn't was when it was about my family, so if someone said something about my dad I'd react there and then I'd face it and get involved and have fights and stuff like that. I could deal with it with me, in a way it wasn't as offensive to me cos I didn't care, it was just words to me but in a way it was directly attacking my family. It made me reactive towards it, more aggressive towards it and it didn't happen often but when it did happen it happened erm and there was fights.

Bilal: There was racism in our school as well, *loads* of it as well, we used to get in fights n that's probably actually when I got respected cos I got respect from the white school know what I mean, I went to a white school and I used to fight them, English [white] lads.

Proactive speaking back

Responses to racism connect to agency and confidence to respond. Responses that are considered and thought out are what we identify as proactive. Young women articulated action to engage, educate and change perceptions, to subvert the dominant representations of them through a process of recognition and resistance to their misrepresentation in everyday encounters with the majoritarian white community. The young people problematized the orientations of their life worlds, named it and understood how to reframe them:

Ruby: I was asked [by white people] if I was Hindu or Bengali, and then the question was what is Hinduism and what is.

Salma: You can be Bengali and Hindu.

Marwa: They [white people] think it's an ethnicity.

Ruby: And then there were questions on both of them and they had no knowledge of, I'd rather people be educated rather than have thoughts.

To limit the impact and reach of racism and the activities of racists, a proactive response is consciously considered. Take for example Rumi's response to her white colleagues whom she considered to have connected with on a personal level. Her proactive response is, quite possibly, linked to the anti-racist training she receives as part of her role as a youth worker:

Rumi: As soon as I put my hijab on, people start looking at me in different ways as if God knows where she has crawled out from, this piece of cloth has changed people's views towards me being racially abusive physically, virtually … yeah like when I put all my photos up on Facebook have had comments from people who I thought were my friends … started to say what is this around her head has she converted to Muslim? oh my god do I know her? … they started to say things about me on this group I could see comments so I blocked myself away from them, so I deleted a few of them, before I deleted them I put up a status saying, should really look at their own characters before pointing and judging others you're not human enough to be my friend. I removed myself from their social media

Proactive responses are informed by knowledge of available measures and resources:

Rumi: One time there was a van, I was trying to pull in and he just rolled his window down and started giving me loads of abuse just over me pulling in, and I'm like it's my way see that arrow there it's my way, and he just wouldn't stop, kept calling me names on I said you know what enough is enough so I got out and rang 111 ... and reported the crime. ... I was on my way to a meeting where we were engaging with the lot of other social groups, lots of police were there, I spoke to one of my colleagues [police] there.

Young people draw on their empowered agency, resilience, and proactive responses of others around them to emulate a similar position:

Sara: Tanya spoke up about what was happening at work, having her in the team gave me a sense of empowerment to speak about my own experiences, if I was on my own I probably wouldn't have said anything, I think if Tanya was on her own she probably would have but I don't think I would have.

Dilshad: I've come to this job, to this line of work because of racism because of my passion against racism that's why I've come to this job, my passion has always been from a 15-year-old to actually fight racism.

Seeing beyond

A consistent and coherent strategy emerging from the data is to see beyond racism. Young people offered solutions to reach out beyond current safe spaces and networks to make meaningful connections:

Aidhan: The school never talks about racism, if you don't talk about a problem how can you solve it?

Tanisha: The Diwali event that happened, we contributed quite a lot to that, we shared some knowledge to people.

Salima: Do more regular events yeh cos we should be sharing knowledge cos there is more people that [are] unaware of what the [our] culture's like.

Tanisha: Yeh but I think we should focus on even more areas.

Saba: Like cross over the bridge as well to like Monkwearmouth [predominantly white area in Sunderland].

Yaser: What brings people together, communities can come together, you might not know each other but with football instant bond, best way is sports activities, everyone is diverse, some areas are not diverse and others are, so you see brown people on one side and white people on the other and it's not nice that's why we go around get to know each other, they might think bad of each other, that person is dangerous that person is dangerous, and once they know each other from football that bond is created.

The struggle of speaking back and seeing beyond

Mehek: Racism happens with all age groups you know, it really hurts when even children do that, they have no fear of consequences, where are those values, Britain is known for those British values. When British values are so embedded then how does racism happen? All these people attend the same schools and have the same teachers. Where does it go wrong?

Rumi: We can't [overcome racism]. It's the minority. No matter what the council do, parties, melas, it's not going to change the views, some are just racist. No matter how hard you try we've done it. We've had Barnes Park meetups, we've even sold rice and curry, people bought the food and eat it but then they'll turn around and still give you abuse, it doesn't change anything.

Mehek: I was scared to go out and get food from a nearby takeaway, it was just literally 2 minutes away, but I am always in fear that I will get attacked.

In a society where whitewashed nationhood occupies so much space, where the idea of diversity is suggestive of problems, and so little of the history of Britain is public knowledge, the question about how hard it is to speak back and see beyond is important. Speaking back and seeing beyond can lead to, feared and actual, repeated forms of attack, physical, psychological, in our public lives including on career pathways and in funding for projects. Transgressing the dominant norms of the occupied spaces of whiteness are brave actions. The lack of governmental support for anti-racist education leaves working class BGM young people and their white peers pitted against each other as they attempt to make sense of the dominator messages that order the conduct of who can belong.

Conclusion

The search for solutions to commonplace racial microaggressions and hateful extremism requires an attentiveness to listen to the lived experience of BGM people about their everyday encounters with racism. These encounters, where a person's sense of belonging to place is denied, are created by the systemic habits of whiteness and the conduct of white people who uncritically believe their rights and entitlement have been taken from them by BGM people (Garner, 2015).

    The narratives in this chapter identify the importance of being cognizant of the situated geographies, the contexts from which the meaning of the lived experience make sense. The voices in this chapter raise the question about the conditions required to speak back and see beyond. One important element in creating these conditions is the actions that develop safe anti-racist space as a necessary condition for young people to learn how to become consciously empowered agents who can challenge the racist marking of the place, they call home (Bowler and Razak, 2020).

The chapter also highlights the importance of nuance in understanding how people come to find their way in and the way out of the problems caused by racism. It identifies the bravery of young people when they ask for localized change in the relationships with their peers (Bowler and Razak 2017). This is not merely seeking a multicultural dialogue across the ordered spatial divides of whiteness. It suggests that people can transcend their spatially divided enclaves and collectively seek shared answers beyond the place allocated in dominator white nation stories.

Critical anti-racist youth work enables a safe space for young people to meet and develop 'aspirational' as well as 'resistant cultural capital' (Wallace, 2018: 470). This approach to engage young people in a critical exploration of their racial realities enables them to connect with the historic challenges to systems of violent control through the 'power of autonomous organising' (Batsleer, 2018: 130). Batsleer (2018: 131) further identifies intersecting connections where ethno-racial realities are woven within the 'sex-gender regime [and both need] to be made visible, if inequalities and oppressive power dynamics are to be addressed'.

One current manifestation of the power of whiteness is the (re)production of culture wars as a deliberate political strategy from contemporary right-wing Governments (Treloar and Begum, 2021). Culture wars perpetuate the idea that 'white culture', whatever this is meant to be, is somehow under attack from the aspirations for equality by BGM people and for a life free from commonplace racial inequalities, microaggressions and acts of violence. As Miri Song (2014) cogently argues, the idea of cultural equivalence denies the reality of whiteness as a system of cultural supremacy. Listening to and making sense of lived experiences of racism offers an informed alternative to the ways that commonplace encounters and everyday interactions can be devoid of any understanding of the 'vertical lines of power or authority' (Lorde, 2017: 15).

In majority white places such as Sunderland the realities of post-industrial decline, alongside the policy of austerity, has left all working class communities depleted of resources and without opportunity structures to rebuild and re-imagine their futures. These precarious realities have enabled the extreme right to fill a void, to offer racist explanations to structural societal problems (Bowler, 2017; Rushton, 2017). In these situated geographies, the places for diversity to thrive are significantly reduced and under-resourced. As Winlow et al (2017: 72) remind us, 'the racial hatred displayed by many of our [white working class] interviewees is ... rooted in the ideology of the British Empire'.

Context in all its forms is a critical factor to understand encounter. Whiteness as the dominant/dominator culture marks territory in local ways. The importance of our focus on Sunderland and Northern English landscapes is to identify them as ordinary and everyday, and not reified as aberrant or more racist in relation to other cities or regions. If racism is everywhere then confronting this reality requires a recognition that all landscapes are racialized and all people including all white people have a racial reality. Speaking back and seeing beyond the normative power of whiteness requires a recognition of how this global force lives out in everyday encounters within the different landscapes where hate is generated.

The young people and youth workers who spoke with us (Razak, 2009; Bowler and Razak, 2017), continue to show both a confidence/concern that their white peers can/cannot challenge white system privilege and engage in a consciously considered dialogue against commonplace racial microaggressions and acts of violence. 'Public space is ... always a contestation over the legitimacy of inclusion and exclusion' (Springer, 2016: 112). It is this 'legitimacy' underpinned by white standards (Bowler, 2018) that we challenge through speaking back and seeing beyond.

In speaking back, we are engaging in moments of change towards seeing beyond the white ignorance and fragility that occupies public space, perpetuating the 'normativity of whiteness' (Preston, 2009: 25). Speaking back highlights the ways that difference is understood and known in the contexts of its occurrence, but difference also emerges from the encounter itself. It is this emergent possibility that our seeing beyond seeks to influence and change. It is this contingent property inherent in the emancipatory possibilities of spatial encounters that maintains hope (Springer, 2016). The absence of engaged and consciously considered dialogue can leave BGM people feeling that there is nothing beyond the persistence of racist trauma. This racial reality is deeply troubling, and society needs to find a solution to it. For young people, safe space affords an opportunity to articulate their world and 'reclaim resistance and agency' (Yancy, 2018: 270) to speak back and see beyond all landscapes of hate.

Notes

[1] Racial microaggressions are: 'brief and commonplace daily verbal, behavioral, or environmental indignities, that communicate hostile, derogatory, or negative racial slights and insults toward people of color' (Sue et al 2007: 273).

[2] The hostile environment is simultaneously causal of racist practices and a legacy of historic racism. In representing this we offer three contemporary scandals involving the British government to illustrate the culture of denial and obfuscation about British racism.

1. The Torture of the Mau Mau (Oxford Human Rights Hub) https://ohrh.law.ox.ac.uk/the-mau-mau-litigation-justice-at-last/ (accessed 20 May 2022).
2. The Windrush Generation Windrush scandal explained, Joint Council for the Welfare of Immigrants (jcwi.org.uk) (accessed 20 May 2022).
3. The Trojan Horse Incident Education experts voice fury over Ofsted's 'Trojan Horse' schools inquiry, Ofsted, *The Guardian*, www.theguardian.com/education/2014/jun/03/education-experts-ofsted-trojan-horse-birmingham-schools (accessed 20 May 2022).

References

Afridi, A. (2018) 'BME community engagement in the UK and public policy: a brief retrospective', in Craig, G. (ed) *Community Development Race and Ethnicity: Theory, Practice and Policy*, Bristol: Policy Press, pp 25–40.

Alcoff, L.M. (2015) *The Future of Whiteness*, Cambridge: Polity Press.

Alexander, C. and Byrne, B. (2020) 'Introduction', in B. Byrne, C. Alexander, O. Khan, J. Nazroo and W. Shankley (eds) *Ethnicity, Race and Inequality in the UK: State of the Nation*, Bristol: Policy Press, pp 1–15.

Aluffi-Pentini, A. and Lorenz, W. (eds) (1996) *Anti-Racist Work with Young People: European Experiences and Approaches*, Dorset: Russell House Publishing.

Barry, A. (2020) *UK Poverty 2019/2020: Work*, Joseph Rowntree Foundation, Available from: https://www.jrf.org.uk/report/uk-poverty-2019-20-work [Accessed 23 May 2022].

Batsleer, J. (2018) 'Undoing sexism and youth work practice. Seeking equality. Unsettling ideology. Affirming difference. A UK perspective', in P. Alldred, F. Cullen, K. Edwards and D. Fusco (eds) *The Sage Handbook of Youth Work Practice*, London: Sage, pp 1127–39.

Bilge, S. (2013) 'Reading the racial subtext of the Québécois accommodation controversy: an analytics of racialized governmentality', *Politikon*, 40(1): 157–81.

Bond, E. and Hallsworth, S. (2017) 'The degradation and humiliation of young people', in V. Cooper and D. Whyte (eds) *The Violence of Austerity*, London: Pluto Press: pp 75–81.

Booth, R. (2019) 'Racism rising since Brexit vote, nationwide study reveals', *The Guardian*, Available from: https://www.theguardian.com/world/2019/may/20/racism-on-the-rise-since-brexit-vote-nationwide-study-reveals [Accessed 19 May 2020].

Bowler, R. (2013) 'The risky business of challenging risk: youth work and young people through the lens of "race"', in J. Kearney and C. Donovan (eds) *Constructing Risky Identities: Consequences for Policy and Practice*, Basingstoke: Palgrave Macmillan, pp 146–62.

Bowler, R. (2017) *Whiteness, Britishness and the Racist Reality of Brexit*, CASS Working Paper, Sunderland: University of Sunderland.

Bowler, R. (2018) 'Critical youth and community work and its struggle with white standards', in G. Craig (ed) *Community Development Race and Ethnicity: Theory, Practice and Policy*, Bristol: Policy Press, pp 41–60.

Bowler, R. and Razak, A. (2017) *Voicing the Needs of YAV's Young People in Sunderland. Project Report*, Sunderland: University of Sunderland.

Bowler, R and Razak, A. (2019) 'Continuities and change: some reflections on 21 years of anti-racist youth work', *Youth and Policy Journal*, May, Available from: https://www.youthandpolicy.org/articles/continuities-and-change-some-reflections-on-21-years-of-anti-racist-youth-work/ [Accessed 23 May 2022].

Bowler, R. and Razak, A. (2020) 'Young people as cultural critics of the mono cultural landscapes that fail them', *Social Policy Review*, 32: 51–70.

Burnett, J. (2017) 'Austerity and the production of hate', in V. Cooper and D. Whyte (eds) *The Violence of Austerity*, London: Pluto Press, pp 217–23.

Chakraborti, N. and Garland, J. (2009) *Hate Crime: Impact, Causes and Responses*, London: Sage.

Chakrabarty, N., Roberts, L. and Preston, J. (eds) (2014) *Critical Race Theory in England*, Abingdon: Routledge.

Cooper, V. and Whyte, D. (eds) (2017) *The Violence of Austerity*, London: Pluto Press.

Craig, G. (ed) (2018) *Community Organising Against Racism: 'Race', Ethnicity and Community Development*, Bristol: Policy Press.

Darling, J. and Wilson, F.H. (2016) 'The possibilities of encounter', in J. Darling and F.H. Wilson (ed) *Encountering the City: Urban Encounters from Accra to New York*, London: Routledge, pp 1–24.

DiAngelo, R. (2019) *White Fragility: Why It's so Hard for White People to Talk About Racism*, London: Allen Lane.

Eddo-Lodge, R. (2017) *Why I'm No Longer Talking to White People about Race*, London: Bloomsbury.

Essed, P. (1991) *Understanding Everyday Racism: An Interdisciplinary Theory*, London: Sage.

Finlay, R., Nayak, A., Benwell, M., Hopkins, P., Pande, R. and Richardson, M. (2020) *Growing up in Sunderland: Young People, Politics and Place*, Newcastle-upon-Tyne: Newcastle University.

Garner, S. (2010) *Racisms: An Introduction*, London: Sage.

Garner, S. (2015) *The Moral Economy of Whiteness: Four Frames of Racializing Discourse*, London: Routledge.

Grierson, J. (2018) 'Hostile environment: anatomy of a policy disaster', *The Guardian*, 27 August, Available from: www.theguardian.com/uk-news/2018/aug/27/hostile-environment-anatomy-of-a-policy-disaster [Accessed 23 May 2022].

Hage, G. (2000) *White Nation: Fantasies of White Supremacy in a Multicultural Society*, London, Routledge.

Hall, S., Massey, D. and Rustin, M. (eds) (2015), *After Neoliberalism? The Kilburn Manifesto*, London: Lawrence and Wishart.

Harries, B. (2018) *Talking Race in Young Adulthood: Race and Everyday Life in Contemporary Britain*, London: Routledge.

Hopkins, P., Clayton, J. and Tell MAMA (2020) *Islamophobia and Anti-Muslim Hatred in North East England*, Newcastle-upon-Tyne: Newcastle University.

hooks, b. (2013) *Writing Beyond Race: Living Theory and Practice*, London: Routledge.

Hughes, G., Copper, C., Gormally, S. and Rippingale, J. (2014) 'The state of youth work in austerity England: reclaiming the ability to "care"', *Youth and Policy*, 113: 1–14.

Hunt, K. (2020) 'How "woke" became the word of our era', *The Guardian*, 21 November, Available from: https://www.theguardian.com/books/2020/nov/21/how-woke-became-the-word-of-our-era [Accessed 23 May 2022].

Jaima, A. (2019) 'On the discursive orientation toward whiteness', *Journal of Intercultural Studies*, 40(2): 210–24.

Khan, S. (2019) *Challenging Hateful Extremism*, Commission for Countering Extremism, Available from: www.gov.uk/government/publications/challenging-hateful-extremism [Accessed 23 May 2022].

Kobayashi, A. and Peake, L. (2000) 'Racism out of place: thoughts on whiteness and an antiracist geography in the new millennium', *Annals of the Association of American Geographers*, 90(2), 392–403.

Lammy, D. (2020) *Tackling Racial Disparity in the Criminal Justice System: 2020*, Available from: https://www.gov.uk/government/publications/tackling-racial-disparity-in-the-criminal-justice-system-2020 [Accessed 23 May 2022].

Lorde, A. (2017) *Your Silence Will Not Protect You*, London: Silver Press.

Lowles, N. and Ryan, N. (2020) *Fear, Hate and Lies in the Wake of the Pandemic*, Issue 42, London: Hope not Hate Ltd.

Maynard, L. and Stuart, K., (2018) *Promoting Young People's Wellbeing through Empowerment and Agency: A Critical Framework for Practice*, London: Routledge.

Meer, N. (2020) 'Race and social policy: challenges and obstacles', in J. Rees, M. Pomati and E. Heins (eds) *Social Policy Review 32: Analysis and Debate in Social Policy*, Bristol: Policy Press.

Naidoo, R. (2008) 'Fear of difference/fear of sameness: the road to conviviality', in S. Davison and J. Rutherford (eds) *Race, Identity and Belonging: A Soundings Collection*, London: Lawrence and Wishart, pp 72–81.

Olusoga, D. (2021) 'The poisonously patronising Sewell report is historically illiterate', *The Guardian*, 2 April, Available from: https://www.theguardian.com/commentisfree/2021/apr/02/sewell-race-report-historical-young-people-britain [Accessed 23 May 2022].

Preston, J. (2009) *Whiteness and Class in Education*, Dordrecht: Springer.

Razak, A. (2009) *South Asian Young Men: Stories, Accounts and Masculinities*, PhD thesis, University of Edinburgh.

Runnymede Trust, (2019) *Class, Race and Inequality in Northern Towns: Policy Brief*, London: Runnymede Trust, Available from: www.runnymedetrust. org/publications/class-race-and-inequality-in-northern-towns [Accessed 23 May 2022].

Rushton, P. (2017) *The Myth and Reality of Brexit City: Sunderland and the 2016 Referendum*, Sunderland: Centre for Applied Social Sciences, University of Sunderland.

Rutherford, A. (2020) *How to Argue with a Racist: History, Science, Race and Reality*, London: Orion Publishing.

Schwarz, B. (2011) *The White Man's World: Memories of Empire*, Oxford: Oxford University Press.

Shire, G. (2008) 'Introduction: race and racialisation in neo-liberal times', in S. Davison and J. Rutherford (eds) *Race, Identity and Belonging: A Soundings Collection*, London: Lawrence and Wishart, pp 7–18.

Social Metrics Commission (2020) *Measuring Poverty 2020*, London: The Legatum Institute, Available from: https://socialmetricscommission.org. uk/wp-content/uploads/2020/06/Measuring-Poverty-2020-Web.pdf [Accessed 23 May 2022].

Song, M. (2014) 'Challenging a culture of racial equivalence', *The British Journal of Sociology*, 65(1): 107–29.

Springer, S. (2016) *The Anarchist Roots of Geography: Toward Spatial Emancipation*, London: University of Minnesota Press.

Sue, D., Capolidupo, C.M., Torino, G.C. et al (2007) 'Racial microaggressions in everyday life', *American Psychologist*, 62(4): 271–86.

Tomlinson, S. (2019) *Education and Race: From Empire to Brexit*, Bristol: Policy Press.

Treloar, N. and Begum, H. (2021) *Facts Don't Lie: One Working Class: Race, Class and Inequalities*, London: Runnymede Trust, Available from: www. nhsbmenetwork.org.uk/wp-content/uploads/2021/04/Facts-Dont-Lie-2021-Begum-Treloar-.pdf [Accessed 23 May 2022].

UN (2021) *UN Experts condemn UK Commission on Race and Ethnic Disparities Report*, United Nations Office of the High Commissioner, Available from: www.ohchr.org/en/press-releases/2021/04/un-experts-cond emn-uk-commission-race-and-ethnic-disparities-report [Accessed 23 May 2022].

Wallace, D. (2018) 'Cultural capital as whiteness? Examining logics of ethno-racial representation and resistance', *British Journal of Sociology of Education*, 39(4): 466–82.

Weale, S. (2020) 'Youth services suffer 70% funding cut in less than a decade', *The Guardian*, 20 January, Available from: https://www.theguardian.com/society/2020/jan/20/youth-services-suffer-70-funding-cut-in-less-than-a-decade [Accessed 23 May 2022].

Winlow, S, Hall, S. and Treadwell, J. (2017) *The Rise of the Right: English Nationalism and the Transformation of Working-Class Politics*, Bristol: Policy Press.

Yancy, G. (2018) 'Afterword', in A. Johnson, R. Joseph-Salisbury, and B. Kamunge (eds) *The Fire Now: Anti-Racist Scholarship in Times of Explicit Racial Violence*, London: Zed Books, pp 266–74.

Yosso, T.J. (2005) 'Whose culture has capital? A critical race theory discussion of community cultural wealth', *Race Ethnicity and Education*, 8(1): 69–91.

12

Rethinking Responses to Hate: Towards a Socio-ecological Approach

Edward Hall

Introduction

Hate crime policy and practice has multiple objectives: to tackle individual acts of harassment and violence, engage with and support communities targeted, and address broader social attitudes and tensions (Hall, 2013; Walters et al, 2016; Home Office, 2018). It is therefore simultaneously narrowly applied and broadly conceived, and therein lies the significant challenge for its effectiveness. This chapter argues that the current dominant criminal justice response to hate – reporting and prosecuting acts of harassment and violence against those in 'protected characteristics' groups – while crucially important for victims and wider communities, does not address the wider ambitions of government to 'build communities that are bound together by the values of tolerance, equality and mutual respect, and in which there is no room for hate' (Home Office, 2018: 3; see also Chakraborti, 2018). Further, the chapter argues this is because the micro and local contexts and situations, and wider structural factors, that shape the incidence of hate, are not adequately acknowledged or engaged with in the conceptualization, design and enacting of policy. Indeed, these contextual factors are arguably obscured from view to distract from the need to address deeply-embedded challenging issues of exclusion and discrimination. The chapter proposes that an appreciation of the complexity and breadth of landscapes of hate will enable a more effective police and criminal justice, and wider social justice, response to hate, working in partnership with victims of hate, local community groups and other agencies. To do this, a 'socio-ecological' model (Cramer et al, 2020), similar to that employed in studies of social determinants of health, is adopted to examine the different scales of influence that shape the incidence of hate, and to identify potential points and spaces for intervention. The socio-ecological model connects to an emerging public health, preventative response to hate (Iganski and Sweiry, 2016; Cramer et al, 2020).

Critiquing responses to hate

The particular history of hate crime in the UK has determined how hate has been conceptualized in policy. The racist murder of Stephen Lawrence in 1993, and subsequent high-profile violent deaths of others from minority groups, and the inadequate criminal justice response (as noted in Chapter 1), transformed policy and practice on discriminatory harassment and violence. They were 'watershed moment[s]' (Hall, 2103: 34) in several ways. First, the weight placed on the duty of police to record hate incidents and crimes, and for this data to be collated and published in annual public reports to represent the extent of the issue. Second, a broadened scope of hate incidents, so that all are recorded and not just those likely to be classified as crimes (Chakraborti, 2015: 1742). Third, the reporting of a hate incident to be either from the victim or a bystander/witness. Fourth, the recording of minor, 'low-level', 'non-crime' incidents that cumulatively can result in a violent outcome if not addressed (as was evidenced in the Pilkington/Hardwick case, noted in Chapter 1 and discussed later). In sum, hate incidents post-Lawrence demanded of the police a more sophisticated, nuanced and contextualized understanding of and response to bigotry and prejudice. However, reporting of incidents and crimes, and campaigns to encourage victims and communities to report, has become the chief focus for police action. For example, Police Scotland's Annual Plan 2021/22 has a key priority to 'Improve public and stakeholder confidence to enhance reporting of crime, especially domestic abuse, sexual crime, *hate crime*, and human trafficking' (Police Scotland, 2021a: 29, emphasis added). The public-facing page on its website on hate crime has reporting at its centre:

> Police Scotland takes hate crime very seriously and will do everything we can to bring those responsible to justice. If you have been targeted because of your disability, race, religion, sexual orientation or transgender identity, or are aware of someone else who has been targeted, we want you to report it. *Reporting hate crime is important. If you report it, we can deal with it, we can prevent the same thing happening to someone else and together we can work to rid Scotland of hate.* (Police Scotland, 2021b, emphasis added)

The stated potential of reporting to address and even end hate is supported by government policy statements; for example, in the Foreword to the

UK government's 'Action Against Hate' (2016), the then Secretary of State for Communities and Local Government emphasized its central importance: 'Together, if we report every incident of hate crime, we can drive it from our streets' (Home Office, 2016: 5, cited in Chakraborti, 2018: 393).

The number of reported hate crimes has risen steadily since data was first recorded in 2013 (in England and Wales; 2011 in Scotland). In the most recent data (year ending March 2021), 124,091 hate crimes were recorded by police forces in England and Wales (excluding Greater Manchester), an increase of 9 per cent on the previous year. The majority (74 per cent; 85,268) were 'race'-related hate crimes; though lower in total number, there were increases in reported sexual orientation (to 17,135), transgender identity (to 2,630) and disability (to 9,208) hate crimes (Home Office, 2021). These increases have in part been due to 'improvements in [police] recording practices' in the last few years (Home Office, 2020: 5). However, there remains significant evidence of under-reporting of hate incidents and crimes (Corcoran, 2015; Walters et al, 2016; Erentzen and Schuller, 2020). For example, the Crime Survey for England and Wales (Home Office, 2020) estimates almost double the number of hate crimes recorded in police data (190,000 compared to 105,090; it should be noted that there are differences in recording methodology) (Home Office, 2020: 5–6). One explanation is that 'many cases are simply not recognised as hate crimes by the criminal justice agencies, non-governmental organisations, or by victims themselves' (Chakraborti, 2015: 1740), potentially seriously undermining the central tool for addressing hate. The reasons for under-reporting include: lack of trust in the police to take reports seriously, take action and treat victims with respect (Sin et al, 2009); limited confidence that there will be an outcome, based on knowledge of the small number of prosecutions (House of Commons Library, 2020: 29) and others' experiences; victims not recognizing what has happened to them as a hate crime, distinct from 'everyday' discrimination, and/or not wanting to recognize it as such, as this can be self-stigmatizing (Browne et al, 2011); fear of reprisal from the perpetrator; and police recording issues, including incidents identified as 'low level and ongoing disputes', offenders' motivations recorded as related to the 'perceived vulnerability' of the victim rather than hate and the challenges of recording online hate (Walters et al, 2016: 17–18).

Under-reporting due to lack of trust in the police was recognized by the Macpherson Inquiry report (Macpherson, 1999), with alternative sites and mechanisms introduced, known as 'Third Party Reporting' (Wong et al, 2020). There is now a network of Third Party Reporting Centres across the UK, based in Citizens Advice Bureaus, Keep Safe sites and local authority venues, and also reporting services, including 'Stop Hate UK', 'True Vision' and 'Tell MAMA'. Schweppe et al (2020) emphasize the value of civil society organizations playing a role in the monitoring of hate crime. However,

Wong et al (2020) found that many of the Centres were poorly resourced, managed and supported, with staff lacking in training and experience (in part due to low numbers of people reporting). Also, Centres were not present in all areas and, if they were, were not widely known (College of Policing, 2014, cited in Wong et al, 2020). A report by the Scottish Commission for Learning Disabilities (SCLD, 2017) similarly found that active Third Party Reporting Centres in Scotland were concentrated in urban centres and less present in more deprived communities, although evidence suggests that hate incidents are more likely to occur in these areas (Wong et al, 2013, cited in SCLD, 2017: 10). Just under half were inactive with the remainder 'not very active' (SCLD, 2017: 11). In contrast, telephone and online (including smartphone apps) based reporting services, for example run by Stop Hate UK and 'Tell MAMA', have received increases in contacts from people affected and others in communities (Walters et al, 2016; Stop Hate, 2019).

Despite the overall challenge of under-reporting, Donovan et al (2019: 198) emphasize that the increasing number of hate incidents reported is a 'positive sign of growing confidence among targeted groups', though they acknowledge that victims who are better resourced and socially positioned are more likely to report. Referring to the findings of the 'All Wales Hate Crime Research Project' (Williams and Tregidga, 2013), Donovan et al (2019: 198) summarize that people report 'because it was the right thing to do, to stop it happening again, and in the hope that the offender is brought to justice'. Clayton et al (2016: 66) also state the symbolic and political importance of reporting, 'as part of [the] broader historical struggle for recognition and problematisation of forms of inequality and oppression' for people targeted. As Donovan et al (2019: 199) conclude, 'if reporting provides opportunities to experience agency (without necessarily leading to a criminal justice response) and provides socially transformative processes for those victimized, as well as for those considering enacting hate, then this might have impacts that are more wide-ranging than just for the individuals involved'. Reporting can therefore have another important purpose, alongside engaging victims and wider groups in the formal, criminal justice response to hate crime: to strengthen self-esteem and sense of right of presence in society and local spaces.

The central focus on the experience of victims and broader attacks on group identities has been vital for the recognition of discrimination and the building of confidence to report, yet has meant that the hate discourse has been narrowly focused, with far less said about those who enact hate. The dominant discourse of hate in policy, the media and most academic study, is of one-off violent incidents, perpetrated by bigoted individuals, unknown to the victim, perhaps with links to far-right or other extreme organizations. This discourse, with its origins in the 'watershed' events (Hall, 2013) referred to earlier, has framed and justified the criminal justice response. As such, incidents can be identified as crimes, the perpetrators' motivations are clear (in most cases) and crimes can be (it is assumed) addressed effectively by the police and the courts. However, this framing is problematic for addressing the full spectrum or 'continuum' of hate (Kelly, 1988). First, it can be a barrier to reporting, as victims may not recognize an incident as hate if it did not involve violence but rather is part of a pattern of everyday, 'normal', discriminatory experiences (Hall, 2019). Second, the act may have been committed not by a stranger but by someone known to them, for example a family member, neighbour or 'friend' (harassment and exploitation by 'friends', known as 'mate crime', is a particular issue for disabled people [Thomas, 2011]). Third, in labelling perpetrators as violent extremists, when evidence indicates that the majority of offenders do not fit this image or have these motivations, many incidents are not recognized as hate (McDevitt et al, 2002).

Iganski (2008, cited in Hall, 2019) argues that most people who become perpetrators of what can be identified as hate crimes are 'ordinary people' who act not through some plan or premeditation but spontaneously, via a 'trigger' event or moment, perhaps in the context of broader social attitudes and/or specific situations. Chakraborti (2015: 1747) explains these spontaneous actions as underpinned in most instances not by 'entrenched prejudice' but rather by 'banal motivations, be it boredom, jealousy, or unfamiliarity with "difference"'. Significantly, Chakraborti (2015: 1746) concludes that the 'failure to recognise the "ordinariness" of much hate crime' is 'a shortcoming of conventional policy frameworks', as it both fails to recognize the (cumulative) harm done by the ordinary acts of hate by many and the non-individual motivations of the majority of offenders. Attention needs to be turned towards the immediate and broader contexts of individuals and communities, and the spatio-temporal events that Iganski (2008) and Chakraborti (2015) have identified as the 'triggers' for acts of hate and the 'hate relationships' between victims and perpetrators (Macdonald et al, 2021).

Spatializing hate: a socio-ecological model of hate crime

There are numerous studies of hate crime, in particular in the US, showing the spatial patterning of incidence, and the unevenness and inequality between areas, commonly related to 'race' and deprivation (for example, Jendryke and McClure, 2109), that reveal landscapes of hate. Iganski's (2008: 55) study of London also evidences the patterning of hate associated with ethnic group make-up and mix of the city, with areas with lower proportions of people from Black and Minority Ethnic communities more likely to see incidents of hate. In addition, Iganski's (2008) study suggests that incidence is related to the spatial configuration of the city, for example, more acts of hate occurring on high streets where there are more people moving and mixing, with the potential for what is termed 'friction' and 'everyday conflicts' (2008: 60). He describes the spaces of streets and neighbourhoods where hate incidents happen as the 'mediator' that 'generat[e] encounters between victims and offenders' (Iganski, 2008: 45, cited in Hall, 2019: 252). Clayton et al (2016) have also studied hate incidence, drawing on the 'ARCH' (Agencies against Race Crime and Harassment) reporting database in the North East region of England. The database reveals the significance of 'low-level', everyday harassment; it is noted that such acts, though they 'may not be criminal, may not be perceived as "violent", or perhaps assumed not to be criminal, are those that are most often reported' (Clayton et al, 2016: 69). Importantly, while incidence occurred in every district across the region, there were concentrations in certain areas and communities and, within these, at particular sites, including in neighbourhoods and people's homes (Clayton et al, 2016). Clayton et al (2016) identified an association between incidence and the level of deprivation in an area. However, they emphasized that no definitive conclusions can be drawn about causation, as this can obscure immediate and broader scale factors, including specific sets of relationships between individuals and groups in an area, limited employment opportunities, lack of affordable housing, closure of community sites, and a wider sense of unfairness and precarity generated by budget cuts and economic uncertainty (exacerbated more recently by events such as the Brexit referendum and the COVID-19 pandemic). Notably, the study found that levels of deprivation did not relate to patterning of incidence of LGBTQ+ harassment and violence; these are often linked more to particular sites and spaces and times, including the night-time economy (see Chapter 6). Socio-economic 'background structural' factors (Iganski, 2008: 45, cited in Hall, 2019: 252) can be seen to be expressed in the 'foreground of offending and victimisation', 'mediated' through specific local geographies. Clayton et al (2016: 70) conclude that, drawing on Poirier (2010), the patterning of hate incidence 'can only be explained through a multi-scalar and relational approach' (see also Hall, 2019), from individual encounters to community contexts, national policies and media representations.

Given that most perpetrators of hate are 'ordinary people' committing acts of hate in the course of their 'everyday lives' (Iganski, 2008: 23, cited in Hall, 2019: 252), and that there is a patterning to incidence, it can be argued that attention must be re-focused onto the specific situations and events that make acts of hate more likely, and not just on the specific group identity of the victim (Chakraborti, 2015). For example, a disabled person is targeted in a hate incident not only because of their disability but also because of the specific immediate and enduring locations and situations they are in, including 'their isolation, their routine activities, their lack of physical presence, or the type of area they live in – not directly related to their identity' (Chakraborti, 2015: 1749). While it is important to map incidence of hate, and to recognize that there are concentrations in certain areas, this can lead to overly straightforward conclusions being drawn regarding an association, even causal relationship, between hate and deprivation or other social features of an area. Local socio-economic factors, including deprivation, ethnic mix, age profile, health and disability, *are* elements in the explanation of hate, but there are many other factors that shape incidence, at a range of scales. Further, many hate incidents *do not* occur in all, for example, deprived areas, but are distributed across *all* communities, in spaces where people meet and encounter one another, and also many acts of hate are committed by people known to the victim (family, acquaintances and 'friends') irrespective of local social contexts (Walters and Hoyle, 2012; Clayton et al, 2016).

A relational and contextual perspective understands incidents of harassment and violence as emerging as two or more people come together in an encounter in a specific spatial context and temporal moment (Hall, 2019). The space may have particular features that shape the encounter, such as a narrow entrance or the layout of a bus stop or shop (see Chapter 8) or features that connect to the victim's group identity, for example a disability parking space, a religious building, a bar or area of a city (see Chapter 6). Timing can also be crucial, with crowded or empty buses, whether people have been drinking alcohol, weekends or holidays, shaping the dynamic of encounters in specific spaces. There are also the public spaces in communities and spatial configuration of neighbourhoods, and forms of local housing, which can determine the nature and frequency of encounters (Iganski, 2008). Finally, there are the local, national and structural factors that 'set the scene' and can provide a 'trigger' for, or legitimize or normalize, people's attitudes and behaviours. Donovan et al (2019), citing the sharp rise in hate crime reports after the 2016 Brexit referendum (BBC News, 2017), conclude that hate incidents are 'almost inevitable' in societies with 'structural differences [that] shape, reflect, and reinforce hierarchies of power based on 'othering' minoritized groups ... hate crime is ... as much a result of socio-historic-economic-cultural factors as it is the result of an individual's decision to enact hate' (Donovan et al, 2019: 191). Arguably, the UK Conservative government's creation in 2012 of a 'really hostile environment for illegal migration' (Kirkup and Winnett, 2012, cited in Griffiths and Yeo, 2021: 522), and austerity-driven cuts to welfare benefits and local services, may also contribute to this inevitability (Healy, 2020).

Cramer et al (2020) conceive of hate crime as a 'threat' to public health, building on emerging work that connects experiences of hate to mental and physical health and wellbeing, and broader community impacts (Iganski and Sweiry, 2016; Roussos and Dovidio, 2018; Williams et al, 2019). They propose a 'socio-ecological model of violence' to think through the range of factors at various scales that shape what they refer to as the 'hate-motivated behaviour' of perpetrators (Cramer et al, 2020: 2): 'structural (for example, social norms, laws), interpersonal (for example, peer groups, family support), and individual (for example, demographics, attitudes). The levels interact with and affect one another'. Other versions of the model include a fourth level – community – placed between interpersonal and structure/society, to describe the physical and social sites, spaces and settings where people live and interact (Centers of Disease Control and Prevention, CDC, 2021). A small number of studies have framed hate crime in socio-ecological terms. Witten (2004) examines the mid-life challenges for those in the transgender and intersex community, arguing that these are shaped by experiences of harassment, violence and abuse, which in turn are the product of factors at a range of scales – individual identity, relationships with partners and children/family, community, healthcare, attitudes in employment contexts and broader socio-economic status, stigma and exclusion – what the author refers to as a 'landscape of systemic actual and perceived violence and abuse' (Witten, 2004: 2).

A socio-ecological framework has been applied more recently to intimate partner violence (Ranganathan et al, 2021), with four levels of factors (with examples) described as: societal (gender discrimination, macro-economic factors); community (local norms about gender roles and behaviours, and deprivation); interpersonal (violence as the 'norm', social isolation); and individual, for both female victim (age, childhood experiences of violence, disability, low social support) and male perpetrator (age, childhood experiences, alcohol use, attitudes) (Ranganathan et al, 2021: 2). Importantly, these factors being present does not necessarily mean that violence will occur but that the risk is heightened; Ranganathan et al (2021) further argue that these factors, and associated violence, are distributed unevenly across areas and neighbourhoods. Here, it is argued that such insights provide opportunities and appropriate spaces, scales and relationships, at which to intervene – to support victims, address perpetrator behaviour, tackle causal factors and ultimately to seek to prevent hate (CDC, 2021) (see following section). Numerous public health studies have demonstrated the role of place, in particular local neighbourhoods, in shaping attitudes and behaviours, including those leading to discrimination and hate (for example, Benier, 2019).

Considering the disability hate-related deaths of Fiona Pilkington and Francecca Hardwick in 2007 (Ralph et al, 2016), we can think through how the socio-ecological interpretation can provide insight into the emergence of hate and suggest potential interventions (explored in more detail in the following section). Fiona Pilkington lived with her two children, both of whom had disabilities, in the village of Barwell, Leicestershire, UK. Between January 2004 and October 2007, Fiona, as well as her mother and some neighbours, reported a series of incidents of harassment and verbal abuse directed at her children by a small group of young people in the local area. Because of the sustained harassment, the impact it was having on her children and herself, and frustrated by the inadequate police response, Fiona set her car alight, killing herself and her daughter (*The Guardian*, 2009). The Independent Police Complaints Commission (IPCC) (2009) criticized the local police force officers for not appreciating the connected and cumulative nature of the incidents, which were identified by the officers as low-level anti-social behaviour; for not acknowledging and examining the severity of the impact on the family; and for not engaging properly (beyond speaking to), in partnership with local agencies, with the young people involved. In the socio-ecological framework, there are 'individual' level factors that potentially increase vulnerability to hate for the victims (in this case, issues of disability, income constraint, being unable to move house and previous experiences) and increased risk of offending for the perpetrators (significantly, very little was reported about them). The interpersonal or 'hate relationships' (Donovan et al, 2019) between the Pilkington family and the group of young people who harassed them developed over the three-year period – the IPCC report (2009) noted that as well as the young people knowing who the family were and where they lived, Fiona Pilkington and her children also knew who they were, their families and where they lived. Such relationships between victims and perpetrators are often interpreted by police and other agencies as anti-social behaviour or neighbour disputes, and hence not prioritized (Donovan et al, 2019). The continued dominance of the 'stranger' and the violent incident in hate crime discourse means that a series of 'low-level' non-violent incidents involving people who are known to each other and live nearby are commonly not taken seriously and understood as hate. Despite support from Fiona's mother and some neighbours reporting incidents, the family experienced increasing social isolation (Chakraborti, 2015). There was also evidence of social and economic deprivation among families in the area (Chakraborti, 2015), although the relationship between deprivation and hate is complex and contested, and reduced funding of social infrastructure may also play a role (Clayton et al, 2016). Societal attitudes towards disabled people, both longstanding negative perceptions and representations, and produced by contemporary government policy towards disabled people (Healy, 2020), shape perpetrators' attitudes and sense of legitimacy for their actions, and the attitudes of police and agencies. This can result in apparently low-level incidents being given less priority and victims not being taken seriously, further perpetuating a broader perception that little can be done about such anti-social behaviour.

Rethinking responses to hate

The deaths of Fiona Pilkington and Francecca Hardwick were a defining moment in the recognition and labelling of disability hate crime (Hall, 2013). In particular, the importance of listening to victims and taking their concerns seriously, the significance of cumulative impacts of hateful actions, and the importance of relational, spatial and temporal, contexts in assessing and addressing the harassment and violence experienced. In this final section, some current and emergent approaches being adopted by police forces and other agencies, which are engaging with the insights discussed earlier, will be examined. Despite significant government and criminal justice efforts, reports of hate incidents and crimes continue to increase; a new approach is needed.

Police forces across the UK have established partnership working with local governments (and specific departments, including housing, communities and social work), and other public and voluntary agencies (for example, healthcare, drug and alcohol services, and victim support), to address a range of community safety issues, including anti-social behaviour, vandalism, road safety and hate crime (Liddle and Diamond, 2013; Harkin, 2018; Menichelli, 2020). 'Community Safety Partnerships' (CSPs) were first recommended in the 'Morgan Report' (shorthand for 'Safer Communities: The Local Delivery of Crime Prevention through the Partnership Approach'; Home Office, 1991). By the mid to late 1990s, when hate crime emerged as a key issue of community safety, CSPs had become very much 'part of the local landscape of crime prevention policy and practice' in the UK (Hughes and Edwards, 2002: 26). The incorporation of multiple organizations and involvement of communities offers potential for addressing hate, as the inherent complexity and specific dynamics of the incidence and causation of hate – housing and neighbourhoods, deprivation and anti-social behaviour – are acknowledged. And, further, the field of potential perpetrators is broadened beyond hate-motivated groups to include 'ordinary' members of communities, yet within specific sets of local and wider contexts (Berry et al, 2011; Menichelli, 2020). To take one CSP in the UK as an example: the Dundee Community Safety Partnership (as set out in the Dundee Community Safety Outcome Improvement Plan 2017-22), includes hate crime as part of its 'Vulnerability' theme, with the key outcome of 'Improved Protection for Vulnerable Groups' to 'keep them safe from harm'. The commitment to respond to hate crime, under a 'Hate Incident Multi-Agency Panel' (HIMAP) is summed up as:

> The Community Safety Partnership will support the development of working practices and share, examine, report and monitor hate crime incidents, crimes and trends to the sector. Third Sector representation at these multi-agency meetings to ensure that victims are supported is key

to the process. We will develop, with partners, preventative approaches and action plans to tackle identified trends, support victims and manage appropriately those who have offended. (Dundee Community Safety Partnership, 2017, 12)

This statement reflects the standard approach to managing hate crime in local areas in the UK: a multi-agency approach including, sharing of information and practices; support for victims as central (with police and voluntary organizations playing a key role); and inclusion of plans to better 'manage' perpetrators of hate, alongside other preventative approaches (Home Office, 2016). However, the key form of response remains the reporting and monitoring of hate incidents and crimes. It is crucial to 'dismantle barriers to reporting' (as identified earlier in the chapter) (Chakraborti, 2018: 392), to make it more accessible and 'victim-friendly' (395), including advocacy and support through the criminal justice process. The increased availability of online and app-based reporting has helped significantly (Walters et al, 2016). However, some of the enduring reasons people do not report, including fear of not being taken seriously, may be better addressed in part by strengthened empowerment among affected individuals and groups, in partnership with local organizations and through the national scale campaigning and awareness raising of organizations such as 'Tell MAMA', including innovative use of social media (Chakraborti, 2018).

Locally focused approaches, and involvement of multiple agencies and communities, such as CSPs, can facilitate 'joined-up' decision-making and resource allocation in local areas to respond to identified 'hot spots' of hate incidents, and relate this to associated problems of anti-social behaviour, housing problems and lack of social support, with the opportunity to put in place a locally based response (Walters et al, 2016). However, according to Hughes and Edwards (2002) there are issues with this shift of emphasis from national state to local communities in responsibility for addressing community-related crimes (along with other social challenges). As Hughes and Edwards (2002) put it (when discussing Stenson's [2002] chapter in their edited collection), the move 'from a universal provision of public services to their targeting of "hot-spots" of crime and social disadvantage' (Hughes and Edwards, 2002: 12) constrains the understanding of and responses to hate, as it 'forget[s] the effect that the diverse social, economic and political histories and the consequent cultural milieu of particular localities have on the generation of social problems such as crime and disorder and on the governmental responses to these problems' (Hughes and Edwards, 2002: 11). The socio-ecological approach would extend this recognition of the role of context to include broader social, economic and cultural factors, and political decisions, that also shape the character and dynamics of local places and communities, including 'setting the scene' (for example, on welfare benefit entitlement and immigration policy) for the legitimization and normalization of hate. At present, Laverick and Joyce (2020) argue, there is an 'apparent contradict[ion]', as anti-discrimination policy 'coexists with discriminatory immigration legislation' (89) and the broader 'role of the state … in fostering of conditions conducive to illiberalism' (92) … 'underpinning … the perpetration of hatred' (96).

A feature of the community safety approach to hate experienced by disabled people and others, in many cities in the UK, has been the establishment of 'safe spaces'. They have emerged as a response to discrimination in mainstream spaces (for example, in universities; see Chapter 9), with people subject to harassment and aggression seeking separate environments away from the oppressive behaviour of others, who dominate and determine the nature of 'normal', mainstream spaces. Networks of 'Keep Safe' sites have been set up by local authorities and charities (for example, 'I Am Me' in Scotland), including local shops and cafes, and community sites such as libraries and museums (indicated by a sign on the door and supported by a smartphone app), where older, vulnerable or disabled people can go if they are scared, lost or frightened, or if they have experienced a hate crime (Terras et al, 2019; Scottish Community Safety Network, 2021). As with Third Party Reporting Centres (discussed earlier), staff at the sites are trained to engage with people when they arrive, provide support, call a named contact and if appropriate report a hate incident (I Am Me Scotland, 2021). The emergence of and support for identified safe spaces, as part of broader community safety responses to hate, can be seen as supportive and proactive, recognizing (disabled and older) people's fear of harassment when present in public spaces, and empowering people to navigate potentially unsafe environments. Hall and Bates (2019) found that people with learning disabilities in a city in Scotland had a broader and more nuanced notion of safe spaces, which had developed alongside the formal network of 'Keep Safe' sites. Many had built up their own network of 'safe' or in many cases more positively 'welcoming' spaces, as part of their 'mental map' of fear and inclusion in the city. These spaces included the public library (also a formal designated Keep Safe space), voluntary disability organization sites, local cafés, where they would likely 'bump into' friends and more temporary spaces, such as newspaper stands. These 'moorings', as Hall and Bates (2019) refer to such sites, crucially featured people, both professional staff and acquaintances (such as newspaper sellers and buskers), known to be friendly and supportive, emphasizing the importance of relationships in preventing (as well as causing) acts of hate. However, Healy (2020) notes that some of the participants in her study of disability hate crime experienced abuse and harassment in supposedly 'safe' spaces, including doctor surgeries' waiting rooms and supermarkets. Identifying specific spaces as 'safe' can provide support, refuge and potentially empowerment for people (in particular, when they are identified and developed by people themselves in relation with others; Hall and Bates, 2019), and does foreground the importance of local community and public space contexts in the experience and production of hate. In another example, Browne et al (2011) in a study of LGBT communities in Brighton, UK, argue for the effectiveness of initiatives by those impacted, rather than looking to formal, police and community safety actions on hate. Their argument is summarized by Clayton et al (2016: 66): 'the treatment [Browne et al's study's] participants receive in their everyday lives is better combatted through a range of more informal techniques of avoidance, collective security and community safety'. However, in this transfer of responsibility (if only unintentionally) to those at risk of hate, there is not only the implication, and even acceptance, of broader spaces as unsafe, but also the avoidance by government and other agencies of the serious and sustained challenge of, and action needed to address, the factors that produce such landscapes of hate.

Developing a challenge to structural policies and broader contexts or 'atmospheres' (Chapter 5) that generate or legitimize hate is not straightforward. Healy (2020), among others, calls for changes to welfare benefit rules (for example, in the UK, 'Work Capability Assessments') and policy and media language that stigmatize disabled people (Briant et al, 2011, cited in Victim Support Scotland, 2017). Further, there are some emerging initiatives seeking to do just that with specific proposals. Gyamerah et al (2021: 9) identified the multiple structural factors linked to being a victim of transphobic hate, in San Francisco, US: 'lower educational attainment, housing instability, homelessness as a child and an adult, a history of sex work, incarceration, and being undocumented'. Importantly, the study examined how trans and social justice activists and campaigning groups in the San Francisco area have 'put forward various demands' for changes to high-level social policy and legislation to address these structural causal factors, including 'decriminalisation of trans people; an end to structural, symbolic, and physical forms of transphobic violence and the social conditions that perpetuate these' (as identified earlier) (Gyamerah et al, 2021: 12–13). At a more local scale, also concerned with challenging the dominant set of attitudes or 'atmosphere', Chana (2020) reports on a series of community initiatives (led by local authorities) to respond to anti-Muslim hate crime in the UK, including ' "Places of Welcome" which is a multi-faith initiative to create interactions between those of different faiths, [and] the "Love your Neighbour" initiative which attempts to bridge the gap between cultural differences' (83). However, there was the concern expressed in the study that being initiated by local government had led in many cases to a disconnect with the communities and individuals that experience hate, and the schemes are often short-lived and under-resourced. Chana (2020), drawing on Fung (2009), argues that the most effective hate crime initiatives are those set up and run by local communities and groups (as noted by Browne et al, 2011, discussed earlier). The short-term and perceived by many to be 'tokenistic' (Chana, 2020: 84) nature of local government initiatives can also be seen as a reluctance or even avoidance to commit to longer-term actions, as doing so would highlight the embedded and enduring nature of hate (as identified in the Gyamerah et al, 2021 study).

A public health or socio-ecological approach to hate 'lays emphasis on prevention, rather than solely trying to ameliorate the effects of the problem' (Iganski and Sweiry, 2016: 105). Local preventative initiatives (discussed earlier) place emphasis on the relationships between people within communities, broadening out the dominant focus of hate crime on a narrowly defined set of potential victims and perpetrators (although, as discussed earlier, the latter receive less policy and scholarly attention). In seeing communities, broadly conceived, as the setting for exclusion and hate, Chana (2020: 83) notes that community initiatives were intended to '[get] individuals to meet those from different cultural backgrounds to address the lack of contact and knowledge between cultural and religious groups'. This acknowledges that, first, there are social and spatial differences and structural inequalities within communities; and, second, lack of engagement and understanding are factors (alongside, Chana [2020] emphasizes, broader employment, income, educational and welfare policy contexts) in producing potential incidents of hate. The effectiveness of such initiatives is uncertain, as Chana (2020) notes, but the emphasis placed on social relations and community spaces, as where hate is produced and where it can, in part, be addressed, is positive. However, it is important to critique the geographically determined notion of 'community' commonly cited in policy as the scale of intervention. In his study, Chakraborti (2018: 396) noted that people affected by hate 'spoke in much more positive terms about smaller, voluntary and community-based services – their mental health support group, their locally-run women's network – ... with whom they felt safe, supported and able to talk openly about their experiences'. In sum, community-based partnerships *are* important, but need to focus on listening to those affected and supporting (and funding) the broad work of local community organizations (not just that focused on hate).

While hate can occur anywhere in a community, there are certain sites and contexts with particular symbolic associations that could generate heightened potential for hate incidents (for example, a disabled person parking space) (Hall, 2019). Identification of and intervention in such spaces could play a role in preventing hate. Davis (2020) highlights the role of such 'environmental factors', noting in particular public transport as a space where (in the study, 'race') hate crimes are more likely to occur (see Chapter 8). Davis (2020: 100), while acknowledging the importance of structural and attitudinal change, argues for the value of a 'deterrent approach ... grounded in realism', including, for example, 'simple, inclusive and insight-driven messaging on public transport and other shared spaces' that could 'could stifle the impulse of a would-be perpetrator' (Davis, 2020: 100).

Until very recently (as noted in Chapter 1), there was no specifically named hate crime legislation in the UK; the criminal justice response has been built on the 'enhancement' of penalties for non-hate related criminal behaviour, to symbolize society's rejection of hateful actions (Hall, 2013). Walters (2014) examines the limitations of the 'punitive approach', including the relative absence of a focus on victims, and emphasizes that current legislative techniques do 'little to challenge individuals' hate motivated behaviours' and further 'may actually antagonise (would-be) offenders who see certain groups as receiving unequal protection from the state' (Walters, 2014: 244; also citing Jacobs and Potter, 1998). As seen earlier, evidence has shown that few hate crime perpetrators are 'motivated by an ideology of hate', it being 'more common for offenders to hold ... superficial or low-level prejudices' (Walters, 2014: 249). Walters (2014) further argues that 'restorative justice' has significant potential to change low-level attitudes and prevent actions of hate through, for example, facilitated engagement between individuals and communities affected by hate and those who offend. However, there are risks involved, which must be carefully managed, most importantly the protection of and support for victims. Importantly, restorative justice is place or context based; as Walters (2014) notes, and as discussed earlier, many (potential) incidents are related to particular landscapes of hate – temporal and spatial moments and social relations in very local contexts, such as shops, housing and public spaces. Crucially, those affected by hate are often 'receptive to ... use of alternative interventions beyond conventional punitive measures' (Chakraborti, 2018: 398–9), including education initiatives focused on diversity in schools and communities. However, the use of such preventative interventions 'remains relatively limited' (Chakraborti, 2108: 399; see also Walters et al, 2016).

Conclusion

The chapter has argued for a rethinking of responses to hate. Legislative, policing and criminal justice framings of hate incidents are important, both for those individuals and communities affected, and for broader society to state its rejection of hate and to deter potential offenders. However, the chapter has, first, through an examination of the limitations of these approaches and, second, by advocating a socio-ecological model of hate (Cramer et al, 2020), demonstrated the need to reimagine the nature, relationships, sites and multi-scalar contexts and causal factors, of the landscape of hate in society. This is a crucial moment – reports of hate crime are increasing, prosecution rates remain low, there is an awareness of heightened social and cultural tensions in UK society, and police resources are constrained. At the same time, there is evidence of growing confidence among some groups and communities impacted by hate; a greater awareness of the links between broad-scale policy rhetoric and actions and local-scale attitudes, relationships and events; and an embracing of public health conceptualizations of a range of social challenges, including hate (Iganski and Sweiry, 2016; Cramer, 2020). There needs to be a 'shift in the balance of resources away from a narrow criminal justice response ... towards civil society and community action' (Iganski and Sweiry, 2016: 105). There is no doubt that there is stigmatization and discrimination, and hateful attitudes and actions are present in our society, and too many people still experience harassment and violence. Yet, there is much to be hopeful for too, as individuals, communities, local organizations, and some policy makers and state practitioners, build new preventative interventions and effective responses to hate.

References

BBC News (2017) 'Record hate crime after EU referendum', 15 February, Available from: https://www.bbc.co.uk/news/uk-38976087 [Accessed 21 February 2022].

Benier, K. (2019) 'The people or the place? An analysis of the protective factors of hate crime in multi-ethnic neighbourhoods in Australia', *Australian Journal of Social Issues*, 54: 157–72.

Berry, G., Briggs, P., Erol, R. and van Staden, L. (2011) *The Effectiveness of Partnership Working in a Crime and Disorder Context: A Rapid Evidence Assessment*, London: Home Office.

Briant, E., Philo, G. and Watson, N. (2011) *Bad News for Disabled People: How the Newspapers are Reporting Disability*, Strathclyde Centre for Disability Research and Glasgow Media Unit, Available from: www.gla.ac.uk/media/media_214917_en.pdf. [Accessed 21 February 2022].

Browne, K., Bakshi, L. and Lim, J. (2011) '"It's something you just have to ignore": understanding and addressing contemporary lesbian, gay, bisexual and trans safety beyond hate crime paradigms', *Journal of Social Policy* 40(4): 739–56.

Centres for Disease Control and Prevention (CDC) (2021) *The Social-Ecological Model: A Framework for Prevention*, Available from: https://www.cdc.gov/violenceprevention/about/social-ecologicalmodel.html [Accessed 30 July 2021].

Chakraborti, N. (2015) 'Re-thinking hate crime: fresh challenges for policy and practice', *Journal of Interpersonal Violence*, 30(10): 1738–54.

Chakraborti, N. (2018) 'Responding to hate crime: escalating problems, continued failings', *Criminology & Social Justice*, 18(4): 387–404.

Chana, S. (2020) 'Working towards a better understanding of Islamophobia', *British Journal of Community Justice*, 16(2): 72–91.

Clayton, J., Donovan, C. and Macdonald, S. (2016) 'A critical portrait of hate crime/incident reporting in North East England: the value of statistical data and the politics of recording in an age of austerity', *Geoforum*, 75: 64–74.

College of Policing, National Policing Hate Group (2014) *Hate Crime Operational Guidance* (C118/0514), Coventry: College of Policing Limited, Available from: https://www.college.police.uk/What-we-do/Support/Equality/Documents/Hate-Crime-Operational-Guidance.pdf [Accessed 30 July 2021].

Corcoran, H., Lader, D. and Smith, K. (2015) *Hate Crime, England and Wales 2014/15*, Report, Home Office, October, Available from: http://report-it.org.uk/files/ho_hate_crime_statistics_201415.pdf [Accessed 10 September 2021].

Cramer, R., Fording, R., Gerstenfeld, P. et al (2020) 'Hate-motivated behavior: impacts, risk factors, and interventions', *Health Affairs Health Policy Brief*, 9 November, Available from: https://www.healthaffairs.org/do/10.1377/hpb20200929.601434/full/ [Accessed 30 July 2021].

Davis, E. (2020) 'Race hate crime and the criminal justice response', *British Journal of Community Justice*, 16(2): 92–102.

Donovan, C., Clayton, J. and Macdonald, S. (2019) 'New directions in hate reporting research: agency, heterogeneity and relationality', *Sociological Research Online*, 24(2): 185–202.

Dundee Community Safety Partnership (2017) *Dundee Community Safety Outcome Improvement Plan 2017–22*, Available from: https://www.dundeecity.gov.uk/sites/default/files/dundee_community_safety_outcome_improvement_plan_2017-2022.pdf [Accessed 30 July 2021].

Erentzen, C. and Schuller, R. (2020) 'Exploring the dark figure of hate: experiences with police bias and the under-reporting of hate crime', *Canadian Journal of Criminology and Criminal Justice*, 62(2): 64–97.

Fung, A. (2009) *Empowered Participation: Reinventing Urban Democracy*, Princeton: Princeton University Press.

Griffiths, M. and Yeo, C. (2021) 'The UK's hostile environment: deputising immigration control', *Critical Social Policy*, 1–24, DOI:10.1177/0261018320980653

Guardian, The (2009) 'Incident diary reveals ordeal of mother who killed herself and daughter', Available from: www.theguardian.com/uk/2009/sep/24/fiona-pilkington-incident-diary [Accessed 6 June 2022].

Gyamerah, A.O., Baguso, G., Santiago-Rodriguez, E. et al (2021) 'Experiences and factors associated with transphobic hate crimes among transgender women in the San Francisco Bay Area: comparisons across race', *BMC Public Health*, 21: 1053.

Hall, E. (2019) 'A critical geography of disability hate crime', *Area* 51(2): 249–56.

Hall, E. and Bates, E. (2019) 'Hatescape? A relational geography of disability hate crime, exclusion and belonging in the city', *Geoforum*, 101: 100–10.

Hall, N. (2013) *Hate Crime*, London: Routledge.

Harkin, D. (2018) 'Community safety partnerships: the limits and possibilities of "policing with the community"', *Crime Prevention and Community Safety*, 20(2): 125–36.

Healy, J. (2020) '"It spreads like a creeping disease": experiences of victims of disability hate crimes in austerity Britain', *Disability & Society*, 35(2): 176–200.

Home Office (1991) *Safer Communities: The Local Delivery of Crime Prevention through the Partnership Approach*, London: Home Office.

Home Office (2016) *Action Against Hate: The UK Government's Plan for Tackling Hate Crime*, London: Home Office.

Home Office (2018) *Action Against Hate: The UK Government's Plan for Tackling Hate Crime – 'Two Years On'*, London: Home Office.

Home Office (2020) *Hate Crime, England and Wales, 2019 to 2020*, Available from: www.gov.uk/government/statistics/hate-crime-england-and-wales-2019-to-2020/hate-crime-england-and-wales-2019-to-2020 [Accessed 6 June 2022].

Home Office (2021) *Hate Crime, England and Wales, 2020 to 2021*, Available from: https://www.gov.uk/government/statistics/hate-crime-england-and-wales-2020-to-2021/hate-crime-england-and-wales-2020-to-2021 [Accessed 21 February 2022].

House of Commons Library (2020) *Hate Crime Statistics*, Briefing Paper Number 8537, 10 December.

Hughes, G. and Edwards, A. (2002) *Crime Control and Community*, Abingdon: Willan.

I Am Me Scotland (2021) Available from: https://iammescotland.co.uk/ [Accessed 10 September 2021].

Iganski, P. (2008) *Hate Crime and the City*, Bristol: Policy Press.

Iganski, P. and Sweiry, A. (2016) 'How "hate" hurts globally', in J. Schweppe and M. Walters (eds) *The Globalization of Hate*, Oxford: Oxford University Press, pp 96–107.

IPCC (2009) *IPCC Report into the Contact Between Fiona Pilkington and Leicestershire Constabulary 2004–2007*, London: IPCC.

Jacobs, J. and Potter, K. (1998) *Hate Crimes*, New York: Oxford University Press.

Jendryke, M. and McClure, S. (2019) 'Mapping crime – hate crimes and hate groups in the USA: a spatial analysis with gridded data', *Applied Geography*, 111, DOI: 10.1016/j.apgeog.2019.102072

Kelly, L. (1988) *Surviving Sexual Violence*, Oxford: Policy Press.

Kirkup, J. and Winnett, R. (2012) Theresa May interview: 'We're going to give illegal migrants a really hostile reception', *The Telegraph*, 25 May, Available from: www.telegraph.co.uk/news/0/theresa-may-interview-going-give-illegal-migrants-really-hostile/ [Accessed 6 June 2022].

Laverick, W. and Joyce, N.P. (2020) 'Reinterpreting the UK response to hate crime', *British Journal of Community Justice*, 16(1): 82–102.

Liddle, J. and Diamond, J. (2013) 'Community safety: partnerships across boundaries in England', in J. O'Flynn, D. Blackman and J. Halligan (eds) *Crossing Boundaries in Public Management and Policy: The International Experience*, London: Routledge, pp 263–79.

Macdonald, S., Donovan, C. and Clayton, J. (2021) '"I may be left with no choice but to end my torment": disability and intersectionalities of hate crime', *Disability & Society*, DOI: 10.1080/09687599.2021.1928480

Macpherson, Sir W. (1999) *The Stephen Lawrence Inquiry: Report of an Inquiry by Sir William Macpherson of Cluny*, London: The Stationery Office, Available from: https://www.gov.uk/government/publications/the-stephen-lawrence-inquiry [Accessed 30 July 2021].

McDevitt, J., Levin, J. and Bennett, S. (2002) 'Hate crime offenders: an expanded typology', *Journal of Social Issues* 58(2): 303–18.

Menichelli, F. (2020) 'Transforming the English model of community safety: from crime and disorder to the safeguarding of vulnerable', *Criminology and Criminal Justice*, 20(1): 39–56.

Office for National Statistics (ONS) (2020) *Crime Survey for England and Wales*, Available from: https://www.crimesurvey.co.uk/en/index.html [Accessed 30 July 2021].

Poirier, M.R. (2010) 'The multiscalar geography of hate crimes', August 6, *Seton Hall Public Law Research Paper*, No. 1654350.

Police Scotland (2021a) *Annual Plan 2021/22*, Available from: https://www.scotland.police.uk/spa-media/njykirkq/annual-police-plan-21-22.pdf [Accessed 30 July 2021].

Police Scotland (2021b) *Report Hate Crime and Third Party Reporting*, Available from: https://www.scotland.police.uk/contact-us/report-hate-crime-and-third-party-reporting/ [Accessed 30 July 2021].

Ralph, S., Capewell, C. and Bonnett, E. (2016) 'Disability hate crime: persecuted for difference', British *Journal of Special Education*, 43(3): 215–32.

Ranganathan, M., Heise, L., Peterman, A., Shalini, R. and Hidrobo, M. (2021) 'Cross-disciplinary intersections between public health and economics in intimate partner violence research', *SSM – Population Health*, 14, DOI:10.1016/j.ssmph.2021.100822

Roussos, G. and Dovidio, J.F. (2018) 'Hate speech is in the eye of the beholder: the influence of racial attitudes and freedom of speech beliefs on perceptions of racially motivated threats of violence', *Social Psychological and Personality Science*, 9(2): 176–85.

Schweppe, J., Haynes, A. and MacIntosh, E.M. (2020) 'What is measured matters: the value of third party hate crime monitoring', *European Journal on Criminal Policy and Research*, 26: 39–59.

Scottish Commission for Learning Disabilities (SCLD) (2017) *Mapping and Scoping Exercise for Third Party Reporting Centres*, Glasgow: SCLD.

Scottish Community Safety Network (2021) *Keep Safe Practice Exemplar*, 6 July, Available from: https://www.safercommunitiesscotland.org/keep-safe-practice-exemplar/ [Accessed 10 September 2021].

Sin, C.H., Hedges, A., Cook, C., Mguni, N. and Comber, N. (2009) *Disabled People's Experiences of Targeted Violence and Hostility*, Research Report 21, Manchester: Equality and Human Right's Commission.

Stenton, K. (2002) 'Community safety in Middle England: the local politics of crime control', in G. Hughes and A. Edwards (eds) *Crime Control and Community*, Abingdon: Willan, pp 109–39.

Stop Hate (2019) *Stop Hate Annual Report 2018/19*, Available from: https://www.stophateuk.org/2019/10/04/stop-hate-uk-annual-statistical-report-2018-2019/ [Accessed 10 September 2021].

Terras, M., Hendry, G, and Jarret, D. (2019) The challenges of safety and community integration for vulnerable individuals', *Safety*, 5: 85, DOI: 10.3390/safety5040085

Thomas, P. (2011) '"Mate crime": ridicule, hostility and targeted attacks against disabled people', *Disability & Society*, 26(1): 107–111.

Victim Support Scotland (2017) *Fostering a Victim Centred Approach to Hate Crime In Scotland*, Edinburgh: VSS.

Walters, M. (2014) 'Restorative approaches to working with hate crime offenders', in N. Chakraborti and J. Garland (eds) *Responding to Hate Crime: The Case for Connecting Policy and Research*, Bristol: Policy Press, pp 243–57.

Walters, M. and Hoyle, C. (2012) 'Exploring the everyday world of hate victimization through community mediation', *International Review of Victimology*, 18(1): 7–24.

Walters, M., Brown, R. and Wiedlitzka, S. (2016) *Preventing Hate Crime*, SSRN, Available from: https://ssrn.com/abstract=2918876 [Accessed 10 September 2021].

Williams, M. and Tregidga, J. (2013) *All Wales Hate Crime Research Project*, Cardiff: Race Equality First and Cardiff University.

Williams, D., Lawrence, J. and David, B. (2019) 'Racism and health: evidence and needed research', *Annual Review of Public Health*, 40: 105–125.

Witten, T.M. (2004) 'Life course analysis: the courage to search for something more: middle adulthood issues in the transgender and intersex community', *Journal of Human Behavior in a Social Environment*, 8(3/4): 189–224.

Wong, K. (2020) 'Reality versus rhetoric: assessing the efficacy of third-party hate crime reporting centres', *International Review of Victimology*, 26(1): 79–95.

Wong, K., Christmann, K., Meadows, L., Albertson, K. and Senior, P. (2013) *Hate Crime in Suffolk: Understanding Prevalence and Support Needs*, Sheffield: Hallam Centre for Community Justice, Sheffield Hallam University.

13

Afterword: Spatializing Hate – Relational, Intersectional and Emotional Approaches

Peter Hopkins

Introduction: spatializing hate

One of the many strengths of this collection is found in the diversity of approaches to understanding the complex landscapes and spatialities of hate that are evident across the chapters. This is seen not only in the different sub-disciplinary approaches of the contributors but also in the varied spatial and temporal contexts that are explored critically in each chapter. In the introduction (Chapter 1), the editors make several useful observations about the utility of using ideas of landscape for appreciating the complex spatialities of hate, and I offer some additional reflections on the spatializing of hate in this afterword.

In Chapter 2, Zoe James and Katie McBride point to the traditional focus of research about hate where attention was paid to the mapping of hate crime. The authors point to the need for critical hate studies to move beyond this focus and to be theoretically critical in its approach to understanding hate. This critical approach is also demonstrated in Chapter 3 where Fiona Vera-Gray and Bianca Fileborn challenge the dominant discourse around recognizing misogyny as a hate crime, pointing to several limitations in adopting such an approach. This highlights the importance of adopting a critical approach that interrogates widely accepted standards and modes of operation; this is about being open to the questioning of widely accepted and dominant ways of thinking about hate, and demonstrating sensitivity to new and emerging – as well as longstanding and deep-rooted – forms of hatred and discrimination, and how these have changed (or not) over time. While there are many good reasons to recognize misogyny as a hate crime, this chapter alerts us to the fact that such recognition is unlikely to provide an all-encompassing solution; furthermore, as noted in Chapter 1, this may not necessarily lead to changes in attitudes towards women and will therefore have limited benefits for them that are perhaps not always clear in campaigns for recognition. This critical and questioning approach is also evident in Chapter 10 where Kath Browne and Catherine Jean Nash overturn the simplistic ways in which heterosexist Christian groups rely upon claims to freedom of speech and discourses of love to espouse views that are hateful and discriminatory. Here, we see the dominant understanding of Christian groups as loving, neighbourly and caring being questioned, critiqued and ultimately turned on its head considering the evidence that is carefully presented by the chapter authors.

Perhaps one of the most obvious ways to think about the relationship between place and hate is through the methods whereby specific spaces become contexts that are hated or that are associated with hate. Such work tends to focus on debates about territorial stigma (for example, Nayak, 2019). Alice Butler-Warke focuses on the production of place-based stigmatization in Chapter 4, demonstrating the ways in which territorial stigma and hatescapes can be reinforced through government policies and political leadership. Here we see how specific spaces – be these neighbourhoods, communities, cities or regions – are labelled as troublesome, cast as a problem and dismissed as beyond recovery. In turn, such places are referred to through a language aligned with hate: distaste, disgust, abhorrence and animosity. In addition to the hate of specific places or contexts, this collection also points to the role of broader geographical and geopolitical matters in the promotion of hate. For example, in Chapter 2, global and state-sponsored neoliberal capitalism is presented as a key explanation for hate with the discussion in Chapter 4 also explaining how such an approach can be reinforced by specific government policies and leadership (such as through Thatcherism).

Furthermore, we learn about the ways in which hate plays out in specific spatial contexts across the chapters. Examples here include references to the ways in which specific built environments such as mosques or nightclubs and venues associated with the LGBT community can be locations associated with hate crime and hatred as explored in Chapter 6 by John Clayton, Catherine Donovan and Stephen J. Macdonald. We also learn about the contested politics associated with university campuses from Matthew Durey, Nicola Roberts and Catherine Donovan in Chapter 5 and related debates about safety on campus from Denise Goerisch in Chapter 9. This chapter also reflects upon the possibilities of virtual spaces – in this context as a source of escape and support – although there is much evidence that such contexts also provide a powerful source for the spreading of hate (for example, Hodge and Hallgrimsdottir, 2020). The role of online contexts is not a major feature of this collection, but the example referred to at the start of this book – of the racist abuse on social media directed at three young

Black players in England's men's football team following the defeat in the European Championship final in 2021 – points to the powerful, hate-filled and damaging role that the online context can open up. Although this presents a significant environment for the spreading of hate and division, it can also be very useful – as Chapter 1 makes clear – for networks of support to be expressed and to mobilize against hate.

Landscapes of hate are not only located in specific fixed geographical contexts but can also be a significant feature of experiences of migration and mobility. A useful example here is the securitization often experienced by Muslims and other ethnic minority groups in their negotiations of airport security. Blackwood et al (2013) explore the experiences of British Muslims negotiations of airport security in the UK reflecting upon the ways in which their national identities, sense of agency as British, and their Muslim identities are put into question in such contexts. Although this may not necessarily be about hate per se, such experiences are part of continuum of negative encounters that are a feature of their everyday landscapes of hate; Ellen Daly and Olivia Smith make specific reference to the important idea of continuum of violence in Chapter 7. Moreover, in Chapter 8, David Wilkin offers an important insight into disability hate crime on public transport pointing to the ever-changing nature of this form of mobility with it also being a necessity for many.

An additional set of spatialities that are important in understanding the complex landscapes of hate are associated with specific events – such as conferences, protests, marches, parades and other public events – which may be one-off or repeated regularly. Such events are often connected with specific organizations or networks of groups who have an online presence alongside the event they are involved in. This context is powerfully addressed in Chapter 10 where Kath Browne and Catherine Jean Nash explore specific contexts in which sexual and gender equalities are resisted and in which heteronormative ideas, such as those associated with heterosexual marriages being the best place to raise children, are actively promoted. Critical here are the ways in which many such groups seek to resist accusations of hate and often employ discourses of free speech and love to do so.

All in all, then, the chapters in this collection spatialize hate from diverse perspectives, utilizing different spatial registers and foci in the process. The most pernicious forms of hate are likely to work through, across and within these diverse spatial contexts and this remains a key challenge for researchers eager to expose and address complex landscapes and experiences of hate. Moreover, Campbell (2016: 71) questions the traditional focus of 'policing spatialities – territories, borders, scales and networks' and suggests instead a focus on 'space as folded, twisted, stretched, and entangled'. Such an approach opens up interesting and important ways to think through the spatiality of hate and the complex geographies involved.

We see some of this complexity, for example, in the operation of Islamophobia and anti-Muslim hatred with experiences of this form of hatred being encountered online, close to specific built environments such as mosques and in educational environments, in supermarkets, on public transport, through global and national geopolitical discourse, and during events organized by racist and Far Right groups (for example, Hopkins et al, 2020). Addressing hate in one specific spatial context – say on university campuses – may be useful in working towards open and equal treatment within such contexts; however, hate may then be experienced in other contexts, such as on the way to and from campus, on public transport or in nearby shopping areas. Moreover, the context itself may be the target of hate – regardless of the social group that utilizes it and so the spatializing of hate requires sensitivity to such diversity.

Intersectional

The chapters in this book explore experiences of hate for a diverse range of different groups and critically reflect upon the specific challenges experienced by marginalized social groups. Chapters 6, 7, 8 and 12 focus wholly or in part on different forms of disability and we learn about experiences of hate directed at the Gypsy and Traveller and transgender communities in Chapter 2, and the experiences of Muslims and LGBT people in Chapter 6. Furthermore, we learn too about race and ethnicity in Chapter 9 and misogyny and the operation of patriarchy in Chapter 3. Overall, chapters tend to consider forms of hate targeted at groups with specific singular forms of identification. In some senses, this is the best way to work as it is important to understand the specific and often-nuanced ways in which hate is experienced and lived out by specific groups, such as those with learning disabilities or those from the LGBT community. With each social group, there are often nuanced and unique ways in which they are targeted, and specialist groups – such as disability rights organizations – have much experience in offering specialist advice and support in relation to the specific forms of marginalization and hate encountered. That being said, Chakraborti and Garland (2012) have argued that we should shift away from looking at victimization based on identity to consider instead issues of vulnerability and difference. Part of their argument is that groups are targeted based on perceptions about their vulnerability rather than this being based on the specific social group to which they belong.

A useful way of adding further sophistication to studies of hate is to consider adopting an intersectional approach. Crenshaw (1991) introduced intersectionality into academic research through her research about Black women's employment experiences and made the point that simply adding racism and sexism together does not address the complex marginalizations experienced by Black women (Crenshaw, 1989). Sensitivity is needed when employing intersectionality, both in relation to its activist and intellectual origins in Black feminism and to ensure that it is not depoliticized and whitened in the process (Hopkins, 2019). Intersectionality is about relationality, social context, power relations, complexity, social justice and inequalities. It is not simply about multiple identities and the adding together of different forms of inequality; such an additive approach to intersectionality overlooks the potential for specific forms of discrimination to change in nature, form and presentation when they work in operation with other forms of prejudice and not only on their own. Some of the chapters in this collection refer to intersectional thinking. For example, in Chapter 3, Fiona Vera-Gray and Bianca Fileborn reflect on the importance of intersectionality and the challenges of single-axis thinking when it comes to understanding complex landscapes of hate. Related to this, Kath Browne and Catherine Jean Nash in Chapter 10 hint at the particular combinations of social positions that are more productive of hateful behaviours such as in the combination of sexuality and religion with heteroactivisms, and in Chapter 11, Rick Bowler and Amina Razak pay specific attention to gendered racisms to explore experiences of racist microaggressions and the complex landscapes of racist hate.

Adopting an intersectional approach – alongside demonstrating a sensitivity to the spatiality of hate – will enable researchers to appreciate the complex, multi-layered and intricate nature of the hate crimes and incidents experienced by individuals and groups. For example, in Chapter 6, John Clayton, Catherine Donovan and Stephen J. Macdonald point to the ways that experiences of hatred focused on specific physical locations can be experienced in similar ways across different groups, pointing to the utility of exploring different groups marginalization in relation to different but important spatial contexts. Moreover, Macdonald et al (2021: 19) note that 'applying an intersectional approach to hate crime may lead to a multi-agency response where the multiple and complex needs of the victims/survivors can be dealt with, not just with a criminal justice consequence but also with a coordinated social service and housing response.'

Relational

Collins and Bilge (2016) identify relationality as a key characteristic of intersectionality, alongside a focus on social context, inequality, justice, complexity and power. In addition to advancing an intersectional approach to the spatiality of hate, researchers could usefully simultaneously demonstrate sensitivity to the relational nature of hate crime. Massey (2005) has discussed the relational nature of space and Hopkins and Noble (2009: 815) observe that 'there exist an array of vectors of relationality'. Furthermore, Ansell et al

(2011: 527) note that relationalities are 'constituted through relationships that are organised and reorganised through networks, flows and mobilities'. As such, part of the process of adopting a relational approach is about being attentive to the spatialities of hate and to the complex networks of relations that operate to generate hate alongside the ways in which such spaces offer support and mediation, or even active challenge and resistance to experiences of, and spaces associated with, hate (for example, Hodge and Hallgrimsdottir, 2020).

Connecting with recent research that emphasizes the potential of relational understandings of hate crime (for example, Donovan et al, 2019; Hall and Bates, 2019), many of the chapters in this book point to the importance of such an approach. Part of this relational approach is about seeking to appreciate the relations – between social groups, actors, agencies, places and events – that operate in complex ways to generate experiences of hate. As Hall and Bates (2019) observe, part of this is about studying the how, who and where aspects of hateful incidents. One of the benefits of adopting a relational approach is that it can assist in appreciating the diverse motivations of specific forms of discriminatory conduct that may not necessarily be about hatred or prejudice. For example, in Chapter 3, Fiona Vera-Gray and Bianca Fileborn make the point that men's engagement in street harassment may be about homosocial bonding, a misplaced sense of entitlement, anxieties about gender diversity or a lack of understanding about appropriate gendered behaviour in public. It may also be about explicit sexism and the reinforcement of patriarchy – but the point here is that there can be complex layers of relations shaping specific behaviours and understanding the sources and motivations of these will enable a more sophisticated understanding of landscapes of hate. This collection only touches briefly on the factors that might drive perpetrators to engage in hateful behaviours; this could present a fruitful avenue for future research that seeks to uncover the complex landscapes of hate.

Emotional

In many respects, the title of this book – *Landscapes of Hate* – evokes powerful emotions. Anderson and Smith (2001: 7) note that 'at particular times and in particular places, there are moments where lives are so explicitly lived through pain, bereavement, elation, anger, love and so on that the power of emotional relations cannot be ignored'. Incidents of hate provide a clear example of this where powerful emotions work in worrying ways to enact violence, verbal abuse and harm on people who are the unfortunate targets of such emotions; likewise, victims of hate crime often experience strong feelings of worry, anxiety and fear. Yet, as Anderson and Smith (2001: 8) also note 'attempting to inhabit these explicitly emotional spaces contrasts with more conventional models of social research whose settings are selected to cast light on political behaviour, economic rationality, class relations and so on – areas of public life whose emotional content is usually (deliberately) played down'. There can be a tendency in understanding landscapes of hate to adopt such an approach – to downplay emotions, to soften passions and to restrain the outburst of anger, fear and resentment. A key challenge in advancing relational and intersectional understandings of landscapes of hate is also about providing space and time to reflect on the emotions that are inevitably involved, a point emphasized in Chapter 1 where the editors reflect not only on the emotions in and of themselves but their role in society and their emplacement on bodies and in specific contexts.

Campbell (2013: 35) observes that '"crime" has affective power which excites, threatens, angers, shocks; it provokes an embodied experience of place and sensibilizes us to change and alterity in everyday settings'. This can be applied to hate crime as well as to forms of hate that fall outside of official definitions of the criminological. Some of the chapters in this collection explore these emotional registers in interesting and important ways, critically interrogating specific concepts or modes of operation that are imbued with feelings, sentiments and moods. For example, in Chapter 2, we learn about the challenges associated with recognition, respect and esteem, discourses of safety are explored in Chapter 9 and the issue of visibility is considered in Chapter 6. Many chapters also consider the issue of stigma – whether this be about its association with specific neighbourhoods or with specific buildings or places such as the gay scene. A challenge here is to allow the power of such emotions to be felt and recollected ethically in research encounters and for these then to be conveyed through academic scholarship.

Relational, intersectional and emotional ...

In conclusion, a key challenge for researchers studying the spatiality of hate is to seek to interrogate landscapes of hate while simultaneously considering the relational, intersectional and emotional aspects of hate. This presents a whole host of ethical and methodological challenges for scholars researching landscapes of hate. An ethically nuanced approach is needed to enable the full range of emotions to come through in research encounters and to employ intersectionality with care and respect. Likewise, a methodologically sophisticated, detailed and attentive approach to research will make it easier to appreciate the complex relationalities involved in landscapes of hate and to enable the critical exploration of these with research participants. Attending to the relational, intersectional and emotional components of hate will advance our understanding of the complex landscapes and spatialities of hate; however, this will not provide a definitive answer or solution to the problem of hate as it inevitably evolves, alters and changes as social norms, values and practices grow and develop, weaken and diminish, and overturn and convert. As we learn in the introduction to this book (Chapter 1) – and in Chapter 12 – a useful response to hate is to consider it in its widest sense and to not only adopt a very narrow approach that attends only to the operation of the criminal justice system. Moreover, although hate is often powerful and can have very damaging consequences, it is not the only emotion to define people's lives; resistance and opposition to hate may also be important features alongside other lived experiences associated with love and joy; perhaps it is in these diverse places, emotions and relations of resistance to hate that hope can be found. This will require ongoing attention from social researchers interested in hate in order that we can continue to seek to appreciate and challenge the evolving landscapes of hate in different contexts and at different times.

References

Anderson, K. and Smith, S.J. (2001) 'Editorial: emotional geographies', *Transactions of the Institute of British Geographers*, 26(1): 7–10.

Ansell, N., van Blerk, L., Hadju, F. and Robson, E. (2011) 'Spaces, times, and critical moments: a relational time-space analysis of the impacts of AIDS on rural youth in Malawi and Lesotho', *Environment and Planning A*, 43: 525–44.

Blackwood, L., Hopkins, N. and Reicher, S. (2013) 'I know who I am, but who do they think I am? Muslim perspectives on encounters with airport authorities,' *Ethnic and Racial Studies*, 36(6): 1090–1108.

Campbell, E. (2013) 'Transgression, affect and performance: choreographing a politics of urban space', *British Journal of Criminology*, 53: 18–40.

Campbell, E. (2016) 'Policing and its spatial imaginaries', *Journal of Theoretical and Philosophical Criminology*, 8: 71–89.

Chakraborti, N. and Garland, J. (2012) 'Reconceptualizing hate crime victimization through the lens of vulnerability and 'difference'', *Theoretical Criminology*, 16(4): 499–514.

Collins, P.H. and Bilge, S. (2016) *Intersectionality*, Cambridge: Policy Press.

Crenshaw, K. (1989) 'Demarginalizing the intersection of race and sex: a Black feminist critique of antidiscrimination doctrine, feminist theory and antiracist politics', *University of Chicago Legal Forum*, 140: 139–67.

Crenshaw, K. (1991) 'Mapping the margins: Intersectionality, identity politics, and violence against women of color', *Stanford Law Review*, 43: 1241–99.

Donovan, C., Clayton, J. and Macdonald, S.J. (2019) 'New directions in hate reporting research: agency, heterogeneity and relationality', *Sociological Research Online*, 24(2): 185–202.

Hall, E. and Bates, E. (2019) 'Hatescape? A relational geography of disability hate crime, exclusion and belonging in the city,' *Geoforum*, 101: 100–10.

Hodge, E. and Hallgrimsdottir, H. (2020) 'Networks of hate: the alt-right, "troll culture", and the cultural geography of social movement spaces online', *Journal of Borderlands Studies*, 35(4): 563–80.

Hopkins, P. (2019) 'Social geography I: intersectionality', *Progress in Human Geography*, 43(5): 937–47.

Hopkins, P. and Noble, G. (2009) 'Masculinities in place: situated identities, relations and intersectionality', *Social and Cultural Geography*, 10: 811–19.

Hopkins, P., Clayton, J. and Tell MAMA (2020) *Islamophobia and Anti-Muslim Hatred in North East England*, Newcastle-upon-Tyne: Newcastle University.

Massey, D. (2005) *For Space*, Sage: London.

Macdonald, S.J., Donovan, C. and Clayton, J. (2021) ' "I may be left with no choice but to end my torment": disabilities and intersectionalities of hate crime', *Disability and Society*, DOI: 10.1080/09687599.2021.1928480

Nayak, A. (2019) 'Re-scripting place: managing social class stigma in a former steel-making region', *Antipode*, 51(3): 927–48.

Index

References to endnotes show both the
page number and the note number (192n4).